£5

О6

A History of the American Avant-Garde Cinema

A film exhibition organized by The American Federation of Arts

The American Federation of Arts is a non-profit, educational institution which organizes and circulates exhibitions and films to museums, universities, schools, libraries and art centers throughout the country. These important services cultivate a greater knowledge and appreciation of historical and contemporary art throughout the United States and of American art abroad.

This film exhibition and catalogue are supported by a grant from the National Endowment for the Arts.

©1976 The American Federation of Arts

Published by The American Federation of Arts
41 East 65th Street
New York, New York 10021

Library of Congress Catalogue Number 76-3966

Designed by Michael Shroyer
Type set by Automated Composition Service, Inc.
Printed by Summit Graphics Corporation

Acknowledgements

The preparation of A HISTORY OF THE AMERICAN AVANT-GARDE CINEMA has involved the cooperative effort of numerous individuals and organizations. In particular, The American Federation of Arts thanks John G. Hanhardt, Associate Curator of Film at the Whitney Museum of American Art and formerly of the Walker Art Center, Minneapolis, for his participation as Guest Curator of the exhibition, his selection of the films and programs, as well as the preparation of the exhibition catalogue's central essay and the accompanying chronology.

We extend our special thanks to the Anthology Film Archives, New York, its entire staff and, especially, Jonas Mekas, General Director, P. Adams Sitney, Director of Library and Publications, Helene Kaplan, Film Curator, and Kate Mannheim, Research Librarian. This film exhibition and catalogue could not have been organized without their research assistance and ongoing work in the preservation, exhibition and study of the avant-garde film.

We also want to acknowledge with appreciation the support and encouragement of the Department of Film of The Museum of Modern Art which presented the premier of the exhibition in May, 1976. Ted Perry, Director, Margareta Akermark, Associate Director, Adrienne Mancia, Associate Curator, and Larry Kardish, Assistant Curator, have aided us at every stage of the project's development.

The publication is the result of the assiduous efforts of the following individuals: Paul S. Arthur, Fred Camper, Ellen Feldman, Lucy Fischer, Lindley P. Hanlon and Stuart Liebman, doctoral candidates in the Department of Cinema Studies of New York University, prepared the essays for each of the seven programs, researched the filmographies and bibliographies, and selected the illustrations accompanying their writing. In addition to their studies and research at NYU, Mr. Arthur has taught film at Rutgers University, NYU, Queens College and now teaches at Bard College; Mr. Camper has taught at Richmond College, NYU and The William Patterson College of New Jersey; Ms. Feldman teaches at NYU; Ms. Fischer teaches at NYU; Ms. Hanlon has taught at The Spence School and NYU; and Mr. Liebman teaches at Queens College.

William G. Simon, Acting Chairman of the Department of Cinema Studies of NYU, has coordinated the preparation of the texts, bibliographies and filmographies as well as the visiting lecturers who tour with the exhibition. Marilyn Singer, editor of the publication, worked closely with all the writers, and also wrote the introduction. Mark Segal, Whitney Museum Film Coordinator, edited Mr. Hanhardt's opening essay. In addition, Francene Keery, official photographer of the Anthology Film Archives, prepared the special frame enlargements and film strips that appear throughout this catalogue.

I would also like to extend my thanks to AFA's Film Department, Steven Aronson, Director, Mary P. Ivers, Program Assistant, Lorie Karlin, Technician, and Arlene Pancza of the AFA staff, for organizing all aspects of the program—the exhibition, the publication, and the visiting lecturers— and to Michael Shroyer, designer of the catalogue.

Finally, The American Federation of Arts gratefully recognizes the generous support of the National Endowment for the Arts which made this entire project possible.

Wilder Green
Director

Trustees

Contents

Preface

The traveling film exhibition A HISTORY OF THE AMERICAN AVANT-GARDE CINEMA has been developed by The American Federation of Arts out of a desire to increase understanding of the art of the film, and particularly that branch of filmmaking that is concerned with the use of the medium as a vehicle for personal expression.

Since 1909, AFA has circulated exhibitions of paintings, sculpture, graphics, drawing and photography. In recent years it has developed programs of films on art and films as art. Two programs now in active circulation are FILMS ON ART/THE ARTS COUNCIL OF GREAT BRITAIN, a selection of documentaries on art and artists, and NEW AMERICAN FILMMAKERS, a group of selected independent films that have been presented in the Whitney Museum of American Art's *New American Filmmakers Series.* Both of these programs have been prepared with the active film programmer and educator in mind. The exhibition described herein, however, has been selected and presented primarily for the institution without an ongoing program of film as art, or without a curator sufficiently well versed in the avant-garde film.

There are three aspects of this presentation that are particularly pertinent. First, the seven programs represent a critical selection by John G. Hanhardt, Associate Curator of Film at the Whitney Museum of American Art. The Whitney Museum is the first in the U.S.A. to devote its film program entirely to the independent American cinema.

Secondly, this exhibition catalogue has been designed not only to accompany the exhibition, but to be of permanent use to students and teachers of the avant-garde film, including as it does, bibliographies, filmographies and chronology, Mr. Hanhardt's essay, and analytical essays for each program.

Finally, the film exhibition is touring the United States accompanied by selected faculty and graduate students from the Department of Cinema Studies at New York University. The avant-garde film is sometimes difficult to appreciate, and it is our belief that a scholar experienced both in understanding and teaching this art form will be useful for orientation of general audiences as well as to assist with study sessions of students and interested members of the community.

It is our hope that this exhibition will be the first in a series of circulating programs to be exhibited by universities, libraries and other organizations and that it will foster an increased awareness of film as an art form.

Willard Van Dyke
Chairman of Film Committee
The American Federation of Arts

Introduction

For each age, for each place, for each time, there has always been an avant-garde. Hector Berlioz, a musician much maligned in his own time, relates that when Beethoven's C# *Minor String Quartet* was premiered, "After a short while, people grew restless and began whispering . . . Eventually, most of them got up and left, protesting aloud that it was meaningless, absurd, unbearable—the work of a madman." James Whistler's *Nocturne in Black and Gold: The Falling Rocket,* today seen as a major work, was lambasted by critic John Ruskin who accused Whistler of "flinging a pot of paint in the face of the public." The public agreed. And Gertrude Stein's "A rose is a rose is a rose," one line from her many writings which strove to re-examine language, was the subject of many a cartoon, the punchline of many a joke. These and other artists were avant-garde; their work was misunderstood, mocked, even banned or destroyed; but eventually, they became familiar, acceptable, sometimes even traditional, or reactionary. As Amos Vogel said in his introductory remarks at the 1975 American Film Festival Film as Art presentation:

> It appears that in every generation there exists an amazing dichotomy between artists and audiences; what is involved is a new, and there-fore disturbing approach to form and content. The artists, as usual, are ahead of their audience. They see further. They are more sen-sitive. The audience is shocked: it does not know what to think. The critics—a by-product of the artists—usually represent an earlier stage of development and want to hold on to what they have finally decided to accept: yesterday's art; more comfortable, more comfort-ing, less disturbing.

All of this figures for the art form of cinema. As Vogel continued, "It is structured in terms of frame-area, composition, color or contrast be-tween black and white, light, shadow; shapes, masses, volumes; and, most importantly, time: movement, rhythm, editing." A startling invention, cinema quickly became a convention. John G. Hanhardt, the guest curator of this film exhibition, points out in his opening essay, "The Medium Viewed," that film's status as a mass entertainment medium carries with it certain expectations of style, technique and genre which have changed minimally in popular cinema's eighty-year history. But cinema is no more "fixed" than any art—a point the avant-garde film-makers seized on in Europe (and sporadically in America) in the 1920's, and the 1930's, and in America from the 1940's to the present. The avant-garde film explores the modernist concerns of time, space and movement with which other modern arts are involved. As Hanhardt shows, these con-cerns, as well as the overthrow of realism and linearity, have informed the avant-garde film; a primary concern with the very material of and proper-ties particular to film has led to the discovery of new techniques, new filmic possibilities. Jonas Mekas elaborates in his book *Movie Journal:*

> Movement can go now from complete immobility to a blurred swish vision to a million unpredictable speeds and ecstacies (Brakhage's work, for instance). The classic film vocabulary allows (or recognizes) only the slowly, respectably Brooks-Brothers-suit paced camera move-ments—the steadiness, the immobility which is called a "good," "clear," "steady" image . . . Some American filmmakers have freed motion. The camera movement can now go anywhere—from a clear, idyllic peacefulness of the image to a frenetic and feverish ecstasy of

motion. The full scale of our emotions can be registered, reflected, clarified—for ourselves, if for nobody else.

Lighting . . . can go now from the "properly" exposed and lit image to a complete destruction of the "proper"; from a complete whiteness (wash-out) to a complete blackness . . . Millions of nuances are now open to us, the poetry of shades, of over- and under-exposures. This shows that something good is happening in some of us, otherwise we wouldn't see this happening in cinema at all.

These new happenings in our cinema reveal that man is reaching, growing into new areas of himself, areas which were either deadened by culture, or scared, or sleeping. Add to what I already mentioned the complete disregard of censorship, the abandoning of taboos on sex, language, etc., and you'll have some idea about the scope and freedom of what's going on. More and more filmmakers are realizing that there is no one single way of exposing (seeing) things; that the steadiness or sharpness or clarity (and all their opposites) are no virtues or absolute properties of anything; that, really, the cinema language, like any other language and syntax, is in a constant flux, is changing with every change of man.

Mekas, with Vogel, is saying that at the heart of avant-garde film is *personal expression* by artists of sensitivity, intelligence and vision. This is not to say that commercial filmmakers are not sensitive or intelligent or that they do not inject their own personalities into their works. But such filmmakers are bound by cinematic codes, conventions, taboos, habits, expectations they cannot escape. By contrast, avant-garde filmmakers, as writer Ken Kelman says, "project genuine experience and direct vision." Maya Deren, one of the first American avant-garde filmmakers put it succinctly in "Amateur Versus Professional," *Film Culture, No. 39:*

Cameras do not make films; filmmakers make films. Improve your films not by adding more equipment and personnel but by using what you have to the fullest capacity. The most important part of your equipment is yourself: your mobile body, your imaginative mind, and your freedom to use both.

These filmmakers reflect the periods in which they live and work— their films do not so much represent a movement, but rather they exhibit trends, drifts. The 1940's, influenced by the art movements of Surrealism and Dadaism, by Freudian analysis, by a sense of post-war absurdity, saw psychodramas and Surrealist films. In 1943, Maya Deren (*Meshes of the Afternoon, A Study in Chroreography for Camera*) started to work and talk on films. She stressed the poetic, dream-like qualities of film and the ability of editing to displace a normal sense of time and space. Deren, as Lucy Fischer shows in her essay on program 1, influenced many independent filmmakers through her concerns and her major preoccupation with the conflict between interiority and exteriority. It was Deren's idea of hiring the Provincetown Playhouse, New York, to show her films which inspired Amos Vogel to establish *Cinema 16,* a showcase for experimental films.
    Among the filmmakers who, along with Deren, were instrumental in creating, encouraging and sustaining avant-garde film in the 1940's were Willard Maas (*Geography of the Body*), Marie Menken (*Notebook*), James

Broughton (*Mother's Day*), Sidney Peterson (*The Lead Shoes*), Ian Hugo (*Bells of Atlantis*), Kenneth Anger (*Fireworks, Scorpio Rising*), and Harry Smith (*Early Abstractions*). Maas, Peterson, Hugo and Broughton were involved with works set to or based on poems, ballads or poetic prose. Maas went on to create psychodramas dealing with sexual conflict, such as *The Mechanics of Love* and *Narcissus*. Hugo, a "supreme colorist," as Stuart Liebman notes in his essay on program 2 and a master of superimposition, described himself as "using images as if they were notes in a symphonic composition." Peterson's sophisticated and witty films, rooted in Surrealism, as were those of his one-time collaborator James Broughton, mixed, in P. Adams Sitney's words, "formal commitment with psychological distancing." Peterson was also a teacher of filmmaking at the San Francisco Art Institute, one of the earliest film schools established in the country. Broughton, poet and playwright, has continued to use the poetic voice into the 1970's; his recent works view human events in terms of rituals and cycles, all infused with a bright sense of humor.

Other filmmakers did not base their work on poetry or prose. Marie Menken, wife of Willard Maas, photographed *Geography of the Body*, but went on to create works which vary widely in technique and subject matter—from a microscopic investigation of sperm to a stylized biography of Andy Warhol. However, as Sheldon Renan says in *An Introduction to the Undeground Film,* "They have in common a lyric lightness and a love for jolting visual rhythms." Menken's film *Notebook,* although completed in the 1960's, was begun in the 1940's. A very different filmmaker, Kenneth Anger, was and is involved with what Stephen Dwoskin in *Film Is* calls the theme of "dreams experienced, yet broken," a them exemplified in *Fireworks* which Anger made at the age of seventeen. His later works fuse Magick, myth and symbolism through editing and superimposition. Of his work, Dwoskin writes:

> He treats inner dreams and fantasies as the essential living being in a way that makes others feel afraid. But he also presents his own fear, his inner self; the film becomes an act of voodoo, a transference of the inner self to form, a myth of its own, but existing openly.

Harry Smith, unlike the other filmmakers of the 1940's, was not involved with poetry or psychodrama or the filming of simple, everyday things. He is an animator and his earliest works involve formal composition and illusory depth through color and shape and an interest in the textural surface of the film material. His later works—particularly *Heaven and Earth Magic Feature (No. 12)*—use cutouts to create striking and arcane images based on Smith's studies in alchemy and psychology.

The 1950's, as Liebman discusses, saw a period of transition between the initiatives of the 1940's and the coming maturity of the avant-garde film in the 1960's. "The period's best films," says Liebman, "moved away from dramatic narrative towards freer thematic organization." In the 1950's, television took over; apathy seemed a way of life. But during that time, the Beats, the Abstract Expressionists and rock-and-roll infused all the arts with new spirit, paving the way for the "underground" film of the 1960's. Among the film artists who began to produce in the 1950's were Shirley Clarke (*Bridges-Go-Round*), Bruce Conner (*A Movie*), Robert Breer (*Recreation, 69*), Stan Vanderbeek (*Science Friction*, which was begun in 1958), Ken Jacobs (*Little Stabs at Happiness, Window*) and Stan Brakhage (*The Wonder Ring, Anticipation of the Night, Prelude, Dog Star Man, Fire of Waters, Riddle of Lumen*). A dancer, Clarke has described all her works as "dances"; in fact, *Bridges-Go-Round* uses superimposition and a continuously moving camera to choreograph New York City's bridges. Clarke's later works include two unusual narratives—*The Connection* and *The Cool World*—and the brilliant and controversial cinema-verité work, *Portrait of Jason.* Bruce Conner, assemblage sculptor, uses found footage and the collage approach in his filmmaking, laying emphasis on juxtaposition, film movement and rhythm. In many ways, Conner's early work anticipated the Pop Art movement. Stan Vanderbeek's work is allied to Conner's in his use of collage, but Vanderbeek uses animation as well as found footage and has gone on to create environmental works, like the Movie-Drome, which, as Sheldon Renan says, are "collages of media." Vanderbeek's involvement with the technology of visual language, with the film as a method of communication has led him toward what Gene Youngblood, in his book *Expanded Cinema,* calls "synaesthetic cinema," and his early works looked forward to the "mixed media" events of the 1960's.

Breer, Jacobs and Brakhage represent three different and important styles of filmmaking. A painter and sculptor, Breer saw film as an extension of ideas he was pursuing in painting. He has animated lines, shapes, human and animal figures, and objects and has used collage and rotoscope techniques. Of all his work, he says, "I'm interested in the domain between motion and still pictures." P. Adams Sitney, in his book, *Visionary Film,* describes Breer's work as "graphic cinema" and says, "There is always a distance between him and the subjects of his films; he is an extreme formalist." He is also a wit and his films reflect his sense of humor.

The early works of Ken Jacobs (*Little Stabs at Happiness, Blonde Cobra*) have been called Baudelairean by Jonas Mekas. They portray, writes Mekas, "A world of flowers of evil, of illuminations, of torn and tortured flesh; a poetry which is at once beautiful and terrible, good and evil, delicate and dirty." These works, like those of filmmakers Jack Smith and Ron Rice, are very much a part of the underground films of the 1960's, even though they were started in the late 1950's. Jacobs' later works are structural, and deal with the material and properties of film. His masterwork, *Tom, Tom, the Piper's Son,* is, as Lois Mendelson and Bill Simon say in their essay on the film in *New Forms in Film,* "with Vertov's *Man with a Movie Camera,* one of the two great works of reflexive cinema whose primary subject is an aesthetic definition of the nature of the medium."

"Historically," writes Sheldon Renan, "Stan Brakhage is the major transitional figure in the turning away of experimental film from literature and Surrealist psychodrama, and in its subsequent move toward the more purely personal and visual." Prolific and articulate, Brakhage has been an inspiration to many independent filmmakers. His lyrical films, based on incidents, people, fears, desires, and symbols from his own life, transform actual life and make us re-see images, colors and, particularly, light. Largely silent, Brakhage's films involve the totality of seeing. Brakhage's seminal book *Metaphors on Vision* suggests that for him, as P. Adams Sitney writes:

> Seeing includes what the open eyes view, including the essential movements and dilations involved in that primary mode of seeing, as well as the shifts of focus, what the mind's eye sees in visual memory and in dreams (he calls them "brain movies") and the perpetual play

of shapes and colors on the closed eyelid and occasionally on the eye surface ("closed-eye vision"). The imagination, as he seems to define it, includes the simultaneous functioning of all these modes.

This view permeates Brakhage's films. It is the reason Dwoskin says, "Brakhage's poetry is really the pure experience of vision."

In the 1960's, the avant-garde film matured under the influeces of the "new freedom," of the Pop Art movement, of Oriental philosophy, of "happenings," of the idea, fostered by John Cage, that art is "a way of waking up to the very life we are living." Such diverse filmmakers as Tony Conrad, (*The Flicker*), George Landow (*Diploteratology or Bardo Folly, Film in Which There Appear Sprocket Holes, Edge Lettering, Dirt Particles, Etc.*), Bruce Baillie (*Castro Street, Mass for the Dakota Sioux*), Michael Snow (*Wavelength*), Standish D. Lawder (*Runaway*), Jonas Mekas (*Notes on the Circus*), Paul Sharits (*T,O,U,C,H,I,N,G*), Robert Nelson (*Bleu Shut*), Larry Jordan (*Our Lady of the Sphere*), Hollis Frampton (*Nostalgia*), Barry Gerson (*Endurance/Remembrance/Metamorphosis*) and Ernie Gehr (*Serene Velocity*) came to the forefront in the 1960's (and 1970's). James Whitney (*Lapis*) and Jordan Belson (*Samadhi*), who began working in films some years before, produced their finest works to date in this fruitful period. Jonas Mekas began producing films based on footage shot in the 1950's. He has said of his work, "I make home movies because I live." His works, based on personal events, show, as Fred Camper, in his essay on program 5, shows Mekas' belief that subject is the product of instantaneous viewing.

On the West Coast, Jordan, Baillie, Belson and Whitney were all influenced by Eastern philosophy, Belson and Whitney in particular are serious students of Buddhism. Belson's works are similar in style, using subtly mutating "gaseous" masses of color. Belson will not tell how his films are made, but he does describe them as meditative quests, as representations of actual states of consciousness. Whitney, whose early work was co-directed by his brother, John, a master of computer animation, also creates meditative works, but his are tantric, *Lapis* being a classical mandala. Larry Jordan, influenced by Joseph Cornell and Max Ernst, is also an animator like Belson and Whitney, but he uses cut-outs from Victorian engravings to create Surrealistic collages portraying a dream-or underworld, a *bardo* world between the states of life and death. Baillie, on the other hand, makes lyrical films in which the Eastern influece is, as in Jordan's works, less obvious. His is a truly "American" cinema of open spaces and characteristic landscapes, of images of travel. Paul Arthur, in his essay on program 3, discusses one of the chief themes and tensions in Baillie's work, the "outsider," who is "incapable of sustaining meaningful contact with either the victims of a culture he condemns or with his nostalgic intimation of a pastoral existence."

Also living on the West Coast is Robert Nelson, whose films are influenced by a sense of the absurd, by the picaresque. Unlike the work of other West Coast filmmakers represented here, Nelson's harkens back to the ironies of Peterson and Broughton. His film *Bleu Shut* is, in Sitney's words, "a prime example of the participatory film," playing games with the audience and encouraging active participation in it.

The end of the 1960's was, as Paul Arthur points out in his essay on program 6, a restless, tense period raising a wealth of political and artistic issues. In cinema, this period saw the growth of the structural film. All of these works reflect themselves as films through their awareness and utilization of the properties and material of film. Tony Conrad's work (along with that of Austrian avant-garde filmmaker Peter Kubelka) with the stroboscopic "flicker" effect, created by mathematical alternations of black and white or color frames, paved the way for later works involving this device. Lindley Hanlon shows in her essay on program 4, the correlation between Conrad's *The Flicker* and serial music's mathematical patterning of musical tones. This correlation applies partially to later structural films.

Michael Snow has been called by Sitney the "dean of structural filmmakers." He uses such formal strategies as the fixed frame, the scanning camera movement, the conversion of space into motion in his works. His viewpoint is disembodied, his art presents, as Sitney says, "a dialogue between illusion and its unveiling." Related to Snow's work are the films of Ernie Gehr and Barry Gerson. Gehr's kinetic works revolve, as Bill Simon says in his essay on Gehr in *New Forms in Film,* around "the ambiguity of what one is seeing." Gehr has written that he tries to break down "the essential contradictions of still and shot." Gerson's films, as Simon points out, "are concerned with the ambiguity of the space of the shot." Gerson speaks of the levels of reality revealed through film—illusions within illusions.

An other type of structural film, in Bill Simon's words, "isolates an idea, a theory, a concept, usually concerning a particular aspect or problem in the cinematic experience, and creates a structure that demonstrates or elucidates it." The films of George Landow and Hollis Frampton are conceptual structural films. Landow uses celluloid itself, the film leader, the abstraction of found images, printed text, etc. in his films. Sitney says of his work, they:

> . . . are all based on simple situations: the variations on announcing and looking (*Fleming Faloon*), the extrinsic visual interest in a film frame (*Film in Which*), a meditation on the pure light trapped in a ridiculous image (*Diploteratology*) and the echo of an illusion (*The Film That Rises to the Surface of Clarified Butter*). His remarkable faculty is as the maker of images, for the simple found objects (*Film in Which* and the beginning of *Diploteratology*) he uses and the images he photographs are radical, superreal and haunting.

Hollis Frampton's films explore the disjunction between image and sound. As Ellen Feldman discusses in her essay on program 7, he is concerned with combating fixity as exemplified by language and with trying to "recapture the complex experience of temporality." In his article on Frampton in *New Forms in Film,* Bill Simon says:

> His films have a sensuous intellectuality; they thrill by their engagement in ideas. If Brakhage's great gift is what he does with light and Snow's what he does with space, Frampton's is what he does with conceptual structures.

Standish D. Lawder's witty structural films use found footage, animation and live action to explore and subvert the traditions of camera movement, the illusion of motion, the material of film, the possibilities inherent in the single frame, etc. Paul Sharits is also interested in the single frame, the film material and the illusion of motion, but he uses looping, the flicker effect and color (sometimes combined with the flicker) to a much greater extent. Of his hallucinatory works, Sharits has said they:

. . . will strip away anything (all present definitions of "something") standing in the way of the film being its own reality, anything which would prevent the viewer from entering totally new levels of awareness.

Sharits' statement forms the basis for a definition of structural film and helps us to understand the works represented here.

But, although films are their own reality, existing independently in time and space, they are, as Deren said, made by filmmakers. As Amos Vogel says, "All of these films are invitations to you to see the world with new eyes, to open your mind to new possibilities, to give your unconscious free rein." The first step in appreciating any art is to maintain an open mind. The second involves exposure. It was with this second step in mind that The American Federation of Arts created this exhibition of *A History of the American Avant-Garde Cinema*. The important word is "A" for there are many histories of avant-garde film, of any art. This particular history selected by John Hanhardt is intended to introduce audiences unfamiliar with avant-garde film to some of the major cinematic achievements of three decades and to allow those familiar with these films to view them once again and gain further insights into and from them.

Just as it is impossible to grasp in full the intricacies of harmony, rhythm, orchestration of a piece of music from one hearing, or to understand the complexities of color, perspective, composition of a painting from one viewing, it is impossible to savor all that an avant-garde film has to offer from one screening. But, even one viewing can suggest the vision of these works and can point the viewer to new ways of examining his/her own perceptions, dreams and understanding of art. And, hopefully, one screening will encourage interest in further viewings. Each film has its own stylistic and structural qualities which lend it its own unique textures, resonances and shades of meaning. Each viewing of a film reveals more about these qualities.

The essays in this publication define and refer to the structural and stylistic qualities, as well as to the content, major concerns and background of the films and their makers. They do not purport to be the "final word" on the films—they, like all criticism, are interpretative; but they, along with John Hanhardt's opening essay on the development and critical response to the avant-garde film, are designed to familiarize the reader/viewer with both the films themselves and with the new criticism necessary for thoughtful discussion of the new cinema.

But, although avant-garde film requires a new criticism and a new way of looking at film, it shares with all art certain essentials of form, structure and tempo. We must seek to recognize these in avant-garde, and all film, but with the knowledge that there is no *one* form, no *one* tempo that is good, right or proper. An open mind, exposure and familiarity with the language of the avant-garde allow us to feel considered appreciation for the avant-garde film, and to say, as Sheldon Renan has:

Some underground films are good. Some are bad. A few are great. But whatever they are, underground films are the film artist's unmitigated vision.

Marilyn Singer
Editor

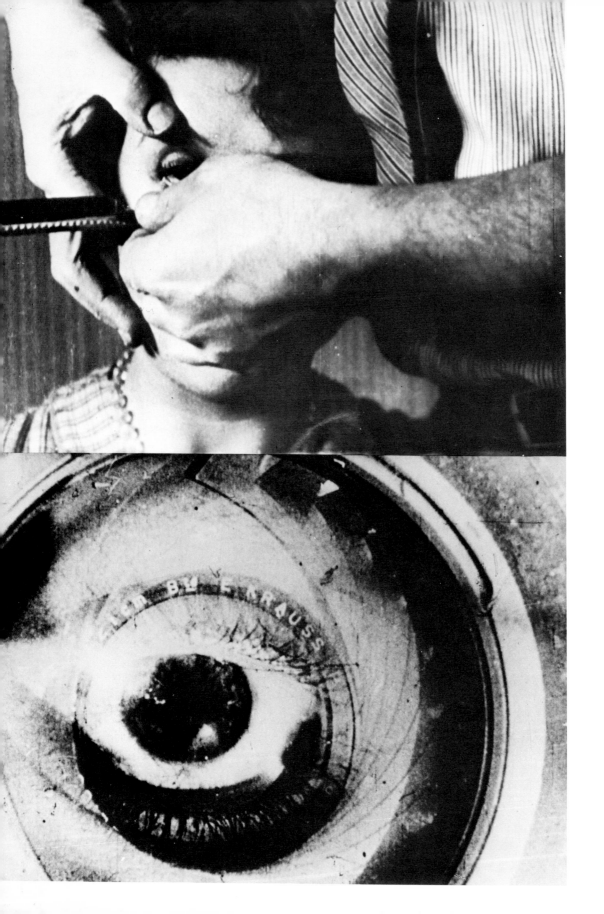

The Medium Viewed: The American Avant~Garde Film

The individual is continuously, and largely unconsciously, casting his environment in the mold of his past experiences through a dynamic interaction between its components and his self-conception. He must perforce classify and interpret himself as well as other things; since no two things (including himself) are ever identical from one moment to the next, he is constantly grouping together sensory and ideological data that are different. Perceptual organization is not a photographic process. It is fundamentally an innovative act; it is an interactive, adjustive relationship between the perceiver and the thing perceived. The two together make up a dynamic creative whole.
H. G. Barnett. *Innovation: The Basis of Cultural Change.*

There must, it seems to me, be some human activity which serves to break up orientations, to weaken and frustrate the tyrannous drive to order, to prepare the individual to observe what the orientation tells him is irrelevant but what may very well be relevant. That activity, I believe, is the activity of artistic perception.
Morse Peckham. *Man's Rage for Chaos.*

And here, somewhere, we have an eye (I'll speak for myself) capable of an imagining (the only reality). And there (right there) we have the camera eye (the limitation of the original liar). . . . And here, somewhere, we have an eye capable of imagining. And then we have the camera eye, its lenses grounded (sic) to achieve 19th-century Western compositional perspective (as best exemplified by the 19th-century architectural conglomeration of details of the "classic" ruin) in bending the light and limiting the frame of the image just so, its standard camera and projector speed for recording movement geared to the feeling of the ideal slow Viennese waltz and even its tripod head, being the neck it swings on, balled with bearings to permit it that *Les Sylphides* motion ideal for the contemplative romantic and virtually restricted to horizontal and vertical movements (pillars and horizon lines) a diagonal requiring a major adjustment, its lenses coated or provided filters, its light meters balanced and its color film manufactured, to produce that picture post card effect (salon painting) exemplified by those oh so blue skies and peach skins.
Stan Brakhage. *Metaphors on Vision.*

Art is a banner calling forth and sustaining the revolted, immediate proof that The Promised Land exists, that man can feel/think his way to vital form.
Ken Jacobs. *New York Film-Makers' Cooperative Catalogue.*

Film That Invents Itself: The Avant-Garde Film

The term "avant-garde" links the films to which it refers with advanced art and ideas in other media and disciplines, and, by definition, with a view of film which is neither traditional nor orthodox. Because most people share a traditional notion of what constitutes a film, films are generally expected to conform to certain conventions. These include strategies of editing and camera movement which confirm a narrative tradition through specific codes of representation. The story and point of view created within this tradition are consistent with the logical development and psychological orientation of its model, the nineteenth century novel, and with the traditions of linear form and illusionistic space. The manner in which these conventions are affirmed or modified affects the viewer's perception of film and motivates the critic's response.

The best-known type of film is the feature-length, commercial, entertainment film. Its premise is that film is mass entertainment requiring certain levels of production and marketing to sustain it as such. These films have standardized running times to permit an optimal number of theatrical showings per day, and utilize supporting conventions of storytelling. In addition, the significant technological developments of sound, color and wide-screen, have been viewed as essential embellishments to a product of an industry constantly seeking to increase its audiences. Motion picture production is thus organized along the lines of a large industry (factory= studio) with highly specialized production crews fashioning the whole film, and sophisticated organizations distributing and marketing it. Film appreciation in general (and in particular its historiography and criticism) has supported this type of film by according it the preeminence it enjoys today while attempting, in the process, to balance its basis in mass entertainment with its justification as art.

There are certain films (once called, interestingly, "art" films) which appear to depart from the conventional model, but which are nevertheless both a reaction to and a confirmation of the established codes of filmmaking. For example, the cinema of the French "New Wave," particularly the films of Jean-Luc Godard, addresses itself to conventions of acting in the American cinema and establishes its own "stars" who become associated with a director's films. There is also a use of color and action which refers to the established iconographies of genres such as the western, romance, and gangster film. At the same time, such films as Godard's *Contempt* (made in 1963 and featuring Brigitte Bardot, Fritz Lang, Jack Palance and Michel Piccoli) employ formal devices of camera movement and editing and reveal narrative strategies which, in their self-referential aspect (referring to the myths and iconography of movie making and culture) break away from the dominant film codes. Alain Resnais' *Last Year at Marienbad* (produced in 1961 with original scenario and dialogue by Alain Robbe-Grillet) bears a more specific relationship to the ideas and forms of the French "New Novel" as represented by such authors as Robbe-Grillet, Michel Butor and Marguerite Duras, ideas which, as part of the intellectual life of Paris, influenced such directors as Resnais and Robert Bresson. The New Novel's manipulation of time and memory finds a correlate in the temporal disjunctions of *Last Year at Marienbad*. While such films as these consciously refer to conventions of production and present instances of radically shifting film time, they do not engage the material of film and the illusion of space (except for such a casual aside as in Godard's *Les Carabiniers* when Michel-Ange tries to peer over the edge of a bathtub in a filmed bathing scene) with the same specific regard as does the avant-garde film.

The avant-garde film of Europe of the 1920's, and in America with increasing activity since the early 1940's, aspires to a radical otherness from the conventions of filmmaking and the assumptions and conditions which inform the dominant view and experience of film. Thus these independent films are made primarily in 16mm (and sometimes in 8mm), not the 35mm of commercial filmmaking, and they involve the filmmaker directly through a tactile, "hands on" approach or an assertive point of view that is the expression of an artist engaged in such vanguard aesthetic movements as surrealism, cubism, abstract expressionism or minimalism. This cinema subverts cinematic convention by exploring the medium and its properties and materials, and in the process creates its own history separate from that of the classical narrative cinema. It is filmmaking that creates itself out of its own experience.

The fact that a critical discourse exists in painting and sculpture that embraces modernism in general and such recent specific movements as minimal art, process art and conceptual art, while no such discourse exists, except marginally, for film, indicates the special manner in which consideration of the avant-garde is held back by the attention given traditional standards of film production and appreciation. In addition to the use of 16mm and more direct involvement with film's materials, there are running times which vary from less than a minute to more than six hours, and formats which range from conventional audience-screen relationships to installations which challenge such conventional relationships. Even the earlier terms identifying these films—underground and experimental—imply a tentative, subversive, clandestine activity.

There exists a tacit complicity of expectation and definition between the viewer and maker of conventional movies which informs film appreciation and supports the established economics and aesthetics of film production. To be successful, a film must be appreciated by certain critics and audiences, and such appreciation presupposes adherence to certain economic and historical definitions of the medium. The avant-garde film is situated outside the dialogue between the commercial entertainment film and its audiences, a dialogue which takes place through the form and content of the films and with critics monitoring the condition of the films and historians offering ideological support for both roles. The enormity of the avant-garde's challenge, and its attendant complexity, is to address the economic, production, distribution, exhibition, critical discourse and historiography which have virtually dominated film production and appreciation. The avant-garde seeks nothing less than to challenge the dominant coordinates of film appreciation—the linear story film and its subject matter as codified by styles and genres in the traditional cinema, and standards of professionalism and production values which are held to be the cinema's norm. This is not to deny the very real achievement of the traditional cinema and its discourse, but to explore the tenacity of the ideology and mythology which support the dominant thinking on film to the exclusion of the avant-garde by defining it from the outset as a subgenre of little interest.

The basis of film is the process of photography, an invention of mid-nineteenth century science and industry. The urge to invent the photograph and motion picture was sustained by the desire for the "solution" to the presumed "problem" of creativity—the reproduction of the perceived

A Hollywood studio

world. As Marcelin Pleynet points out in *Debat: Economique, Ideologique, Formel:*

> It is interesting to note that it is precisely when Hegel is summing up
> the history of painting, when painters are beginning to be aware that
> the scientific perspective which determines its relation to the figure
> is the product of a special cultural pattern . . . that it is precisely at
> that moment that Niepce invents photography. Niepce (1765-1833),
> a contemporary of Hegel (1770-1831), is called upon to confirm the
> Hegelian view, to provide a mechanical reproduction of the ideology
> contained in the perspectival code, its norms and their effects on
> censorship.[1]

Science, and more specifically technology, were considered the underpinning of a developing economic and social/cultural world view, capitalism, which, in the twentieth century, was to create its architecture of production in the assembly line. The assembly line offered the perfect linear correlate for a linear world view of mass production and mass markets. That view sought justification and preservation in the photograph and the cinema, and it found both. The Daguerretype became a new mechanical mirror to be held up to all and to be seen for its power to reproduce self and environment, and to confirm an immortality on both. The photograph was to serve the illusion of democratizing the powers of creation through technology, while retaining the element of mystery, present in the technology. Science, technology, and capital had created their illuminated manuscript, their medium. The process of projecting a film resembled, as in film production, an assembly line, each frame, seen in rapid succession, creating a moving image. Implicit in the medium was its drive to create a coherent world view.

The animation of the photograph and its transformation into motion pictures developed rapidly. The Frenchmen Louis and Auguste Lumière set out in the late 1890's to reproduce the world on a new map called film. They traveled the globe filming the events of daily living—a train entering a station, workers leaving a factory, and such social events as coronations. The Lumières were among the first film documentarians, and they employed a variety of camera movements and placements to reveal and explicate diverse events. Another Frenchman, George Méliès, began to create a cinema of fantasy at the turn of the century. Méliès recognized the magical quality of film, its ability to make objects and people disappear, the possibilities it presented for fashioning illusion. Born of a theatrical tradition, Méliès recognized the unique potential and properties of the medium. However, the ability of film to appear to reproduce the known world and to preserve spatial illusionism became dominant as film turned into an entertainment commodity with standardized formats. As the assembly line was to be an answer to the maximization of commodity production and standardization, so the monopoly/technology and organization of production of the motion picture industry in Southern California was to create a new mass entertainment which quickly became one of this country's largest industries.

The fact that the avant-garde film has not been seriously considered in the predominant thinking on film rests in part on the traditional histories devoted to film. As with all written history, the historical explanation of the development of film is guided by metahistorical considerations. Historians have wrestled with the ambition of making the writing of history a science. But whereas scientists can agree on a scientific problem and scientific explanation, no such understanding has ever existed in historiography. As Hayden White has written in his book *Metahistory:*

> This may merely reflect the protoscientific nature of the historical enterprise, but it is important to bear in mind this congenital disagreement (or lack of agreement) over what counts as a specifically historical explanation of any given set of historical phenomenon. For this means that historical explanations are bound to be based on different metahistorical presuppositions about the nature of the historical field, presuppositions that generate different conceptions of the *kind of explanations* that can be used in historiographical analysis.[2]

> Unlike literary fictions, such as the novel, historical works are made up of events that exist outside of the consciousness of the writer. The events reported in a novel can be invented in a way they cannot be (or are not supposed to be) in a history. This makes it difficult to distinguish between the chronicle of events and the story being told in a literary fiction. . . . Unlike the novelist the historian confronts the veritable chaos of events *already constituted,* out of which he must choose the elements of the story he would tell. He makes his story by including some events and excluding others, by stressing some and subordinating others. This process of exclusion, stress, and subordination is carried out in the interest of constructing a story of a particular kind. That is to say he "emplots" his story.[3]

Hayden White here presents the dilemma of the film historian and the assumptions contained in the definitions of film which have informed so much of its written history. Because the traditional cinema is structured or emploted, along linear narrative lines, it is interpreted and placed within literary contexts. In addition, since it is a large entertainment industry, it assumes in some histories an exclusively social and cultural role based on its economics. These factors have resulted in the organization of film histories around self-contained national cinemas, genres, and historical periods which are defined by developments in the industry and by narrative/iconographic similarities. Criticism and history have also been guided by a desire to impute authorship of the entertainment film to the director, screenwriter, cinematographer and studio. Such surface readings of film have ignored code, and more formal organizations of the narrative film. Clearly the film historian has not established the historiographical tools to embrace the avant-garde film and the modernist ambition.

It is in the context of these general historiographical problems that we now turn to some specific manifestations of historical and/or critical methods. One such approach is the "auteur theory," which locates authorship of the Hollywood film with the director. Originally promulgated as the *politique des auteurs* in France, the auteur theory was articulated in this country by Andrew Sarris "not so much a theory as an attitude, a table of values that converts film history into directorial autobiography,"[4] as Sarris has written in *The American Cinema.* As directorial autobiography of the Hollywood movie, the auteur theory has served as a model for approaches to such films through the screenwriter, cinematographer and others, and has had an enormous impact on the writing of film history and criticism. As effective as it has been in revealing certain subtleties of the narrative film, the auteur theory has excluded the avant-garde film. The avant-garde is considered in terms of whether it has anything to offer the "movies," and it is defined in terms of content—" . . . [the avant-garde] impulses seem to be channeled toward the shattering of content taboos, political, religious, and sexual . . . "[5] Thus are the formal and aesthetic concerns of the avant-garde dismissed as they cannot be handled by the vocabulary established for evaluating the Hollywood entertainment film.

Some writers have attempted to probe more deeply into the nature of film on a theoretical level, but have been guided, and limited, by certain assumptions regarding the relationship between film and photography and, by implication, between film and "reality." Siegfried Kracauer, for example, considers film "a redemption of physical reality." Kracauer writes in his preface to *Theory of Film* that he is "concerned with content. It rests upon the assumption that film is essentially an extension of photography and therefore shares with this medium a marked affinity for the visible world around us. Films come into their own when they record and reveal physical reality."[6] This model of film sees its ultimate achievement in the narrative code of neo-realism and the documentary ideal of Robert Flaherty and cinema-verité.

Similar thinking informed the writing of art historian Erwin Panofsky on *The Cabinet of Dr. Caligari*, a highly stylized work emanating from Berlin and heavily influenced by German Expressionism. Panofsky attacked the film for its artificiality and "pre-stylizing of reality" and saw the fruitful potential of film "in the problem of manipulating and shooting unstylized reality in such a way that the result has style."[7]

Stanley Cavell, Professor of Philosophy and Aesthetics at Harvard University and author of *Must We Mean What We Say?*, attempts in his recent book *The World Viewed: Reflections on the Ontology of Film,* to develop a theoretical interpretation of film which, however carefully worked out, presupposes the relationship of film to reality via photography:

> The material basis of the media of movies (as paint on a flat delimited support is the material basis of the media of painting) is, in the terms which have so far made their appearance, *a succession of automatic world projections.* "Succession" includes the various degrees of motion in moving pictures: the motion depicted; the current of successive frames in depicting it; the juxtapositions of cutting. "Automatic" emphasizes the mechanical fact of photography, in particular the absence of the human hand in forming these objects and the absence of its creatures in their screening. "World" covers the ontological facts of photography and its subjects. "Projection" points to the phenomenological facts of the viewing, and to the continuity of the camera's motion as it ingests the world.[8]

The "absence of the human hand" which Cavell feels characterizes the art and ontology of film ignores the avant-garde's exploration of the materials, processes and properties of the film medium. Avant-garde film has, indeed, revealed the artist's hand, much as contemporary painting, for example, has revealed the materials and exposed and reflected upon traditional supports for imagery. In fact, the avant-garde has demonstrated that a film need not have frames, that it may bypass altogether the photographic process, that it may not have as its subject the "world" as Cavell uses that term, and that it may involve viewing situations which do not utilize the conventional projection process.

"A photograph is *of* the world," according to Cavell, and the fact "that the projected world does not exist (now) is its only distance from reality."[9] He adds that the function of photography is to "maintain the presentness of the world by accepting our absence from it." He sees this, by extension, as the basis of the film experience. We have here a "kind of explanation" implicit in many of the narratives of film history, the organization of that history around its relation to photography and to society as a mass entertainment art untouched by the "elitism" of the theatre and other arts. The chaos of the outside world which the historian organizes and interprets is precisely what the film historian perceives of film as doing—as distancing the outside world on the screen through narrative forms and traditions preserving and ordering it. Thus, traditional film historians and theoreticians and filmmakers support and inform each other's work in a common view of film.

In recent years, the French and Anglo-American structuralists have made significant contributions to the methodology of film analysis, but primarily with reference to the narrative film.[10] They have attempted to establish causal relationships between society/culture and the content of movies as mediated by the motion picture industry. Theirs is a view of film as mass entertainment having an investment in the status quo. But as Annette Michelson has argued in her essay *Art and the Structuralist Perspective,*[11] structuralism's basis in structural linguistics and Levi-Strauss' structural anthropology has not equipped it to deal with certain advanced art, particularly work, the experience of which cannot be grasped outside of operational time and space.

Structuralism attempts to locate the "universals," the "distinctive features," common to all of man's social and cultural expressions. In order to locate the distinctive features of film, the structuralist has modeled his approach on that of linguistics, which offers the model of linear, narrative forms. Even while the previous rigidity in terms of the linguistic model is loosening, the avant-garde film and its non-narrative structures are beyond the methodology of most structuralist theory. The most fruitful area of linguistic-based theory appears to be semiology, which is concerned with the definition of image/signs and cinematographic codes. The definition of narrative codes on all levels of the image-message would appear to offer informative contrast to the forms of the non-narrative film.

However, the confusion which has been created in structuralist criticism and theory in terms of the avant-garde is illustrated in the following exchange between the editor of *Screen* magazine, a British journal concerned with structuralist theory and criticism, and filmmakers Peter Wollen and Laura Mulvey:

Screen: Nevertheless, the importance of language and the way it is used in your film is very different from the kind of irrational, mythic overtones of the Anglo/Saxon avant-gardes, such as Sharits, Wieland, Frampton, and so on. I see your film as closer to a materialist conception of language such as, e.g., modern French theories of writing.

Wollen: That's an absolutely false characterization of those films. For instance, Hollis Frampton's *Zorns Lemma* (1971) is based on mathematical transformations in relation to the alphabet . . .

Screen:	Which again comes from mysticism and the Kabbala.
Wollen:	But by that token, Kabbalism is also very strong, e.g., in Robbe-Grillet. . . . I see *Zorns Lemma* on the Straub side of the interface rather than the Brakhage side. Though it does have a neoplatonist aspect concerning light.
Screen:	Maybe we should talk about that some other time. [12]

The films under discussion appear "irrational" when language and image sequencing are evaluated and grounded in traditional semantic/information/communication capacities and within the parameters of syntactical rules.

The writing of film's history generally presents a development from the experiments with successive motion to the theatrical tableaus and gestures of the first story films to a gradually evolving standardization (grammar) of editing, camera movement, compositions, lighting and shots. The cinema evolved through the work of D. W. Griffith, Thomas Ince, Erich von Stroheim, F. W. Murnau, and Orson Welles, a complex of styles and strategies used to explicate what the historian and critic see as a series of world views, or narrative organizations, in which subject/content and photography serve as the basis. The successive phases in the history of the world's cinema are taken as a loosening of the techniques of filmmaking and story-telling from the restraints of theatrical models to seeking allegiance to the predominant traditional literature and, to a much larger extent, and primarily in Europe, to the modernist novel and criticism. Film is not permitted, in this view, to transcend the narrative model of traditional literary forms but must instead carry on the tradition of the popular novel. Those achievements of the world's cinema which are revolutionary in their conscious appraisal and reformulation of the materials of film, such as the Soviet cinema in the 1920's and particularly the films of Dziga Vertov, and the American avant-garde are traditionally viewed as anti-humanistic and "unproductive" in their approach. The assumption is that there is a norm which does not question the procedures of filmmaking and which is congruent with a cultural and ideological order, and, further, that this norm must be preserved.

The radical approaches in recent years to performance, dance, painting, sculpture and film reveal an eclectic attitude toward the arts in which forms and expectations are broken down and reconstituted. This situation has been considered in the writing and teaching of Annette Michelson, whose efforts, based on phenomenological models and modernist concerns, constitute an important revision in thinking about film. In her writing, the perceptual coordinates of the creating and viewing experience are related to abstract expressionism, minimal and post-minimal painting and sculpture, the art and ideas of Marcel Duchamp, the music and writing of John Cage and Pierre Boulez, the theater of Richard Foreman, the performance/dance of Yvonne Rainer, the philosophical writings of Jean-Paul Sartre, Maurice Merleau-Ponty, Edmund Husserl, and Jean Piaget, among others. Her work has included a restitution of the revolutionary Soviet cinema, in particular the work of Dziga Vertov, and an approach to traditional film aesthetics and criticism informed by modernism and the American avant-garde film.

An example of Michelson's approach to traditional film aesthetics and criticism is her perceptive reading of the French theoretician André Bazin, one of the most influential writers on film. As co-editor of *Cahiers du Cinema,* he had a seminal influence on the thinking of the directors of

the French "New Wave" (Godard, Resnais, Francois Truffaut, Claude Chabrol, et. al.). Bazin's ontology of film posited a "seamless" image, a cinema which could enclose in its frame a world view of order confirmed by the realism implicit in photography. Thus Bazin became a champion of Erich von Stroheim's detailed and ambitious aspirations of re-creation and of veracity-through-art of the Italian neo-realists:

> More fundamentally . . . Bazin was unable to accept the modernist questioning of an external "reality" or "order" as such and their restitution within the framework of the work of art itself. Prompted, no doubt, by Sartre's rejection of the artist-as-god, developed in essays on Mauriac, he proposes as models of cinematic "authenticity" both Murnau, "who composed his images without montage, revealing its structural depth without in any way cheating" and von Stroheim, who rejected "photographic expressionism and the tricks of montage."[13]

Michelson is addressing an ontology of film which sees the medium as sustaining an illusion of reality through an "uncorrupted" cinematic (photographic) ideal. In another article, Michelson discusses Bazin and Eisenstein as the creators of two cinematic ontologies—"Bazin positing the response to spatio-temporal continuity of neo-realism as that of the existential freedom viewed as choosing in ambiguity, Eisenstein offering to his spectators the experience of revolutionary consciousness unfolding in the apprehension of the dialectic." Bazin and Eisenstein join "in common recognition of the cognitive experience as central to the strategies and ends of art" and offer, at the same, "the terms of a debate on the *politics of illusion.*" Michelson goes on to state the problem faced by the avant-garde in the face of Bazin's ontology:

> For someone like myself, working as an art critic during the late 50's and early 60's, Bazin's taste and theory tended to sever film from the modernist tradition; his allegiance to the notion of film as only and irretrievably a "mass medium" effected a breach between one's experiences and expectations of the work of advanced painters and musicians on the one hand, and of the filmmakers on the other. He had, in his filmic ontology, precluded the interest and the development of processes of abstraction, of reflectiveness and the critical examination, by and through the art itself, of the terms of its illusionism. All this was unacceptable.[14]

The avant-garde film addresses the "material discontinuities attendant upon the filmic process"[15] and thus subverts the dominant codes which assumes linearity and spatio-temporal cohesiveness and traditional narrative structures. Daguerre's first photographs of the streets of Paris, which were a precursor to Eugene Atget and the surrealists, serve as a metaphor for the elusive nature of film. The first photographs by Daguerre showed Paris streets empty of people except for one in which a man is frozen in time. He held still to have his shoes polished, and so unconsciously preserved his image while everyone else disappeared from the film stock which was not fast enough to preserve movement. The view in that photograph appears as an ordinary world view, but inspection leads us to realize that the people filling the streets are there, but not there, on celluloid.[16] This implicit manifestation of the properties of the photographic process, properties which embrace far more than an ordered

and cohesive world view, was also evident in the earliest cinema. Noël Burch and Jorge Dana have written:

> We believe it can be shown that the pre-Griffith period of cinema contained a potential for non-linearity which is often perceptibly manifest: "uncentered" tableau shots in Lumière, "mobile" close-ups in *The Great Train Robbery*, "a-chronological" editing in *The Life of an American Fireman*—both by Porter—, acknowledgement of the depth-illusion in the films of Méliès.[17]

It is the implications of the Daguerre photograph and of the early films discussed by Burch and Dana which have been largely ignored in mainstream film criticism and history but which have informed the work and thinking of avant-garde filmmakers.

The History of the American Avant-Garde Film: Origins and Models

The precursors and models of the American avant-garde film are the avant-garde films produced in Europe during the 1920's and 1930's and the cinema of the Soviet Union produced in the late 1920's. Made by artists who, for the most part, had reputations in other media, the films were independent productions created outside the ascending mainstream of commercial film production and distribution. The European avant-garde demonstrated how the tenets and strategies of modernist art could be re-articulated in the medium of film. As Standish Lawder has written in *The Cubist Cinema:*

> The avant-garde film movement of the twenties is that chapter in the history of film created, for the most part, by painters and poets whose principal medium of expression was not film. Their films were non-commercial undertakings, and usually non-narrative in form. Through the medium of film, they sought to give concrete plastic shape to inner visions rather than manipulate images of external reality for dramatic effect. In its broadest outlines, the avant-garde film movement followed a course similar to modern painting in the twenties, that is, from a rigorously geometric and abstract style, as in De Stijl or Bauhaus aesthetic, to the hallucinatory content of surrealism in the late twenties.[18]

These filmmakers were concerned with the properties of filmic movement, editing, and the fantastic juxtapositions and gestalts that could be created through manipulation of photography or the graphic animation of abstract forms. Such films as Robert Wiene's *Das Cabinet des Dr. Caligari* (*The Cabinet of Dr. Caligari*) (1920); Fernand Leger's *Ballet Mechanique* (1924); Hans Richter's *Rhythmus 21* (1921); and Luis Buñuel and Salvador Dali's *Un Chien Andalou* (1929) reflect the diversity of concerns in the European avant-garde films and point to the variety of forms which would be manifested in the American avant-garde.

Unlike the other films under discussion here, *The Cabinet of Dr. Caligari* is a studio-made film. However, it has become associated with, and has had considerable impact upon, the avant-garde. The influence of German Expressionism is apparent in the stylized decor and distortion of perspective, in the exaggerated gestures of the actors' characterizations, and in the scenario of dreams and madness. *The Cabinet of Dr. Caligari* is

Ballet Mechanique by Fernand Leger

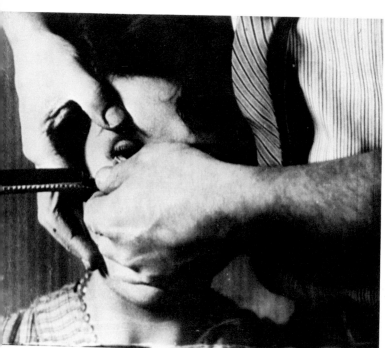

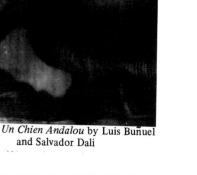

Un Chien Andalou by Luis Buñuel
and Salvador Dali

largely a static film whose expressiveness is based on the artificial expressionism of the theatre. In this regard, it was criticized by Erwin Panofsky, as noted earlier, but the film served as a model for the early American avant-garde, with the figure of Cesar the somnambulist anticipating what P. Adams Sitney calls the "Trance" film. Moreover, the very theatricality of the film helped subvert the traditional notion of the "illusion of continuity," and marked it as a radical work warranting attention within the avant-garde.

Ballet Mechanique is an independently made avant-garde film which comes directly out of Leger's concerns in painting, particularly from his "mechanical" period of 1920-24. As an artist, Leger was involved with the issues of cubism, and was developing his work along a theory, the subject of which was the examination of vision. The film's preoccupation with edited rhythms and its explorations of filmic space were joined by, as Sitney writes, "the rapid intercutting of static scenes to give the impression of motion—a hat stretched out to a shoe or a triangle jumping into the shape of a circle—and perhaps the very first to combine fragments of actual motion into purely rhythmic figures."[19] It also utilizes the printed text, as did cubist painting, to generate a specific temporal and perceptual operation—the perception of flat letters and of language—within the edited rhythms of juxtapositions and metaphoric extensions of objects and mechanics. *Ballet Mechanique* demonstrated that abstraction can be derived from ordinary objects through perceptual and rhythmic ordering of objects in a manner determined by the film itself, rather than by properties of the objects. The film exists outside the traditional narrative and formal concerns of cinema.

As a painter, Hans Richter was involved with cubism and expressionism, and a preoccupation with volumes and solids, colors and shapes, was to inform his film work. Like all his films, *Rhythmus 21* is an abstract composition, of which the content was "essentially rhythm, the formal vocabulary was elemental geometry, the structural principle was the counterpoint of contrasting opposites, and in which space and time became interdependent."[20] The legacy of Richter's cinema for the animated, graphic film of the American avant-garde was a concern with the materials of animation based on the abstraction of shapes and movement joined in rhythms. Richter's is a non-narrative animation—not a cartoon—which composes in time within the spatial coordinates of the screen and the ambiguity/illusion of film space.

Rooted in surrealism and dadaism, *Un Chien Andalou* by Luis Buñuel and Salvador Dali is a film of free-association and discordant juxtapositions working with and against the traditional expectations of the viewer. The linear sequencing of outrageous images was calculated to confront film's presumed verification of reality. The images and their ordering verify instead the "unconscious" world of Freud and of dreams. It is a view into dreams without a dreamer, a plunge into a narrative with familiar structure but without familiar meanings. Unlike *Rhythmus 21* or *Ballet Mechanique*, *Un Chien Andalou* is not rooted in the abstraction of images or in their creation; and unlike *The Cabinet of Dr. Caligari,* its images are located in a real (familiar) world of streets and people, not an artificial one.

The Soviet cinema as represented by Sergei Eisenstein and Dziga Vertov entered into a dialogue with the European avant-garde film through mutual influence and a shared concern with the expressive potential of the medium of film. Eisenstein's importance in a consideration of the avant-garde resides in his films (*Potemkin* was a favorite of the surrealists)

and in his theoretical writings, which elaborated his ideas about editing (montage), composition, and a range of other basic issues. Standish Lawder discusses an interesting and remarkable passage from Eisenstein's film *Old and New*, which indicates the possible influence of the European avant-garde on the Soviet director:

> It is tempting to see in Eisenstein's *Old and New* of 1929 certain echoes of . . . *Ballet Mechanique.* In the cream separator scene, for instance, the patterns of machinery in motion—seen through the eyes of the skeptical peasants who ask, "Will it work?"—are transformed into a dazzling arabesque of light playing on metallic surfaces. Even closer to the spirit of . . . Leger is the freedom with which Eisenstein edited this visually sensuous passage, for intercut with these poetic images are spectacular shots of pirouetting shafts of light which, on closer inspection, can be seen to be nothing more than a spinning bicycle wheel! This passage in Eisenstein's film is by far the most abstract he ever made, and quite likely he was stimulated to experiment along these lines by the European avant-garde films that Ehrenburg had shown him in 1926.[21]

It is important to remember, however, that for Eisenstein abstract imagery was used only in service of the narrative, not as an end in itself.

Dziga Vertov's *The Man with the Movie Camera* is on one level a day in the life of a Soviet cameraman. The film shows him at work, experimenting with his equipment and creating a dialectic between his experience and the medium of film. The viewer witnesses the procedures of filming, processing, editing and projecting the film. The very complexity of the work in terms of editing, idea and ideology plots an ontology of film through its self-referential strategies. Vertov's film is especially important in discussion of the avant-garde film since it came out of Soviet Russia at a time when the interaction among artists working in all media comprised a euphoria of exploration. Constructivism in painting and sculpture and formalism in literary theory bracket an aesthetic and a context in which the artists worked. Constructivism's abstraction, employment of materials, and activization of space, and formalism's examination of literary texts in formal and structural terms, influenced the Soviet cinema. Thus Vertov's film was created in a context of change, in which process and method were part of the social and aesthetic/artistic enterprise. The radical Soviet cinema is similar to the avant-garde film of Europe in the 1920's and of America in the 1940's and later insofar as it operated within contexts of modernism and radical ambitions.

In a seminal appreciation of *The Man with the Movie Camera,* Annette Michelson writes:

> . . . . If the filmmaker is, like the magician, a manufacturer of illusions, he can, unlike the prestidigator and in the interests of instruction of a heightening of consciousness, destroy illusion by that other transcendentally magical procedure, the reversal of time by the inversion of action. He can develop, as it were, "the negative of time" for "the communist decoding of reality." This thematic interplay of magic, illusion, labor, filmic techniques and strategy, articulating a theory of film as epistemological inquiry is the complex central core around which Vertov's greatest work develops[22]. . . . In a sense most subtle and complex, he was, Bazin to the contrary, one of those directors

"who put their faith in the image;" that faith was, however, accorded to the image seen, recognized as an image and the condition of that faith or recognition, the consciousness, the subversion through consciousness, of cinematic illusionism.[23]

The European avant-garde directly confronted the medium of film by engaging the issues of its illusionism and its temporal and material qualities while affirming a source in, but distance from, the iconography of the popular entertainment film, especially comedy and melodrama (e.g. the surrealists' enthusiasm for the comedies of Chaplin and the serial adventures of the French director Louis Feuillades). This at once serious and playful/anarchic attitude signified a liberation from the traditional, academic culture at a time when the arts were undergoing a radical change. However, outside the cineclubs and special expositions the films were little shown, and they were seldom presented in a gallery or museum context, which might have affirmed their origins in the other arts and thereby validated and encouraged the aesthetic issues they raised. Failing to affirm a world view congruent with that of film historians, critics, and general viewers, the avant-garde films of the 1920's became curiosities in the film histories and problems in some film theories, as evidenced in the following footnote by Stanley Cavell on the French avant-garde:

Dadaists and surrealists found in film a direct confirmation of their ideologies or sensibilities, particularly in film's massive capacities for nostalgia and free juxtaposition. This confirmation is, I gather, sometimes taken to mean that dadaist and surrealist films constitute the *avant-garde* of filmmaking. It might equally be taken to show why film made these movements obsolete, as the world has. One might say: Nothing is more surrealist than the ordinary events of the modern world; and nothing less reveals that fact than a surrealist attitude. This says nothing about the value of particular surrealist films, which must succeed or fail on the same terms as others.[24]

This passage makes quite clear the author's inability to establish access to the formal innovation of the films under consideration or to separate them from the narrative traditions, to say nothing of the fact that art critics and historians might dispute the obsolescence of a movement like dadaism, which has profoundly influenced recent art. On the other hand, Annette Michelson's "rediscovery" of Vertov and the placement of his achievement within a modernist context, and her efforts to bring the European and American avant-garde into an aesthetic discussion in the pages of an art journal (*Artforum*) have been among the most significant developments in recent thinking on film.

The history of the American avant-garde film begins in the early 1940's. Hans Richter and many compatriots in the other arts left Europe during the second world war and came to the United States, where they played an important role in this country's cultural life. Their influence was most visible in screenings of their and other avant-garde films given at film societies such as *Cinema 16* in New York and *Art in Cinema* in San Francisco. These screenings were attended by the new generation of filmmakers. In addition, writings on and by these filmmakers appeared alongside the criticism and manifestoes of the emerging avant-garde in *Film Culture* magazine, which became, in the late 1950's, the house organ of the independent, New American cinema. The emergence of the avant-garde in film in this country is in part a function of the larger shift of the center of artistic activity from Europe to the United States during and after World War II.

A determining factor in the development of the avant-garde film was the nature of the motion picture industry in Hollywood, which excluded individuals wishing to make films outside the parameters set by the commercial cinema's tradition of production and distribution. Because the economics of 35mm production were prohibitive of creative experimentation, artists turned to the increasingly available 16mm film and equipment format. Relatively inexpensive 16mm production developed in the 1940's, 1950's, and 1960's into increasingly portable cameras and improved film, both of which permitted a greater range of situations in which to develop imagery. The portability of 16mm equipment encouraged its private use by artists who shared it with others who sought to liberate their visions and ideas through the manipulation of the camera apparatus, lenses and celluloid.

The freeing of the avant-garde filmmaker from the constraints of tradition and functionalism can be traced through each of the seven programs being presented here. They have been organized chronologically to offer a continuing history while at the same time containing within each the diversity of concerns being expressed at the time. After a decade of activity, the American avant-garde filmmakers realized that financial support and public recognition would not be forthcoming as they had been for the other arts. Museums and art galleries virtually ignored this cinema, as film did not appear to function within the economics of collecting and its attendant support system of galleries, museums, and critical journals. In the absence of assistance from private foundations, the film industry and the art marketplace, filmmakers were left to their own collective efforts and individual perseverance. The *New York Film-Makers' Cooperative* was established in 1962, seven years after the founding of *Film Culture* magazine. Both were initiated and greatly aided by the efforts of Jonas Mekas. *Film Culture*'s position viz a viz the avant-garde shifted from a generally European orientation and critical approach to the avant-garde to a full embrace of the independent film in the late 1950's. Mekas, whose vision and enthusiasm for the avant-garde constitute the single most important force in its recognition and support, began a weekly column in the *Village Voice* (New York) entitled "Movie Journal." In that enormously and internationally influential forum he voiced a passionate declaration of the achievements of the avant-garde.

Cooperatives, which are non-profit operations run by the filmmakers themselves, sprang up around the country and offered outlets for the independent film. The filmmaker's control over his/her film extended to selection of copy used in the catalogues to describe the films, and monitoring of the condition of the prints. The cooperatives remain the major distributors of the avant-garde film. The traditional, non-theatrical distributor has not been able to "market" the work of the avant-garde except when a particular film or filmmaker enjoys a large reputation.

The proliferation of courses and degrees in film production and appreciation in colleges and universities is a recent development in American education. The support of the avant-garde filmmaker in the academy as an instructor and artist-in-residence is another recent and welcome sign of the infusion of new ideas into the film curriculum. (The brilliant but all-too-brief exception in the early years of the avant-garde was the San Francisco Art Institute and the efforts of Sidney Peterson, who produced, with his students, a series of films, including *The Lead Shoes* (1949), which is being presented in the second program.)

New York and San Francisco have been the traditional centers for independent filmmaking, with a number of filmmakers organizing themselves in both cities around film societies and cooperatives. New York's cultural ties to Europe and its central position in post-war American art and intellectual life made it a natural place for the film artist to settle. The presence of critics and museums led to growing support for the medium through historical appreciation and exhibition, and sustained an avant-garde in film that was linked to contemporary achievements in painting, sculpture, performance and criticism. In San Francisco, the influence of Eastern ideas and philosophy and the less urban situation of the Pacific coast resulted in a more freewheeling film with its imagery and editing rooted in eastern iconography and western surrealism.

It was not until 1974 that a history of the avant-garde film was written which attempted to organize and interpret its development—P. Adams Sitney's *Visionary Film.* As critic and teacher, Sitney has been an influential voice in the development of the avant-garde. He serves on the Board of New York's Anthology Film Archives, whose archival and exhibition program is performing the essential function of lending focus to the history of the avant-garde film and linking its traditions to the cinemas of Europe and other countries through its exhibition and research programs.

In his introduction to the *Film Culture Reader,* which he edited, Sitney offers some comments on the history of the avant-garde film: "Avant-garde filmmaking in the United States has never been a movement; the individualism of the artists prevented that. Yet there have been collective drifts, general tendencies (always with contemporary exceptions, of course), around which the film historian can structure his observations." [25] While the writing of history is seldom so simple, Sitney's reading of the early history of the American avant-garde film does reveal the cohesiveness of tendencies shared by filmmakers at various points in time. In his book *Visionary Film,* Sitney seeks out the "visionary strain within the complex manifold of the avant-garde." He sets out a series of terms (Trance film, mythopoeic, Structural, and Participatory) to describe a historical morphology of the avant-garde film. Sitney offers that:

> Just as the chief works of French film theory must be seen in the light of Cubism and Surrealist thought, and Soviet theory in the context of formalism and constructivism, the preoccupations of the American avant-garde filmmakers coincide with those of our Post-Romantic poets and Abstract Expressionist painters. Behind them lies a potent tradition of Romantic poetics. Wherever possible, both in my interpretation of films and discussion of theory, I have attempted to trace the history of Romanticism. I have found this approach consistently more useful and more generative of a unified view of these films and film-makers than the Freudian hermenutics and sexual analyses which have dominated much of the previous criticism of the avant-garde. [26]

The historical patterns which Sitney saw emerge are presented as confirmation of a visionary strain in the avant-garde film.

In the *Film Culture Reader* Sitney posits a distinction between the "graphic" and "subjective" film. The graphic film evolved more "calmly" than the subjective:

> After the initial exploration of the flat surface and the hard-edge forms, the graphic was vitalized by the development of the hand-painted film and quite recently has entered the area of imagery generated by computers and electrically modified (through television tape). The appearance of the flicker film (black and white or pure color alternations) bridges the division between animated and directly photographed film by its critical reduction of both to a common atomism.[27]

The subjective film dates from the 1940's, when the filmmaker often played a central role in heavily symbolic visual contexts. These early films were like dreams, or dream-like states, reflecting the cultural influence of Freud. Sitney sees a shift away from the Freudian base to a Jungian one, from the psychodrama to the mythopoeic epic. The single somnambulistic "Trance" figure yielded to multiple characters with mythic personae.

Greater attention was given to editing and flat and literal symbolic codes gave way to more complex formal strategies. Within this line of development are the picaresque films, based on the psychodrama and distinguished by an anarchic sensibility and by humor and sexual fantasy. There also developed the lyrical film in which the field of vision became the subject of the film, to the total exclusion of actors. More recent developments are the directly self-referential diary film and the "structural" film, the latter concerned with filmic space and the screen surface as mediated by temporal distensions.

This brief outline of Sitney's history does not do justice to his thesis. His reading of the Trance and Mythopoeic and Lyrical films of Maya Deren, Kenneth Anger, Stan Brakhage, Bruce Baillie, Sidney Peterson, James Broughton, Gregory Markopoulos, and the animated (graphic) films of Harry Smith and Robert Breer, to name but a few, are perceptive. His situating this cinema within a modernist context has informed some excellent interpretations of films and of relationships between the arts, most effectively with reference to the earlier films. *Visionary Film* also posits a Romantic notion of the filmmaker/artist and places the film enterprise within the broader Romantic trend of contemporary art. Art historian Edward Fry has elaborated on the "privateness of the modern tradition" in a catalogue for an exhibition of environmental works titled *Projects in Nature:*

> The privateness of the modern tradition as a whole is coeval with supremacy of Romanticism since the early nineteenth century . . . even so supposedly public a statement as *Guernica* is predicated on Picasso's private concerns and mythologies. The privateness of the romantic heritage, successfully challenging the public traditions of classicism and the academies of the state has governed the aspirations of culture for the past 150 years, during a period when the Protestant nations of northern Europe were also creating the social structures of industrial capitalism. Modern northern romantic culture is the exact analogue of those structures, a culture created of, by and for an alienated and disaffected segment of their middle classes. The only subject of the northern romantic tradition is of course nature; or more specifically, the response of the individual to both external nature and

the "Nature" within himself. It is a totally private matter, the partial recompense available to the alienated individual within an alienating social structure. If we thus conjoin the privateness of the modern tradition, the virtual identity of that tradition with Romanticism, and the intensification of romantic individualism in American life; and if we add to these elements the romantic, and subsequently liberal, view of history as dynamic, evolutionary, and self-critical; we will have a partially adequate framework for understanding the recent activities of artists . . . .[28]

Fry's statement sheds some interesting light on the avant-garde film and on Sitney's interpretation of its history, particularly the privateness of the filmmakers' experience, and the intensity of the films which they project onto the world while at the same time absorbing that world through their art. Sitney's application to this experience of literary and Romantic "Visionary" qualities, led to a subtle reading of the Lyric and Mythopoeic forms and ambitions, but found greater difficulty in dealing with the "structural" film, which he characterizes as "a cinema of structure in which the shape of the whole film is predetermined and simplified, that is, that shape which is the primal impression of the film."[29] He writes:

> In the elaborate chain of cycles and epicycles which constitutes the history of the American avant-garde film the Symbolist aesthetic which animates the films and theories of Maya Deren returns, with a radically different emphasis, in the structural cinema. Although dream and ritual had been the focus of her attention, she advocated a chastening of the moment of inspiration and a conquest of the unconscious, a process she associated with Classicism. The filmmakers who followed her pursued the metaphors of dream and ritual by which she had defined the avant-garde cinema, but they allowed a Romantic faith in the triumph of the imagination to determine their forms from within. From this aesthetic submission grew the trance and mythopoeic film. When the structural cinema repudiated that credo that film aspires to the condition of dream or myth, it returned to the Symbolist aesthetic that Deren had defined, and in finding new metaphors for the cinematic experience with which to shape films, it reversed the earlier process so that a new imagery arose from the dictates of the form.[30]

The shape of the structural film is "simplified" only if other imagery is by definition more complex. Predetermination of form does not determine complexity or simplicity of image. A more suitable context in which to consider the structural film is that of epistemological inquiry. The structural film implies that perception is the primary process by which the world is known. The films draw attention to themselves, as in Andy Warhol's *Empire*, which stares for twelve hours at the Empire State Building, and to the activity of perceiving through a camera and on a screen. The complexity of the structural film lies in its modulation of a condition where perception and cognition are interactive on the level of film's ontology in representing the materials and experience of viewing film. It acts upon the viewer by asserting the congruence of the perception of itself and learning.

> If cinema is to take its place beside the others as a full-fledged art form, it must cease merely to record realities that owe nothing of

their actual existence to the film instrument. Instead, it must create a total experience so much out of the very nature of the instrument as to be inseparable from its means.[31]

Deren's comment places film firmly within the modernist context of new forms and materials in the other arts. The work of artists such as Robert Morris, Carl Andre, and Frank Stella challenges traditional visual conditions and the traditional basis of art in craft and a limited range of materials and activities. Andre and Morris' sculpture engages materials through the manipulation of spatial and iconographic distinctions and properties. Stella's paintings explore surface through geometric abstraction and the interaction of color. The structural film bears a relationship to the recent ideas and activities in the other arts and a consideration of that art's achievement reflects on the history of the avant-garde film and will, hopefully, offer new access to it and our perception of it.

The Broken Mirror: Materials And Oppositions

Cinema is a Greek word that means "movie". The illusion of movement is certainly an accustomed adjunct of the film image but that illusion rests upon the assumption that the rate of change between successive frames may vary only within rather narrow limits. There is nothing in the structural logic of the filmstrip that can justify such an assumption. Therefore we reject it. From now on we will call our art simply: film. (Hollis Frampton)[32]

To tell a story has become strictly impossible. Yet it is wrong to claim nothing happens any longer in modern novels. Just as we must not assume man's absence on the pretext that the traditional character has disappeared, we must not identify the search for new narrative structures with the attempt to stress any event, any passion, any adventure. (Alain Robbe-Grillet)[33]

The avant-garde film has been presented here as addressing itself to the history and materials of film, and to the process of its own perception. In recent years, the avant-garde has enjoyed increased recognition of its accomplishments, with filmmakers presenting new works in gallery and museum contexts as well as in traditional theatrical situations. The work of Paul Sharits, Tony Conrad and Anthony McCall indicates some directions in which the avant-garde is now moving.

Sharits' "locational" pieces utilize a number of projected images aligned in a gallery space to create tensions between them. Continuous projections, they break down the traditional coordinates of an auditorium with the screen on stage and the film experience having a defined beginning, middle, and end.

Nothing is timeless but its an idea that haunts us . . . something that exists in my own work. In one way, all we know is now . . . The work must be experienced in terms of its material presence. The tense of memory is the present, and the tense of prophesy is now. Time is an illusion. The now is inescapable. (Carl Andre)[34]

Sharits' "locational" pieces offer the material presence of film in a continuous, non-narrative, multi-screen situation in which time is experienced as continuous presentness. Sharits also exhibits strips of film between

Synchronousoundtracks by Paul
Sharits

Film Sukiyaki by Tony Conrad

42

plexiglas, again presenting the materials of film but in such a way that they can be analysed, frozen in time. One comes face to face with the substance of celluloid, and one also discovers the overall composition of the film.[35]

At the Walker Art Center (Minneapolis) in 1974, Tony Conrad presented an evening of film projects and events that included a display of film strips being pickled in mason jars; the actual projection of films which had previously been cooked as part of a recipe; the preparation of a dish on stage followed by the projection (throwing) of the cooked film onto the screen; and the presentation of a continuous four-projector installation of film loops consisting of abstract images accompanied by taped musical compositions. Conrad's performance/presentation orchestrated an awareness of what film is—a celluloid material—by creating a series of metaphors for the production and projection of film. Throughout the evening the audience could examine and handle the film.

In his film *Line Describing a Cone,* Anthony McCall deals with the perception of projected light. A projector is placed in a gallery and against a wall is projected a gradually inscribed circle which creates between the projector and wall a cone of light which the audience can "touch," and through and about which it can move. In this instance, the film is perceived not only as a projected image, but also as a projected beam of light, capable of enclosing and defining actual space.

The avant-garde continues to explore the physical properties of film, and the nature of the perceptual transaction which takes place between viewer and film. It challenges theories of film which posit as its basis its photographic/illusionistic/representational properties. The traditional coordinates of film/screen/projection are being questioned by "artists who have denied the material and analytical basis of this judgment, not by ideology, but by materiality itself. Such paintings [films] do not lend themselves to this kind of physical analysis of the object, but to a gestural analysis of the art activity per se."[36] Thus the materials, activities, and properties with which Sharits, Conrad and McCall are concerned transgress the familiar limits of the film-viewing situation. In light of this, it is interesting to read Ken Jacobs describing his reaction to seeing Joseph Cornell's film *Rose Hobart,* which he borrowed to show Jack Smith:

> I was seeing Jack again and I told him, "Jack, you've got to see this movie." We looked at it again and again, and we were both knocked out. Jack tried to act at first like a little bit removed, like I was overstating it, and then he broke down and said, "No, it's very good." We looked at it in every possible way: on the ceiling, in mirrors, bouncing it all over the room, in corners, in focus, out of focus, with a blue filter that Cornell had given me, without it, backwards . . .[37]

This playful approach to projection, the tactile involvement with projector and film, create a performance metaphor for Jacobs' *Tom, Tom, the Piper's Son* (1969), which "experiences" an early American film through various analytic strategies which re-choreograph the original film's action.

When discussing new art it is important not to use a "vocabulary derived from the old position."[38] Take, for example, the question of time. People often react to avant-garde film by saying it is too long. One cannot, or one is not supposed to, walk away from it as one can from a painting. It is to be expected that when a film work is presented in an unfamiliar context one's perception of it is affected by preconditioned ideas and habits. Yet there is nothing in length or running time which is inherently good or bad. One effect of the avant-garde film and the new directions described briefly here has been to open up the medium to new conditions of temporal experience.

In her catalogue essay on the artist Robert Morris, Annette Michelson writes:

> It is, I think, a prime quality of Morris' work that it offers through a series of exploratory enterprises, the terms of a sharpened definition of the nature of the sculptural experience, and that it does so in a manner wholly consistent with a commitment to the secularist impulse and thrust of modernism. I mean by this to suggest its mixture of modesty and ambition. Staking out areas of intensive exploration of the qualities of shape, scale, size, placing, weight, mass, opacity and transparency, visibility and obscurity, this work urges reflection on the present, concrete options of sculpture, as on the general terms and conditions of its perception. Cognitive in its fullest effect, then, rather than "meaningful," its comprehension not only demands time; *it elicits the acknowledgement of temporality as the condition or medium of human cognition and aesthetic experience.*[39]

Michelson's point applies as well to some of the recent concerns and achievements of the avant-garde film.

The avant-garde film, whether consciously or not, organized its output in relation to certain preoccupations in the other arts. The perceiver brings certain expectations to the experience of a work of art. As has been discussed, in film one commonly expects a photographic medium allied to cognitive (cultural and conditioned) assumptions regarding the function of that medium, namely to give order, through narrative forms, and thereby confirm a world view.

The experience of the avant-garde film can be disorienting. Film has only an eighty-year history and so does not exhibit ruptures with dominant codes as does the history of most disciplines, including painting, and physics, among others. One is therefore less prepared for the unfamiliar in film than in other areas. Consider, then, the thesis of Morse Peckham in his book *Man's Rage for Chaos:*

> Man desires above all a predictable and ordered world, a world to which he is oriented, and this is the motivation behind the role of the scientist. But because man desires such a world so passionately, he is very much inclined to ignore anything that intimates that he does not have it. And to anything that disorients him, anything that requires him to experience cognitive tension he ascribes negative value. Only in protected situations characterized by high walls of psychic insulation, can he afford to let himself be aware of the disparity between his interests, that is, his expectancy or set of orientation, and the data his interaction with the environment actually produces . . . Art offers precisely this experience.[40]

The absorption of film by the artist into the modernist and romantic nature of the aesthetic object/experience creates a hermenutics with technology (film). The wresting of film from the public sphere into a highly personal one forces cognitive tensions on the viewer accustomed to the "insular" walls of the confirming experience of traditional film. The resistance to the avant-garde film by the cultural institution, be it a current aesthetic or program, affirms a profound allegiance that film has to an affirmative world view.

> We rehearse for roles all our lives, and for various patterns of behavior. We rehearse our national, our local, and our personal styles. These things we rehearse so that we may participate in a predictable world of social and environmental interaction. But we also must rehearse the power to perceive the failure, the necessary failure, of all those patterns of behavior. Art, as an adaptational mechanism, is reinforcement of the ability to be aware of the disparity between behavioral patterns and the demands consequent upon the interaction of the environment. Art is rehearsal for those real situations in which it is vital for our survival to endure cognitive tension, to refuse the comfort of validation by affective congruence when such validation is inappropriate because too vital interests are at stake; art is the reinforcement of the capacity to endure disorientation so that a real and significant problem can emerge. Art is the exposure to the tensions and problems of a false world so that man may endure exposing himself to the tension and problems of the real world.[41]

It is the power of the avant-garde film to question the "predictable world of social and environmental interaction" through its basis in a recording medium that provides a unique source of tension for the artist, and ultimately for the perceiver, in his/her quest.

Film theory, criticism, and history must meet the challenge to expose the problems of that "false world" with terms posited by the medium itself. Literary, linguistic and mechanistic models are not, exclusive of each other, capable of meeting the challenge. The examination of what film is, formally and structurally, is the first step toward ascertaining what film is as a biological/social experience for the viewer. What vital interests and instincts are at stake in viewing the avant-garde, and all forms, of film? Very real and significant problems can emerge from such a question. It is a question we must ask.

John G. Hanhardt
Guest Curator

Footnotes

1. Marcelin Pleynet. "Debat: Economique, Ideologique, Formel," *Cinethique*, No. 3. Quoted by Annette Michelson in "Screen/Surface: The Politics of Illusionism," *Artforum*, September 1972, p. 62.

2. Hayden White, *Metahistory: The Historical Imagination in Nineteenth Century Europe.* Baltimore: The Johns Hopkins University Press, 1975, p. 13.

3. Ibid., p. 6n.

4. Andrew Sarris. *The American Cinema, Directors and Directions 1929-1968.* New York: E. P. Dutton & Co., Inc., 1968, p. 30.

5. Ibid., p. 23.

6. Siegfried Kracauer. *Theory of Film: The Redemption of Physical Reality*, New York: Oxford University Press, 1965, p. ix.

7. Erwin Panofsky. "Style and Medium in the Moving Pictures," in *Film: An Anthology*, Compiled and Edited by Daniel Talbot, Berkeley and Los Angeles: University of California Press, 1967, p. 32.

8. Stanley Cavell. *The World Viewed, Reflections on the Ontology of Film*, New York: The Viking Press, 1971, pp. 72–73. For two informative reviews of Cavell's book see: Noel Carrol, "Books Reviewed," *Film Comment*, January–February, 1973, p. 62; Rosalind Krauss, "Dark Glasses and Bifocals, A Book Review," *Artforum*, May 1974, pp. 59–62.

9. Ibid., p. 24.

10. For an introduction and bibliography on structuralism, semiology and film, see: John Hanhardt and Charles Harpole, "Linguistics, Structuralism, Semiology, Approaches to Cinema, with a bibliography," *Film Comment*, May–June 1973, pp. 52–59.

11. Annette Michelson. "Art and the Structuralist Perspective," *On the Future of Art*, New York: The Viking Press, 1970.

12. *Screen.* Autumn 1974. Cited by Peter Gidal, "Theory and Definition of Structural/Materialist Film." *Studio International*, November/December 1975, p. 194.

13. Annette Michelson. "Book Review," (*What is Cinema?* by André Bazin, edited by Hugh Gray, University of California Press, 1967), *Artforum*, Summer 1968, p. 70.

14. Annette Michelson. "Screen/Surface: The Politics of Illusionism," *Artforum*, September 1972, p. 62.

15. Nöel Burch and Jorge Dana. "Propositions," *Afterimage*, 1975, p. 49.

16. "For, says Brecht, the situation is 'complicated by the fact that less than at any time does a simple *reproduction of reality* tell us anything about reality. A photograph of the Krupp works or GEC yields almost nothing about these institutions. Reality proper has slipped into the functional. The reification of human relationships, the factory, let's say, no longer reveals these relationships. Therefore something actually has to be *constructed*, something artificial, something set up.' It is the achievement of the surrealists to have trained the pioneers of such photographic construction," Walter Benjamin, "A Short History of Photography," *Screen* (London), Spring 1972, p. 24.

17. Burch and Dana. *op. cit.*, p. 65n.

18. Standish D. Lawder. *The Cubist Cinema*, New York; New York University Press, 1975, p. 35.

19. P. Adams Sitney, *Visionary Film, The American Avant-Garde*, New York: Oxford University Press, 1974, p. 314.

20. Lawder. *op. cit.*, p. 52.

21. Ibid., p. 188.

22. Annette Michelson. *"The Man With the Movie Camera:* From Magician to Epistemologist," *Artforum*, March, 1972, p. 66.

23. Ibid., p. 69.

24. Cavell. *op. cit.*, pp. 163–164n.

25. P. Adams Sitney, editor. *Film Culture Reader*, New York: Praeger Publishers, 1970, p. 4.

26. Sitney, *Visionary Film*, p. ix.

27. Sitney, *Film Culture Reader*, p. 5.

28. *Projects in Nature.* Introduction by Edward Fry, Eleven Environmental Works Executed at Marriewold West, Far Hills, New Jersey, New Jersey: Marriewold West, Inc., 1975, n.p.

29. Sitney. *Visionary Film*, p. 407.

30. Ibid., p. 435.

31. Maya Deren. "Cinematography: The Creative Use of Reality," *Daedalus*, Winter 1960, p. 167. Cited in Sitney, *Visionary Film*, p. 43.

32. Hollis Frampton. "For a Metahistory of Film: Commonplace Notes and Hypotheses," *Artforum*, September 1971, p. 35.

33. Alain Robbe-Grillet. *For A New Novel: Essays on Fiction*, New York: Grove Press, Inc., 1965. p. 33.

34. Marcia Tucker and James Monte, *Anti-Illusion: Procedures and Materials*, New York: Whitney Museum of American Art, 1969, pp. 36–37.

35. Annette Michelson. "Paul Sharits and the Critique of Illusionism: An Introduction," *Projected Images*, Minneapolis: Walker Art Center, 1974.

36. Tucker and Monte. *op. cit.*, p. 27.

37. Sitney. *Visionary Film*, p. 387.

38. Annette Michelson. *Robert Morris*, Washington: The Corcoran Gallery of Art, 1969, p. 17.

39. Ibid., p. 23.

40. Morse Peckham. *Man's Rage for Chaos: Biology, Behavior and the Arts*, Philadelphia: Chilton Books, 1965, p. 313.

41. Ibid., p. 314.

Chronology

The asterisked titles denote those films included in this exhibition. The Chronology makes clear that the history of the independent film is comprised of the efforts of many filmmakers and this listing is by no means complete. With every year, more and more films were produced; some were screened at *Cinema 16* or at the open screenings at the *Film-Makers' Cinematheque,* and while many were lost or forgotten, certain films and filmmakers were considered in the criticism and discussion of the day. This listing includes many of the films and filmmakers that were important at various stages in the avant-garde film's history. Included in the Chronology are the films of European filmmakers such as Peter Kubelka who have been influenced by, and been important to, the American avant-garde movement. Also included are films such as *Primary* by Ricky Leacock, a documentary (cinema-verité) film not often associated with the avant-garde. It is listed because it was recognized as an important development in filmmaking and given the Third Independent Film Award (1961) by *Film Culture* magazine, the leading critical journal of the avant-garde film.

The dates of the Chronology refer to the time of a film's completion, thus a film finished and released in 1970 may have been worked on since 1965. Also one should recognize that many dates are difficult to pin down. Filmmakers change their minds or cannot remember, and accurate records are not kept. This indicates the importance of research being done today into the origins and history of the avant-garde film. Certainly the Anthology Film Archives, New York, under its director Jonas Mekas, has been outstanding in the areas of film preservation and the collection of primary and secondary material on films and filmmakers. Their research center, along with that of The Museum of Modern Art's Department of Film, have been and will continue to be important resources for new perspectives on the history of the avant-garde film.

Included in the Chronology are certain events, such as the founding of the *Film-Makers' Cooperative,* which were important to the development and particular direction which the avant-garde film took. They are events which at the time were considered of great importance and have remained today focal points in discussion of the avant-garde's history. Not included here are the premiere screenings of particular films in New York and other parts of the country because of the problems in pinpointing them with any degree of accuracy. However, it should be remembered that these premiere screening events, the actual showing of the films, were important occasions. In any case, it is hoped that a Chronology of dates for the films will indicate the scope, diversity, and creativity of the avant-garde film. (J.G.H.)

1943
The Nest (Anger)
Meshes Of The Afternoon (Deren and Hammid)
Color Sequence (Grant)
Geography Of The Body (Maas)
Film Exercise No. 1 (Whitney)

1944
Escape Episode I (Anger)
At Land (Deren)
Rena Scence (Harrington)
Film Exercises No. 2 and 3 (Whitney)

1945
Drastic Demise (Anger)
A Study In Choreography For Camera (Deren)
Visual Variations On Noguchi (Menken)
Film Exercises No. 4 And 5 (Whitney)

1946
Escape Episode II (Anger)
Glen Falls Sequence (Crockwell)
Ritual In Transfigured Time (Deren)
Fragment Of Seeking (Harrington)
The Potted Psalm (Peterson and Broughton)
Dreams That Money Can Buy (Richter)

1947
Fireworks (Anger)
Transmutations (Belson)
The Long Bodies (Crockwell)
The Cage (Peterson)
Clinic Of Stumble (Peterson)
Horror Dream (Peterson)
Art In Cinema Film Society established in San Francisco.
Cinema 16 Film Society established in New York.

1948
Improvisations #1 (Belson)
Mother's Day (Broughton)
Meditation On Violence (Deren)
Image In The Snow (Maas)
Merry-Go-Round (Maas and Moore)
The Quiet One (Meyers, Loeb)
Du Sang De La Volupte Et De La Mort: Psyche; Lysis; Charmides (Markopoulos)
Ah, Nature (Peterson and Hirsh)
Mr. Frenhofer And The Minotaur (Peterson)
The Petrified Dog (Peterson)
Sausalito (Stauffacher)

1949
Puce Moment (Anger)
On The Edge (Harrington)
The Dead Ones (Markopoulos)
The Lead Shoes (Peterson)
Festival and International Experimental Film Competition, Belgium, established.

1950
Rabbit's Moon (Anger)
Adventures Of Jimmy (Broughton)
Ai-Ye (Hugo)
Cinema 16 Film Library established.

1951
Mambo (Belson)
Four In The Afternoon (Broughton)
Loony Tom, The Happy Lover (Broughton)
Flowers Of Asphalt (Markopoulos)
Swain (Markopoulos)
Celery Stalks At Midnight (Whitney)

1952
Caravan (Belson)
Interim (Brakhage)
Form Phases I (Breer)
Parade C (Eames)
Bells Of Atlantis (Hugo)
In The Street (Levitt, Loeb, Agee)
Color Cry (Lye)
Elodora (Markopoulos)
Notes On The Port Of St. Francis (Stauffacher)

1953
Eaux D'Artifice (Anger)
Le Jeune Homme Et La Mort (Anger)
Bop Scotch (Belson)
Mandala (Belson)
The Boy And The Sea (Brakhage)
Unglassed Windows Cast A Terrible Reflection (Brakhage)
Form Phases II And III (Breer)
The Pleasure Garden (Broughton)
Polka-Graph (Bute)
Dance In The Sun (Clarke)
The Little Fugitive (Engel)
Rhythm (Lye)
The End (MacLaine)

1954

Inauguration Of The Pleasure Dome
    (Anger)
Disistfilm (Brakhage)
The Extraordinary Child (Brakhage)
The Way To Shadow Garden (Brakhage)
Form Phases IV (Breer)
Image By Images I (Breer)
Un Miracle (Breer)
Abstronics (Bute)
Color Rhapsody (Bute)
Mood Contrast (Bute)
In Paris Parks (Clarke)
Pattern For A Sunday Afternoon
    (D'Avino)
Treadle and Bobbin (Gallentine)
Jazz Of Lights (Hugo)

1955

Thelma Abbey (Anger)
In Between (Brakhage)
Reflections On Black (Brakhage)
"Tower House" (Brakhage) became
    Centuries Of June (Cornell)
The Wonder Ring (Brakhage)
Image By Images II And III (Breer)
Bullfight (Clarke)
Aviary (Cornell)
Gnir Rednow (Cornell)
Evolution (Davis)
Lovers And Lollipops (Engel)
Man In Pain (Jordan)
Undertow (Jordan)
Mosaik Im Vertrauen (Kubelka)
Mechanics Of Love (Maas, Moore)
Yantra (Whitney)
Film Culture magazine founded.

1956

Flesh Of Morning (Brakhage)
Nightcats (Brakhage)
Zone Moment (Brakhage)
Cats (Breer)
Image By Images IV (Breer)
Motion Pictures (Breer)
A Legend For Fountains (Cornell)
Theme And Transition (D'Avino)
Trumpit (Jordan)
Narcissus (Maas, Moore)
A To Z (Snow)
On The Bowery (Rogosin)

1957

Daybreak And Whiteye (Brakhage)
Loving (Brakhage)
Jamestown Baloos (Breer)
Recreation I (Breer)
Recreation II (Breer)
A Moment In Love (Clarke)
A Movie (Conner)
Angel (Cornell)
Nymphlight (Cornell)
Pastorale D'Ete (Hindle)
Saturday Afternoon Blood Sacrifice:
    TV Plug: Little Cobra Dance (Jacobs)
Visions Of A City (Jordan)
Waterlight (Jordan)
Adebar (Kubelka)
Glimpse Of The Garden (Menken)
8 x 8 (Richter)
Early Abstractions (Films #1-#5, #7
    & #10) (Smith, H.)
N.Y., N.Y. (Thompson)
Astral Man (Vanderbeek)
Mankinda (Vanderbeek)
What, Who How (Vanderbeek)

1958

Flight (Belson)
Anticipation Of The Night (Brakhage)
A Man And His Dog Out For Air (Breer)
Par Avion (Breer)
Shadows (Cassavetes)
Brussels "Loops" (Clarke)
The Big O (D'Avino)
Weddings And Babies (Engel)
Melodie Inversion (Hugo)
The One Romantic Venture of Edward
    (Jordan)
Triptych In Four Parts (Jordan)
Schwechater (Kubelka)
Free Radicals (Lye)
Come Back Africa (Rogosin)
A La Mode (Vanderbeek)
Wheels No. 1 (Vanderbeek)
Yet (Vanderbeek)
Jonas Mekas begins writing his "Movie
    Journal" column in *The Village
    Voice.*
Creative Film Society founded.

N.Y., N.Y. by Francis Thompson

Free Radicals by Len Lye

Lifelines by Ed Emshwiller

1959
Raga (Belson)
Seance (Belson)
Handwritten (Boultenhouse)
Cat's Cradle (Brakhage)
Sirius Remembered (Brakhage)
Wedlock House: An Intercourse
    (Brakhage)
Window Water Baby Moving (Brakhage)
Eyewash (Breer)
Trailor (Breer)
Bridges-Go-Round (Clarke)
Skyscraper (Clark, Jacoby, Van Dyke)
The Room (D'Avino)
The Very Eye Of Night (Deren)
Dance Chromatic (Emshwiller)
Transformation (Emshwiller)
Weddings And Babies (Engel)
Pull My Daisy (Frank, Leslie)
Achoo Mr. Keroochev (Vanderbeek)
Dance Of The Looney Spoons
    (Vanderbeek)
Science Friction (Vanderbeek)
Wheels No. 2 (Vanderbeek)

1960
The Dead (Brakhage)
Inner And Outer Space (Breer)
A Scary Time (Clarke, Hughes)
A Trip (D'Avino)
Lifelines (Emshwiller)
Finds Of A Fortnight (Jordan)
Minerva Looks Out Into The Zodiac
    (Jordan)
Pictograms (Jordan)
Arnulf Rainer (Kubelka)
Primary (Leacock)
The Flower Thief (Rice)
Blacks And Whites, Days And Nights
    (Vanderbeek)
Skullduggery (Vanderbeek)
Lemon Hearts (Zimmerman)
The New American Cinema Group
    founded.
Canyon Cinema founded.

1961
The Gymnasts (Baillie)
Mr. Hayashi (Baillie)
On Sundays (Baillie)
Allures (Belson)

Films By Stan Brakhage: An Avant-Garde
    Home Movie (Brakhage)
Prelude: Dog Star Man (Brakhage)
Thigh Line Lyre Triangular (Brakhage)
Blazes (Breer)
Kinetic Art Show-Stockholm (Breer)
The Connection (Clarke)
Cosmic Ray (Conner)
The Sin Of Jesus (Frank)
Venice Etude No. 1 (Hugo)
The Death Of P'town (Jacobs)
The Monkey (Jordan)
Pussy On A Hot Tin Roof (Kuchar)
Serenity (Markopoulos)
Guns Of The Trees (Mekas)
Arabesque For Kenneth Anger (Menken)
Snapshots Of The City (Vanderbeek)
Catalogue (Whitney)

1962
Everyman (Baillie)
Have You Thought Of Talking To The
    Director? (Baillie)
Here I Am (Baillie)
News #3 (Baillie)
Blue Moses (Brakhage)
Dog Star Man: Part I (Brakhage)
Dog Star Man: Part II (Brakhage)
Horse Over Tea Kettle (Breer)
Pat's Birthday (Breer)
Shoot The Moon (Burckhardt, Grooms)
Stone Sonata (D'Avino)
Thanatopsis (Emshwiller)
Jewel Face (Jordan)
Tootsies In Autumn (Kuchar)
Moonplay (Menken)
Senseless (Rice)
Heaven And Earth Magic Feature (Film
    #12) (Smith, H.)
Scotch Tape (Smith, J.)
Film-Makers' Cooperative founded.

1963
Scorpio Rising (Anger)
A Hurrah For Soldiers (Baillie)
To Parsifal (Baillie)
Dionysius (Boultenhouse)
Mothlight (Brakhage)
Oh Life-A Woe Story-The A Test News
    (Brakhage)
Breathing (Breer)
Jerry (Brooks)
The Cool World (Clarke)
Pianissimo (D'Avino)

Journey Around A Zero (De Hirsch)
Totem (Emshwiller)
Non Catholicam (Hindle)
The Gondola Eye (Hugo)
Baud'larian Capers (Jacobs)
Blonde Cobra (Jacobs)
*Little Stabs At Happiness (Jacobs)
Twice A Man (Markopoulos)
Film Magazine Of The Arts (Mekas, J.)
Halleljujah The Hills (Mekas, A.)
Go! Go! Go! (Menken)
*Notebook (Menken)
Plastic Haircut (Nelson)
The Queen Of Sheba Meets The Atom
    Man (Rice)
Christmas On Earth (Rubin)
Flaming Creatures (Smith)
Summit (Vanderbeek)
Andy Warhol Films Jack Smith Filming
    "Normal Love" (Warhol)
Blow Job (Warhol)
Dance Movie (Warhol)
Haircut (Warhol)
Kiss (Warhol)
Salome And Delilah (Warhol)
Sleep (Warhol)
Tarzan And Jane Regained . . . Sort Of
    (Warhol)
Scarface And Aphrodite (Zimmerman)
Canyon Cinema Cooperative founded.

1964
The Brookfield Recreation Center (Baillie)
*Mass For The Dakota Sioux (Baillie)
Re-Entry (Belson)
Dog Star Man: Part III (Brakhage)
Dog Star Man: Part IV (Brakhage)
Songs 1–8 (Brakhage)
First Flight (Breer)
Nightspring Daystar (Brooks)
Lurk (Burckhardt)
Divinations (De Hirsch)
Newsreel: Jonas In The Brig (De Hirsch)
Babo 73 (Downey)
Alone (Dwoskin)
Scrambles (Emshwiller)
The Neon Rose (Gerson)
Night Crawlers (Goldman)

Recommended By Duncan Hines (Gold-
    man)
We Stole Away (Jacobs)
*Window (Jacobs)
The Winter Footage (Jacobs)
Duo Concertantes (Jordan)
Bin Traum Der Liebenden (A Dream Of
    Lovers) (Jordan)
Johnnie (Jordan)
Georg (Kaye)
Fleming Faloon (Landow)
Peaches And Cream (Levine, C.)
Yes (Levine, N.)
The Devil Is Dead (Linder)
Skin (Linder)
Award Presentation To Andy Warhol
    (Mekas)
The Brig (Mekas)
Chumlum (Rice)
New York Eye And Ear Control (A Walk-
    ing Woman Work) (Snow)
Breathdeath (Vanderbeek)
Batman Dracula (Warhol)
Couch (Warhol)
Empire (Warhol)
Harlot (Warhol)
Henry Geldzahler (Warhol)
Mario Banana (Warhol)
Shoulder (Warhol)
Soap Opera (Warhol)
Taylor Mead's Ass (Warhol)
The Thirteen Most Beautiful Women
    (Warhol)
Film-Makers' Cinematheque founded.

1965
Kustom Kar Kommandos (Anger)
Quixote (Baillie)
Yellow Horse (Baillie)
Phenomena (Belson)
Nothing Happened This Morning
    (Bienstock)
The Art Of Vision (Brakhage)
Black Vision (Brakhage)
*Fire Of Waters (Brakhage)
Pasht (Brakhage)
Songs 9–22 (Brakhage)
15 Songs Traits (Brakhage)
Three Films (Blue White, Blood's Tone,
    Vein) (Brakhage)

Flaming Creatures by Jack Smith

Two: Creely/Mc Clure (Brakhage)
Ten Second Film (Conner)
Vivian (Conner)
Aviary (Cornell)
Centuries Of June (Cornell)
A Finish Fable (D'Avino)
Peyote Queen (De Hirsch)
Chinese Checkers (Dwoskin)
George Dumpson's Place (Emshwiller)
Grandma's House (Fleischner)
Echos Of Silence (Goldman)
Pestilent City (Goldman)
Lisa And Joey In Connecticut: "You've Come Back!" "You're Still Here!" (Jacobs)
Naomi Is A Dream Of Loveliness (Jacobs)
The Sky Socialist (Jacobs)
Hamfat Asar (Jordan)
Petite Suite (Jordan)
Corruption Of The Damned (Kuchar, G.)
Sins Of The Fleshapoids (Kuchar, M.)
Studies And Sketches (Landow)
The Death Of Hemingway (Markopoulos)
Andy Warhol (Menken)
Lights (Menken)
Confessions Of A Black Mother Succuba (Nelson, R.)
Oiley Peloso The Pumph Man (Nelson, R.)
Oh Dem Watermelons (Nelson, R.)
Thick Pucker (Nelson, R.)
Viet Flakes (Schneemann)
Short Wave (Snow)
Phenomenon No. 1 (Vanderbeek)
Colorfilm (Van Meter)
Olds-Mo-Bile (Van Meter)
Afternoon (Warhol)
Beauty #2 (Warhol)
Bitch (Warhol)
Camp (Warhol)
Drunk Warhol)
Face (Warhol)
Fifty Fantastics And Fifty Personalities (Warhol)
Hedy (Warhol)
Horse (Warhol)
Ivy And John (Warhol)
Kitchen (Warhol)
The Life Of Juanita Castro (Warhol)
Lupe (Warhol)

More Milk Yvette (Warhol)
My Hustler (Warhol)
Outer And Inner Space (Warhol)
Paul Swan (Warhol)
Poor Little Rich Girl (Warhol)
Prison (Warhol)
Restaurant (Warhol)
Screen Test #1 (Warhol)
Screen Test #2 (Warhol)
Space (Warhol)
Suicide (Warhol)
The Thirteen Most Beautiful Boys (Warhol)
Vinyl (Warhol)
Diffraction Film (Yalkut)

1966
All My Life (Baillie)
*Castro Street (Baillie)
Port Chicago Vigil (Baillie)
Show Leader (Baillie)
Still Life (Baillie)
Terminations (Baillie)
Tung (Baillie)
The Secret Cinema (Bartel)
Metanomen (Bartlett)
23rd Psalm Branch, Part I (Brakhage)
66 (Breer)
Winter (Brooks)
*The Flicker (Conrad)
Sing Lotus (De Hirsch)
Chafed Elbows (Downey)
Relativity (Emshwiller)
Information (Frampton)
Manual Of Arms (Frampton)
Process Red (Frampton)
Fat Feet (Grooms)
Death In The Afternoon (Hill)
FFFTCM (Hindle)
29: 'Merci, Merci' (Hindle)
The Old House Passing (Jordan)
In The Country (Kramer)
Unsere Afrikareise (Kubelka)
Hold Me While I'm Naked (Kuchar)
Leisure (Kuchar)
Mosholu Holiday (Kuchar)
*Film In Which There Appear Sprocket, Holes, Edge Lettering, Dirt Particles, Etc. (Landow)
Ineluctable Modality Of The Visible (Lipton)
Excited Turkeys (Maas)
Galaxie (Markopoulos)
Himself As Herself (Markopoulos)

The Chelsea Girls by Andy Warhol

David Holzman's Diary by James McBride

58

Ming Green (Markopoulos)
Through A Lens Brightly: Mark Turbyfill
    (Markopoulos)
Cassis (Mekas)
Hare Krishna (Mekas)
*Notes On The Circus (Mekas)
Report From Millbrook (Mekas)
Schmeerguntz (Nelson G., Wiley, D.)
Venus And Adonis (Palazzolo)
Water Light/Water Needle (Schneemann)
Piece Mandala/End War (Sharits)
Ray Gun Virus (Sharits)
World Movie/Fluxfilm (Sharits)
Amphetamine (Sonbert)
Hall Of Mirrors (Sonbert)
Where Did Our Love Go? (Sonbert)
Bufferin (Warhol)
The Chelsea Girls (Warhol)
Eating Too Fast (Warhol)
The Velvet Undergound and Nico
    (Warhol)
*Lapis (Whitney)
Le Parc (Yalkut)
Moondial Film (Yalkut)
P+A−I (K) (Yalkut)
Turn Turn Turn (Yalkut)
Us By The Riverside (Yalkut)
The Millennium Film Workshop founded.

1967
Valentin De Las Sierras (Baillie)
Offon (Bartlett)
*Samadhi (Belson)
Scenes From Under Childhood: Section
    No. 1 (Brakhage)
Songs 24 And 25 (Brakhage)
23rd Psalm Branch, Part II And Coda
    (Brakhage)
Letter To D. H. In Paris (Brooks)
Man In Polar Regions (Clarke)
Portrait Of Jason (Clarke)
Breakaway (Conner)
Liberty Crown (Conner)
Looking For Mushrooms (Conner)
Report (Conner)
The White Rose (Conner)
Cayuga Run, Hudson River Diary: Book I
    (De Hirsch)
Shaman (De Hirsch)
Atmosfear (Dewitt)
No More Excuses (Downey)
Naissant (Dwoskin)
Soliloque (Dwoskin)

Heterodyne (Frampton)
Now That The Buffalo's Gone (Gershfield)
Room (Double Take) (Gidal)
Nine Variations On A Dance Theme
    (Harris)
Airshaft (Jacobs)
The Edge (Kramer)
Eclipse Of The Sun Virgin (Kuchar)
*Diploteratology Or Bardo Folly (Landow)
Orgia (Maas)
Bliss (Markopoulos)
The Divine Damnation (Markopoulos)
Eros, O Basileus (Markopoulos)
The Illiac Passion (Markopoulos)
David Holzman's Diary (McBride)
Wildflowers (Mekas)
Thighing (Nauman)
Fog Pumas (Nelson, G., D. Wiley)
The Awful Backlash (Nelson, R.)
Blondino Preview (Nelson, R.)
Grateful Dead (Nelson, R.)
The Great Blondino (Nelson, R., W. Wiley)
Half Open And Lumpy (Nelson, R.)
Hot Leatherette (Nelson, R.)
The Off-Handed Jape (Nelson, R.)
Penny Bright And Jimmy Witherspoon
    (Nelson, R.)
Superspread (Nelson, R.)
7362 (O'Neill)
America's In Real Trouble (Palazzolo)
The Bride Stripped Bare (Palazzolo)
He (Palazzolo)
O (Palazzolo)
Fuses (Schneemann)
Standard Time (Snow)
*Wavelength (Snow)
The Bad And The Beautiful (Sonbert)
Truth Serum (Sonbert)
The History Of Motion In Motion
    (Vanderbeek)
Man And His World (Vanderbeek)
Panels For The Walls Of The World
    (Vanderbeek)
Poem Field No. 1 (Vanderbeek)
See, Saw, Seems (Vanderbeek)
Spherical Space No. 1 (Vanderbeek)
T.V. Interview (Vanderbeek)
**** (Warhol)
Bike Boy (Warhol)
I, A Man (Warhol)
Imitation Of Christ (Warhol)
Lonesome Cowboys (Warhol)
The Loves Of Ondine (Warhol)
Nude Restaurant (Warhol)

Permutations (Whitney)
Hand Tinting (Wieland)
1933 (Wieland)
Sailboat (Wieland)
Cinema Metaphysique No. 5 (Yalkut)
Kusama's Self-Obliteration (Yalkut)

1968

A Trip To The Moon (Bartlett)
The Horseman, The Woman, And The Moth (Brakhage)
Lovemaking (Brakhage)
My Mountain Song 27 (Brakhage)
Song 26 (Brakhage)
Pbl I And II (Breer)
*69 (Breer)
Eel Creek (Brooks)
The Wind Is Driving Him Toward The Open Sea (Brooks)
The Bed (Broughton)
The Secret Life Of Hernando Cortez (Chamberlain)
Third Eye Butterfly (De Hirsch)
Trap Dance (De Hirsch)
Me, Myself And I (Dwoskin)
The Director And His Actor Look At Footage Showing Preparations For An Unmade Film (Fisher)
Documentary Footage (Fisher)
Phi Phenomenon (Fisher)
Maxwell's Demon (Frampton)
Snowblind (Frampton)
Surface Tension (Frampton)
Morning (Gehr)
Wait (Gehr)
Automatic Free Form (Gerson)
Hall (Gidal)
Key (Gidal)
Loop (Gidal)
Wheel Of Ashes (Goldman)
Arc (Herbert)
Outscape (Herbert)
Canaries (Hill)
Billabong (Hindle)
Chinese Firedrill (Hindle)
Ian Hugo: Engraver And Filmmaker (Hugo; revised 1972)
Soft Rain (Jacobs)
Wind (Jonas)
Gymnopedies (Jordan)
3 Moving Fresco Films (Jordon)
13 Fragments And # Narratives From Life (Jost)

The Film That Rises To The Surface Of Clarified Butter (Landow)
Sunday In Southbury (Lawder)
Si See Suni (Levine, C.)
Siva (Levine, C.)
Optured Fraiken Chaitre Joe (Levine, N.)
Zero To 16 (Levine, N.)
(A)lter-(A)ction (Markopoulos)
Die Schachatel (Markopoulos)
Gammelion (Markopoulos)
The Mysteries (Markopoulos)
Diaries, Notes And Sketches (Mekas)
Bouncing Two Balls Between The Floor And Ceiling With Changing Rhythms (Nauman)
Dance Or Exercise On The Perimeter Of A Square (Nauman)
Playing A Note On The Violin While I Walk Around The Studio (Nauman)
Walking In An Exaggerated Manner Around The Perimeter Of A Square (Nauman)
War Is Hell (Nelson, R.)
Kodak Ghost Poems—Part I, The Adventures Of The Exquisite Corpse (Noren)
Screen (O'Neill)
Pigeon Lady (Palazzolo)
Hand Catching Lead (Serra)
Hand Lead Fulcrum (Serra)
Hand's Scraping (Serra)
Hands Tied (Serra)
N:O:T:H:I:N:G (Sharits)
Razor Blades (Sharits)
*T,O,U,C,H,I,N,G (Sharits)
Late Superimpositions (Film #14) (1965–1968) (Smith, H.)
Holiday (Sonbert)
Oh (Vanderbeek)
Superimposition (Vanderbeek)
Vanderbeekiana (Vanderbeek)
Will (Vanderbeek)
Catfood (Wieland)
Rat Life And Diet In North America (Wieland)
Clarence (Yalkut)

1969

Invocation Of My Demon Brother (Anger)
Moon 1969 (Bartlett)
Stand Up And Be Counted (Bartlett, Freude)
Cosmos (Belson)
Momentum (Belson)

American 30's Song (Brakhage)
Scenes From Under Childhood: Section No. 2 (Brakhage)
Scenes From Under Childhood: Section No. 3 (Brakhage)
Song 27 (Part II) (Brakhage)
Song 28 (Brakhage)
Song 29 (Brakhage)
Window Suite Of Children's Songs (Brakhage)
Nuptiae (Broughton)
Permian Strata (Conner)
The Children's Party (Cornell, finished by Jordan)
Cotillion (Cornell, finished by Jordan)
The Midnight Party (Cornell, finished by Jordan)
The Tatooed Man (De Hirsch)
Take Me (Dwoskin)
Tops (Eames)
Image, Flesh And Voice (Emshwiller)
Artificial Light (Frampton)
Carrots And Peas (Frampton)
Lemon (For Robert Huot) (Frampton)
Palindrome (Frampton)
Prince Ruperts Drops (Frampton)
Works And Days (Frampton)
Me And My Brother (Frank)
Reverberation (Gehr)
Transparency (Gehr)
Evolving (Gerson)
Generations (Gerson)
Group I: Grass/Ice/Snow/Vibrations (Gerson)
Group II: Water/Contemplating (Gerson)
Clouds (Gidal)
Heads (Gidal)
Pluto (Herbert)
Watersmith (Hindle)
Through The Magiscope (Hugo)
Nissan, Ariana Window (Jacobs)
Tom, Tom, The Piper's Son (Jacobs)
*Our Lady Of The Sphere (Jordan)
Brandy In The Wilderness (Kaye)
Ice (Kramer)
Institutional Quality (Landow)
Catfilm For Ursula (Lawder)
Eleven Different Horses (Lawder)
Headfilm (Lawder)
Necrology (Lawder)
Road Film (Lawder)
*Runaway (Lawder)
Rape (Lennon, Ono)
Apropo Of San Francisco (Levine, C.)

Bessie Smith (Levine, C.)
Premoonptss (Levine, N.)
Prismatic (Levine, N.)
Index-Hans Richter (Markopoulos)
Moment (Markopoulos)
The Olympian (Markopoulos)
Political Portraits (Markopoulos)
Sorrow (Markopoulos)
My Girlfriend's Wedding (McBride)
Mother Of Five (Mc Laughlin)
Time And Fortune Vietnam Journal (Mekas)
Autumn Winterfilm (Mideke)
Gas Station (Morris)
Mirror (Morris)
Slow Motion (Morris)
Art Make-Up (Nauman)
Black Balls (Nauman)
Bouncing Balls (Nauman)
Gauze (Nauman)
Pulling Mouth (Nauman)
The Wind Variations (Noren)
Your Astronaut (Palazzolo)
Frame (Serra)
Dripping Water (Snow, Wieland)
◄——————► (Snow)
One Second In Montreal (Snow)
Tuxedo Theatre (Sonbert)
La Raison Avant La Passion (Wieland)
Line Of Apogee (Williams)
Beatles Electroniques (Yalkut)
Electronic Moon No. 2 (Yalkut)
Videotape Study No. 3 (Yalkut)

1970

Quick Billy (Baillie)
Lovemaking (Bartlett)
World (Belson)
The Animals Of Eden And After (Brakhage)
The Machine Of Eden (Brakhage)
Scenes From Under Childhood: Section No. 4 (Brakhage)
Sexual Meditation No. 1: Motel (Brakhage)
The Weir-Falcon Saga (Brakhage)
70 (Breer)
The Golden Positions (Broughton)
Comming Attractions (Conrad)
Straight And Narrow (Conrad)
Robert Having His Nipple Pierced (Daley)

Tom, Tom, the Piper's Son by
Ken Jacobs

Moment (Dwoskin)
Times For (Dwoskin)
Branches (Emshwiller)
Carol (Emshwiller)
Film With Three Dancers (Emshwiller)
Fusion (Emshwiller)
Earthspirit House (Finne)
Production Stills (Fisher)
Zorns Lemma (Frampton)
Sweet Dreams (Freude)
Field (Gehr)
History (Gehr)
Serene Velocity (Gehr)
Group III: Sunlight/Floating/Afternoon
    (Gerson)
Group IV: Beaded Light/Dissolving/
    Beyond (Gerson)
Group V: Endurance/Remembrance/
    Metamorphosis (Gerson)
Takes (Gidal)
Blues (Gottheim)
Corn (Gottheim)
Fog Line (Gottheim)
Goulimine (Graves)
200 Stills At 60 Frames (Graves)
May Pops (Herbert)
Apertura (Hugo)
Hildur And The Magician (Jordan)
Canyon (Jost)
Remedial Reading Comprehension
    (Landow)
Corridor (Lawder)
Dangling Participle (Lawder)
Apotheosis (Lennon, Ono)
Horseopera (Levine, C.)
London Bridge Falling Down (Levine, N.)
Break Out! (Macdonold)
Alph (Markopoulos)
Genius (Markopoulos)
Wisconsin (Morris)
Deathstyles (Myers)
Kirsa Nicholina (Nelson, G.)
My Name Is Oona (Nelson, G.)
Bleu Shut (Nelson, R.)
King David (Nelson, R.)
Runs Good (O'Neill)
Premium (Ruscha)
S:Stream:S:S:Ection:S:Ection:S:S:
    Ectioned (Sharits)
(. . . A Continuous . . .) (Shulman)
Spiral Jetty (Smithson)
Side Seat Paintings Slides Sound Film
    (Snow)

Film Form No. 1 (Vanderbeek)
Film Form No. 2 (Vanderbeek)
Found Film No. 1 (Vanderbeek)
Aquarian Rushes (Yalkut)
Anthology Film Archives founded.
The New American Filmmakers Series
    (Whitney Museum of American Art)
    established.

1971
Why Not (Arakawa)
Title (Baldessari)
Serpent (Bartlett)
Meditation (Belson)
The Act Of Seeing With One's Own Eyes
    (Brakhage)
Angels' (Brakhage)
Deus Ex (Brakhage)
Door (Brakhage)
Eyes (Brakhage)
Fox Fire Child Watch (Brakhage)
The Peaceable Kingdom (Brakhage)
Sexual Meditation: Room With View
    (Brakhage)
The Trip To Door (Brakhage)
Wech (Brakhage)
Western History (Brakhage)
This Is It (Broughton)
Four Square (Conrad)
An Experiment In Meditation (De Hirsch)
Fall (De Witt)
Trixi (Dwoskin)
Choice Chance Woman Dance (Emshwiller)
The Secrete Of Life (Faccinto)
Hapax Legomena I: (Nostalgia)
    (Frampton)
Hapax Legomena III: (Critical Mass)
    (Frampton)
Hapax Legomena IV: (Travelling Matte)
    (Frampton)
Still (Gehr)
Group VI: Converging Lines/Assimilation
    (Gerson)
Movements (Gerson)
Bedroom (Gidal)
8MM. Film Notes On 16MM. (Gidal)
Focus (Gidal)
Barn Rushes (Gottheim)
Doorway (Gottheim)
Harmonica (Gottheim)
Izy Boukir (Graves)
Circus Girls (Gutman)
Fig (Herbert)
Film Portrait (Hill)

Later That Same Night (Hindle)
Swamp (Holt, Smithson)
Aphrodisiac (Hugo)
July 1971–In San Francisco, Living At Beach Street, Working At Canyon Cinema, Swimming In The Valley Of The Moon (Hutton)
Paul Revere (Jonas, Serra)
Leah (Jost)
What's Wrong With This Picture? (Landow)
Color Film (Lawder)
Erection (Lennon, Ono)
Imagine (Lennon, Ono)
Story Of A Dot (Levine, N.)
No More Leadershit (Macdonold)
Neo-Classic (Morris)
Easy Out (O'Neill)
Color Aid (Serra)
Inferential Current (Sharits)
La Region Centrale (The Central Region) (Snow)
Carriage Trade (Sonbert)
A Practical Guide To Archery And Other Conjectures (Spence)
6 Loop Paintings (Spinello)
Matrix (Whitney)
Electronic Fables (Yalkut)
Metamedia (Yalkut)
Four Lectures (*The Idea of Morphology, The Idea of Abstraction, The Myth of the Absolute Film, The Myth of the Film-Maker)* delivered by P. Adams Sitney at The Museum of Modern Art (Depatment of Film).
First "Special Film Issue," *Artforum* magazine. (Edited by Annette Michelson.)

1972

For Example (Arakawa)
1970 (Bartlett)
Chakra (Belson)
Eye Myth (Brakhage)
Gift (Brakhage)
The Presence (Brakhage)
The Process (Brakhage)
*The Riddle Of Lumen (Brakhage)
Sexual Meditation: Faun's Room Yale (Brakhage)
Sexual Meditation: Hotel (Brakhage)
Sexual Meditation: Office Suite (Brakhage)
Sexual Meditation: Open Field (Brakhage)

The Shores Of Phos: A Fable (Brakhage)
The Wold-Shadow (Brakhage)
Moment (Brand)
Rate Of Change (Brand)
Zip-Tone-Cat-Tune (Brand)
Gulls And Buoys (Breer)
Dreamwood (Broughton)
Dyn Amo (Dwoskin)
Filet Of Soul (Faccinto)
Aparatus Sum (Frampton)
Hapax Legomena V: (Ordinary Matters) (Frampton)
Hapax Legomena II: (Poetic Justice) (Frampton)
Hapax Legomena VI: (Remote Control) (Frampton)
Hapax Legomena VII: (Special Effects) (Frampton)
Tiger Balm (Frampton)
Yellow Springs (Frampton)
Group VII: Portrait Of Diana/Portrait Of Andrew Noren (Gerson)
Movie No. 1 (Gidal)
Upside Down Failure (Gidal)
Pear I (Herbert)
Pear II (Herbert)
Plum (Herbert)
Aphrodisiac II (Hugo)
Levitation (Hugo)
The Sacred Art Of Tibet (Jordon)
What's Wrong With This Picture (Part II) (Landow)
Construction Job (Lawder)
Raindance (Lawder)
Aspects Of A Hill, Pt. I: The Periphery (Levine, N.)
Front And Back (Lugg, Cohen)
The Liberal War (Macdonold)
Reminiscences Of A Journey To Lithuania (Mekas)
Scenes From Life: Golden Brain Mantra (Noren)
Easy Out (O'Neill)
Last Of The Persimmons (O'Neill)
Lives Of Performers (Rainer)
Neuron (Russett)
Plumb Line (Schneemann)
Irvington To New York (Schneider)
Orbitas (Schneider)
Still Life (Schneider)
Apotheosis (Schwartz)
Googolplex (Schwartz)

Ice by Robert Kramer

Programs

1
1943-1948

Meshes of the Afternoon (Maya Deren and Alexander Hammid)
Geography of the Body (Willard Maas)
Early Abstractions (#1-#5, #7, #10) (Harry Smith)
Fireworks (Kenneth Anger)
A Study in Choreography for Camera (Maya Deren)
Mother's Day (James Broughton)

2
1949-1958

The Lead Shoes (Sidney Peterson)
Bells of Atlantis (Ian Hugo)
The Wonder Ring (Stan Brakhage)
Bridges-Go-Round (Shirley Clarke)
A Movie (Bruce Conner)
Recreation (Robert Breer)
Anticipation of the Night (Stan Brakhage)

3
1959-1963

Science Friction (Stan Vanderbeek)
Prelude, Dog Star Man (Stan Brakhage)
Notebook (Marie Menken)
Little Stabs at Happiness (Ken Jacobs)
Mass for the Dakota Sioux (Bruce Baillie)

4
1963-1966

Scorpio Rising (Kenneth Anger)
Fire of Waters (Stan Brakhage)
Window (Ken Jacobs)
The Flicker (Tony Conrad)

5
1966-1967

Samadhi (Jordan Belson)
Film in Which There Appear Sprocket Holes, Edge Lettering, Dirt Particles, Etc. (George Landow)
Castro Street (Bruce Baillie)
Notes on the Circus (Jonas Mekas)
Lapis (James Whitney)
Wavelength (Michael Snow)

6
1967-1970

T,O,U,C,H,I,N,G (Paul Sharits)
Runaway (Standish D. Lawder)
69 (Robert Breer)
Diploteratology or Bardo Folly (George Landow)
Our Lady of the Sphere (Larry Jordan)
Bleu Shut (Robert Nelson)

7
1970-1972

Serene Velocity (Ernie Gehr)
The Riddle of Lumen (Stan Brakhage)
Endurance/Remembrance/Metamorphosis (Barry Gerson)
Nostalgia (Hollis Frampton)

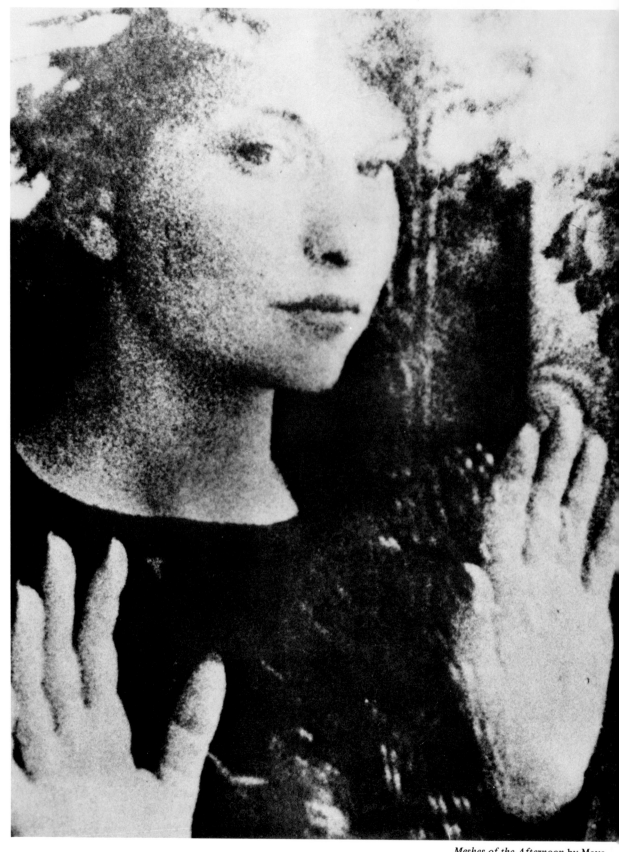

Meshes of the Afternoon by Maya
Deren and Alexander Hammid

1

Meshes of the Afternoon (Maya Deren and Alexander Hammid)
Geography of the Body (Willard Maas)
Early Abstractions (#1-#5, #7, #10) (Harry Smith)
Fireworks (Kenneth Anger)
A Study in Choreography for Camera (Maya Deren)
Mother's Day (James Broughton)

> Each film was built as a chamber and became a corridor, like a chain reaction. You know those puzzle games where if you draw a continuous line from one point to another, consecutively numbered, you end up with a picture? Well . . . I finally drew those points and got a picture.
>
> Maya Deren
> (Letter to James Card)[1]

In writing these lines in 1954, Maya Deren was articulating her desire to take a retrospective glance over the films she had authored since the time of *Meshes of the Afternoon,* the work which in 1943 had signalled the birth of the American avant-garde. Though formulated in regard to her own cinematic oeuvre, Deren's thoughts seem applicable to the critical-historical task of comprehending the work of the generation of which she was a part.

For just as Deren saw her own successive works as delineating a significant pattern, so that notion seems particularly apt for fathoming the even more complex relationships between the works of Deren, Kenneth Anger, Willard Maas, James Broughton and Harry Smith. And just as Deren found compelling the urge to solve the puzzle of her individual career, so one finds intriguing the task of constructing a picture from the group of points that plot the collective work of this group of filmmakers between the formative years of 1943 and 1948.

The work of the early American avant-garde seems fundamentally motivated by an obsession with self-definition. This tendency operates both on a personal level in respect to the psychological identities of the individual artist, and on an aesthetic level in regard to the filmmaker's relation to the other arts.

In the first sphere we find a body of work whose themes collectively exemplify the state of self-consciousness, whose narratives map out alternate routes for psychic exploration. Central to these interior investigations is a vision of the self as painfully fragmented and the films become elaborate, palliative quests for psychic and erotic coherence and resolution.[2]

But the portrayal of interiority within these films exists in dialectical tension with the presence of the outside world. If the films are universally concerned with the isolated self, they are equally conscious of the problematic relation between the self and the exterior universe. This conflict seems most eloquently voiced in the words of René Magritte, in a passage describing his conception for the painting "The Human Condition, I":

The problem of the window led to *La Condition Humaine.* In front of a window seen from the interior of a room, I placed a picture that represented precisely the portion of landscape blotted out by the picture. For instance, the trees represented in the picture displaced the tree situated behind it, outside the room. For the spectator it was simultaneously inside the room; in the picture and outside, in the real landscape, in thought. Which is how we see the world, namely outside of us, though having only one representation of it within us.[3]

It is this poignant sense of the coexistence of worlds, the interior sphere of dream, memory, sexual fantasy and imagination with that of external reality, which informs the thematics of the films of Deren, Maas, Anger, Broughton and Smith. Moreover, it constitutes the central bond between them.

But the propensity for self-definition which operates thematically in the individual cinematic works is in evidence on a broader aesthetic level as well. For just as the filmmakers of this era seemed consumed with notions of personal identity, so too they struggled with establishing their professional identity as cineastes in relation to the other arts.

All of these themes and tensions seem to crystallize in Maya Deren and Alexander Hammid's *Meshes of the Afternoon,* the film that heralded, as well, perhaps, as demarcated, the New American cinema which was to issue from it. The poles of interior and exterior worlds seem immediately invoked in the work by Deren's own description of her cinematic goals. She writes that it was her intention "to put on film the feeling which a human being experiences about an incident rather than to record the incident"[4] itself. The particular experience which Deren tries to capture in *Meshes* is the dream. Although she represents the narrative as beginning with a "real" incident (the entrance of the woman into the house) which evolves into a dream (when the woman falls asleep in the chair), the overall sense we have of the film is rather of the more complex dynamics of a dream within a dream. The manifest content of the dream involves an iconography of keys, assorted persons, knives and mirrors. Its latent content, however, reveals the force of violence, the ambivalence of sexuality and the tension of multiple selves. The theme of interiority versus exteriority seems reflected as well in the "action" of the film. For the recurrent dream fragment involves the repeated passage of an individual from outside the house to inside.

The pivotal and most arresting moment of the film (when Deren falls asleep in the chair) involves a literalization of this conflict. For after a series of alternating shots of Deren's eye in close-up and the view out the window, a camera movement pulls us away from the external world, through a tunnel-like structure into the interstices of her mind.

Another crucial moment of the film seems based upon a parallel dialectic. As one of the multiple Deren figures menacingly arises with dagger in hand to approach a second Deren figure asleep in the chair, she takes a series of steps which Deren carefully edits into a synthetic con-

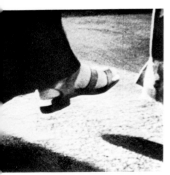

tinuity. In the first shot we see her in the room preparing to move and in
the next shot we see her emerging in an outside landscape. This is followed
by five close-ups of feet walking: the first by the sea, the second on earth,
the third on grass, the fourth on pavement, and the fifth on carpet.

The sequence ends with the character arriving in the room once more.
Although Deren explains this section as symbolically recapitulating the individual's progression from life to death, it seems significant that the movement as depicted incorporates the fluid transition between exterior and interior locales. For here as elsewhere in the film, the opposition of inside
and outside space seems to stand as metaphoric for the poles of interior
and exterior worlds.

But perhaps the most fundamental instance of the dialectic of interiority and exteriority in the work of Deren occurs on the level of the
filmmaking process itself. For Deren, that procedure involves two distinct
phases:

> *photography,* by which actuality is recorded and revealed . . . in its
> own terms; and *editing,* by which those elements of actuality proper
> may be re-related on an imaginative level to create a new reality.[5]

Clearly in this vision of filmmaking, photography is associated with
the external world and editing with the interior province of creativity.
Thus the filmmaking endeavor itself implicitly involves the kind of passage
from one world to another that we find explicit in the narrative of *Meshes.*

For Deren, it is the interior sphere of imagination that takes prece-
dence, and, therefore, editing in her films becomes a privileged formal device. It functions, as she says, to externalize an inner world and create a
universe whose laws of space, time and causality deviate from those of
physical reality. Thus we find in *Meshes* that synthetically connected
panning camera movements around a table create the illusion of two
Derens sitting side-by-side, as does the technique of superimposition,
which places twin images of Deren within the identical frame.

We perceive that time within the film is manipulated—particularly in
the sequence involving Deren's pixilated, staccato movements around the
stairs, and in the series of shots depicting a key falling to the ground in dis-
tended temporality. And we discover that Deren's editing challenges
causal laws as well, as keys turn into knives and the figure of Deren in
goggles metamorphoses into that of Hammid.

Editing is similarly the central agent for creating the repetitions and
displacements of the film, so reminiscent of oneiric structure. A narrative
action (like that of a character entering the house) can be repeated endless-
ly by the connection of footage; and objects can be mysteriously relocated
by the mechanics of a splice. Thus in *Meshes,* a shot of a knife poised in a
loaf of bread may be followed by an image which relocates it under the
covers of a bed.

In delineating the plot structure of *Meshes* Deren has said:

> The very first sequence of the film concerns the incident, but the girl
> falls asleep and the dream consists of the *manipulation of the elements
> of the incident.* (Italics mine.)[6]

In so characterizing the narrative, Deren would seem, perhaps unconsciously, to have given a description of the creative process as well. For

A Study in Choreography for Camera by Maya Deren

Geography of the Body by Willard Maas

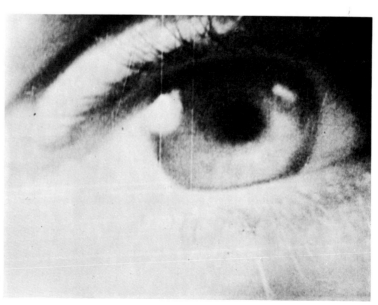

just as Deren the dreamer elaborates the incidents of waking life, so Deren the filmmaker fashions the photographic material of external reality into poetic expressions of interiority.

It is this sense of the ascendancy of the imagination that pervades Deren's third film, *A Study in Choreography for Camera* (1945) in which the movement of a dancer creates "a geography that never was."[7]

Once more this creative geography involves a dialectic of interior versus exterior spaces. In a section which Deren entitles "extension outdoors, close-up indoors" we see synthetically connected shots of dancer Talley Beatty raising his leg in the woods and lowering it into the space of a room. This volatility of space continues even within the interior domain. For by means of match-cutting long-shots and close-ups of Beatty in movement, Deren moves him imperceptibly from one apartment to another, and then finally into the space of The Metropolitan Museum of Art.

Ultimately the film ends with a reversal of its initial directionality as Beatty leaps from interior space back out into the woods. In *A Study in Choreography for Camera* it is as though the five-step walk sequence of *Meshes* had been expanded into the entire dynamic of a film.

Although one finds hints and traces of psychological reference in *A Study* (for example, in the multiplicity of selves created in the opening panning shots which connect four images of Beatty, or in the multi-headed Egyptian statue by which he dances in the hall of the museum) the psychic element is far less emphatic than in *Meshes*. For *A Study* seems primarily involved with proclaiming the strength of the imagination and its power to defy the spatio-temporal coordinates of the external world. This assertion is articulated specifically through the metaphor of dance and the potency of film to explode the rigid constraints of theatrical space. Thus the fluid transitions of Beatty's dance movements seem to stand as analogues for the movements of consciousness, by which (as Deren tells us) "a person is first one place and then another without traveling between."[8]

If *A Study* involves the creation of an imaginary exterior geography, then ironically, *Geography of the Body*, made by Willard Maas in 1943, attempts to imbue the external corporeal surface with a sense of resonant interior space.

Once more the dialectic of external/internal is pivotal to the dynamics of the work. While the images of the film survey the superficies of the body, other elements conjoin to infuse those images with a sense of interior reverberation. On the soundtrack, for example, we have a poetic text by George Barker which serves to parallel the investigation of the physical body with an account of a fantastic psychic journey. The sounds and images are carefully synchronized to create a sense of the equation of the two modes of exploration. Thus, as an image of a female breast appears upon the screen, we have a reference to Sappho, and in conjunction with a female torso, we have the summoning of Venus.

But the central vehicle for creating the impression of an interior mystery housed in the body is the filmmaker's imagistic concentration on bodily orifices which are clearly viewed as magical passageways to inner sanctums. Thus a shot of the ear is accompanied by a text referring to "the entrance to the Hyderabadean temple," and the image of a navel by the inquiry, "What inhabits those mysterious caverns in which a single jewel reminds us that anatomy has its prizes?" Crucial to this iconography is the privileged position of the eye—the bodily opening which seems most poignantly to connect exterior and interior worlds. Significantly, its image

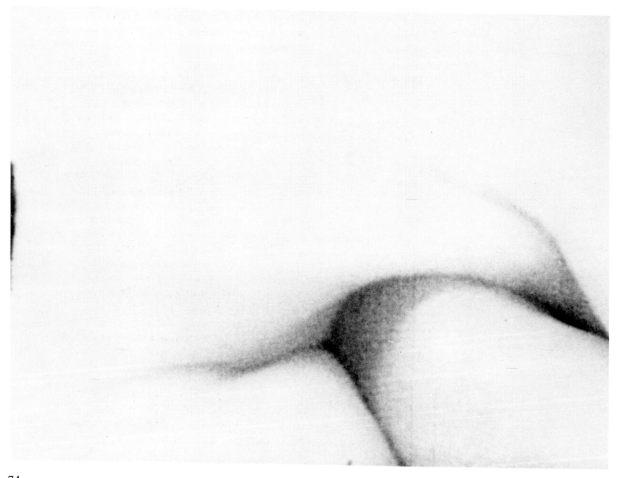

symmetrically opens and closes the film.

The sense of interiority in Maas' vision of the body is also extended by his use of magnifying lenses. Through extreme close-up, these lenses tend to defamiliarize the parts of the body and in so doing invest such images as the thumb with a powerful sexual aura. The technique of magnification thus serves to approximate the heightened state of erotic concentration.

For Maas, as for Deren, editing is the major creative strategy in the filmmaking repertoire. It allows him to connect the interior references voiced in the spoken text with the exterior presence of the body. It allows him as well to create a *composite* body (from those of Maas, Barker and camerawoman, Marie Menken)—a body whose hermaphroditic sexuality arises from its coupling of images of male and female gender. While with Deren we entered the realm of creative geography, it would seem with Maas we approach the domain of creative anatomy. Moreover, in utilizing editing to cement fragmented body parts, Maas seems to have literalized the ideal communicated in the final line of Barker's text which reads: "The desire and pursuit of the whole is called love."

Ultimately, just as Maya Deren used editing to create in *A Study for Choreography* a narrative built on a bodily movement, so Willard Maas in *Geography* forges, through editing, a narrative out of the terrain of the body itself. By fragmenting images of body parts and sequentializing them in time, the sense arises of the body as a navigable landscape and of its comprehension as a psycho-physical journey. One is reminded of the Surrealist painter Matta's characterization of Max Ernst as "a man who had lived two Odysseys: the Odyssey of the erotic and the Iliad of the mind."[9]

Whereas Deren and Maas had both initiated their creative endeavors in other artistic fields (specifically that of poetry and dance), Kenneth Anger was essentially a child of Hollywood. He claims to have appeared in Max Reinhardt's *A Midsummer Night's Dream* (1935) and between the years of 1941 and 1946 had made some five 16mm amateur films. *Fireworks* (1947), which he made at age seventeen, was the first of his works to be exhibited publicly.

Fireworks would seem to merge the world of physical corporeality explored in Maas' *Geography of the Body* with the sense of an oneiric universe created in *Meshes of the Afternoon.*

We find, as in *Meshes*, the inward focus of the dream; but like the Surrealists, Anger conceives the dream as an aggressive answer to the opposing pole of waking reality. As the opening voice-over text informs us:

In *Fireworks* I released all the explosive pyrotechnics of a dream. Inflammable desires dampened by day under the cold water of consciousness are ignited that night by the libertarian matches of sleep and burst forth in showers of shimmering incandescence. These imaginary displays provide a temporary relief.

Fireworks is thus a film whose basic assumption is the repression of interior impulses by the exterior world. Explicitly it portrays the dream as the central mode of release; but implicitly it offers the "imaginary displays" of the avant-garde cinema as a potentially liberating force in itself.

Like the protagonist in *Meshes* the somnambulist in *Fireworks*

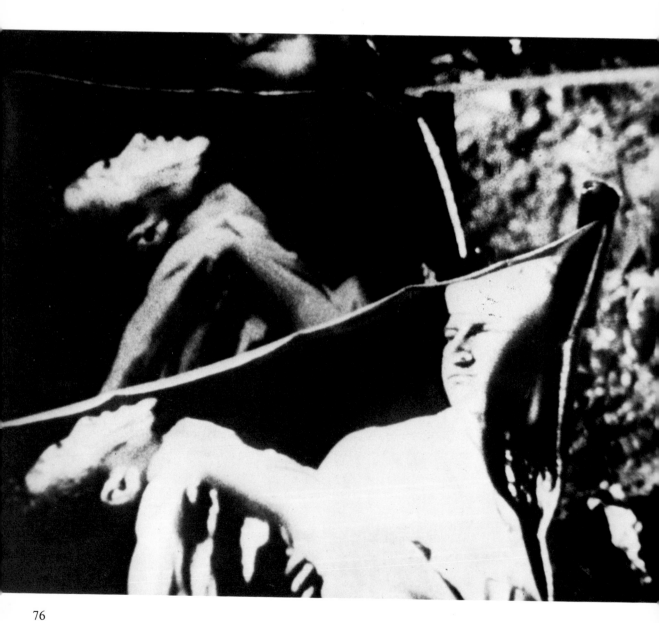

(played by Anger himself) must execute transitions between interior and exterior space. On a narrative level, a dreamer awakens, dissatisfied at finding himself alone in bed, arises with a mock erection and leaves his bedroom for the outside world through a door marked "Gents." As Anger passes a hanging wire sculpture en route to the door, the reference to Cocteau seems apparent, and the space he subsequently enters is reminiscent of that of the Hotel des Folies-Dramatiques in *Blood of a Poet.* The world he encounters is one of ambiguous spatiality, which positions it clearly in the oneiric realm. He meets a sailor against the painted backdrop of a bar. The sailor stands on his hands, and with a Cocteau-like flourish, the image flips right-side-up. By a magical cut, the sailor and Anger are transported from the space of the bar back to that of the bedroom. Continually, the encounter with the sailor is intercut with actual exterior footage involving blurred focus shots of street and car lights at night.

The sense of the body as housing an interior reality reappears with a violent twist in *Fireworks.* Here, the dreamer's confrontation with his love objects (the sailors) leads to a sado-masochistic orgy in which his body is ripped open to reveal his internal organs and a gas meter heart. We are reminded of a line from Cocteau's later film *The Testament of Orpheus* (1959) in which he says: "My film is nothing other than a striptease show consisting of removing my body bit by bit revealing my soul quite naked."[10]

The dream of aggression has as its target not only Anger himself, but the external society which acts as omnipotent repressive force. Thus in its iconography of matches, Christmas trees and roman candles, it satirizes social institutions in the manner of Buñuel's *L'Age d'Or.* As Anger has ironically put it: "This flick is all I have to say about being seventeen, the United States Navy, American Christmas and the Fourth of July."[11]

Fireworks is also a technically stunning work. It utilizes depth-of-focus as an organizing principle of the shot. Thus camera movements track in patterned, symmetrical fashion into or out of the depth of the frame; and characters are blocked dramatically along the diagonal axis. The sense of action-cutting in the film is highly sophisticated, particularly in the montage approach of the sailors and the treatment of the ensuing attack. Anger's plastic sense of composition is also exemplary as he continually varies the angle of framing and the position of the subject within the screen rectangle.

As with *Meshes* the narrative progression of *Fireworks* is complex and involves the mirrored labyrinth of a dream within a dream. It begins with a statuesque pose of a sailor holding a bloodied Anger in his arms and thereafter cuts to the image of Anger the sleeper awakening from that dream and stumbling into another. The existence of the first dream is posited by the appearance of photographs depicting the opening shot—a dream within a dream as articulated by the image of a "still" from a film, within the progression of the film itself. The temporal relations between the dreams become even more enigmatic, however, when we realize that the second dream culminates in the beating of Anger, an event implied by the initial shot.

Of the ending of *Meshes* in which the violence that surfaced in the character's dream seemed ultimately to have climaxed in her actual death, Deren wrote: "It would seem that the imagined achieved for her such force that it became reality."[12] With Anger a similar sense emerges of the potency of the dream. But rather than constituting a

self-destructive force, it seems to offer a mode of qualified alleviation. For when the dreamer awakens from the second dream, he is no longer alone, and the broken plaster cast which we have seen in earlier sequences is miraculously reconstituted whole at the end. As Anger tells us, the dreamer "returns to bed less empty than before."[13]

While Deren and Anger are concerned with the interiority of the dream and Maas with the realm of erotic mystery, James Broughton allows us to enter the "country of emotional memory."[14] *Mother's Day* is a nostalgic comedy which takes a rather perverse backward glance over a childhood dominated by the figure of Mother. As the dream and sexual fantasy held a sacred position in the Surrealist canon, so too did the evocation of childhood. As André Breton wrote:

> If [man] retains a certain lucidity, all he can do is turn back toward his childhood which however his guides and mentors may have botched it still strikes him as somehow charming. There the absence of any known restrictions, allows him the perspective of several lives lived at once.[15]

The notion of "the perspective of several lives lived at once" seems particularly apt in characterizing *Mother's Day*. For as *Meshes* and *Fireworks* elaborate convoluted structures of dreams within dreams, so *Mother's Day* posits the notion of memory encapsulated within memory. Thus not only does the film advance Broughton's remembrance of his childhood, but it postulates simultaneously his mother's recollection of her own ambiguous past.

Because we are in the interior dominion of memory, time within the film is highly abstract and subjective. Chronology is disrupted as we witness a multi-directional temporality in which events flow forward and backward in time. Mother at one moment is seen as young, and at the next as old, at one moment is outfitted in the style of the 1940's and the next in Victorian garb. Broughton's aim is to create a sense of simultaneity—the simultaneity of the psyche which commutes fluidly between the spheres of past, present and future.

Broughton, too, utilizes editing to achieve this internal temporality. But editing is combined with techniques involving the manipulation of mise-en-scene which he inherited from his background in the theatre. The classic sequence employing editing and costume/prop changes is that of Mother at the window surveying her suitors. With each cut back to her, she is dressed in a different fashion; and with each return to the suitors, a Méliès-like magical transformation is accomplished.

Broughton enlists a purely theatrical strategy (that of using adults to play children's roles) in order to render the dual sense of an adult remembering the past and of the child who lives in the adult. Broughton also uses stop-motion to achieve manipulations of foreground and background that approximate the relative dominance of certain images within the mind. Thus in one shot we have a suitor in the foreground and an aged mother in the rear, while in the succeeding shot their positions are reversed.

Mother's Day is also a poignant vision of the life cycle itself as articulated through the metaphor of the mirror. As one of his editing tropes, Broughton intercuts shots of Mother gazing at herself in a hand mirror with images of Mother at an older age within the mirror frame. Cocteau, of course, lurks somewhere through the looking glass and one is

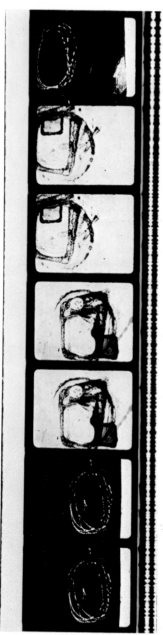

Early Abstractions (#1) by Harry Smith

reminded of Heurtebise's line in *Orphee:* "You have only to watch yourself all your life in a mirror and you'll see death at work like bees in a glass hive." But the mirror imagery in *Mother's Day* extends beyond its literal reference as Mother's children are also viewed as her "reflections." The implication is that they will cyclically repeat in their adult lives the familial and sexual rituals they have rehearsed as youths.

Thus, *Mother's Day* becomes a sexual quest as well. For it is the attempt of an adult male to fathom the awesome sexuality of Mother—a mother who, in Broughton's words, thought herself "a frail Victorian miniature, but [was] actually voluptuous and severe in the flesh." [16] The film is thus, as he puts it, "a malicious rhapsody of the Oedipus complex." [17]

In a sense, *Mother's Day* invokes the Surrealist idealization of childhood only to tarnish it. For it is, like *Fireworks,* a film about repression and it paints a picture of the artist's youth as one in which sexuality was systematically denied, fit into conventionalized roles (like heads into hats), and romanticized into saccharine "loveliness."

As in the films of Deren, Maas and Anger, a central tension between exteriority and interiority permeates the shape of *Mother's Day.* It is, after all, the attempt of an adult standing outside the realm of his youth to re-enter its universe—to cross "the impossible borderline" between the past and the present. It also treads a precarious balance between the two poles in maneuvering a stance somewhere between the distanced glance of irony and the emotionalized regard of melancholy.

In entering the creative orb of Harry Smith we come to the extremity and limit of the interior view. For the initial films on the *Early Abstractions* reel (made approximately between the years of 1939 and 1946) are distinguished by the singular refusal to turn the camera outward upon the vista of the external world. Rather, in these films (#1-#3) Smith either paints or employs a complex batiking process to enable him to fasten images directly on the surface of the film. In *Visionary Film,* P. Adams Sitney has correctly identified Smith as an hermetic artist in terms of his ties to alchemy and magic. But he is also quintessentially hermetic in the more mundane definition of the word: "completely sealed; airtight."

Even Smith's descriptions of his films are couched in ironic, hermetic metaphors of the body. He refers to his films as "cinematic excreta" and says that they have been organized in patterns "derived from the interlocking beats of respiration, the heart and the EEG Alpha component." The length of film #1, he tells us, is that of an orgasm. [18]

Eventually in the later films on the *Early Abstractions* reel, the hermetic seal is somewhat broken. In films #4, #5 and #7, Smith veers from the practice of painting directly on the filmstrip and aims the camera outward, although it is to photograph and animate his own designs. With film #10 (made in the late 1950's), however, the process goes a step further. Rather than utilize his own pictorial creations, Smith employs "found" objects (in the form of cut-out pictures) as the basis of a fantastic collage composition.

Whereas the other filmmakers of this era had had their roots in dance, poetry, theatre or cinema, Smith seems most tied to the legacy of painting. His pure abstractions follow in the neoplastic traditions of Mondrian and Kandinsky and his collages in the Surrealist vein of Max Ernst.

But although on the surface the works of Smith would seem to share little with those of Deren, Anger, Maas and Broughton, their comparative

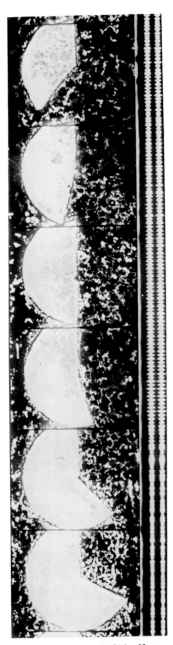

Early Abstractions (#2) by Harry Smith

deep structures reveal significant textual parallels, for the formal mechanics of Smith's films seem to translate into the realm of pristine abstraction, the dynamics which operate representationally in the works of the other filmmakers.

We have seen how the notion of metamorphosis is crucial to the works of Deren, Broughton and Anger. In *Meshes,* we saw keys turn into knives and in *A Study for Choreography*, the exterior space flow into that of interior. In *Fireworks,* a bar becomes a bedroom and in *Mother's Day* one set of costumes transformes into another. In Smith's abstractions, space becomes entirely and deliriously volatile; metamorphosis is the norm, constancy the exception. Sometimes the transitions take place on the level of shape. Thus in #1, a cluster of hand-drawn circles merge into a unified biomorphic form, then gape open to create still another configuration. Subtle permutations occur simultaneously in the parameter of color. In one section, for example, turquoise bleeds gradually and sequentially into batiks of olive green, orange, purple, red, pink, brown, and ultimately black.

Whereas in *Mother's Day,* figure/ground relations had been altered in a representational context, in *Early Abstractions* they are manipulated within the framework of pure form. Continually, colors which are at one moment established as amorphous background suddenly become attached to discrete foreground shapes. In one sequence of #2, for instance, fuschia is at first identified with the stationary background and then suddenly appears as the tonality of a moving circle.

Similar to figure/ground displacements are the transpositions Smith accomplishes in the relationship of parts to wholes. In film #3 a checkerboard pattern is seen at first to comprise the entire surface of the screen. It then breaks down and becomes discrete square units within a larger context.

Just as the engagement of deep space had proven basic to the mise-en-scene of *Fireworks* so its fabrication proves pivotal in Smith's abstractions #3 and #4. #3 (which seems influenced by the canvases of Mondrian and the filmic work of Hans Richter) involves a patterned geometry of squares and rectangles. As they expand and contract, their size in sublime two-dimensionality, they project an impression of receding and advancing in depth—an impression Smith augments by proper choice of coloration.

Other techniques disorient the spectator and keep him/her perceptually off-balance. In abstraction #2 (a rigorous and exhaustive study of circular forms), for example, off-screen space is continually implicated as spheres float by from every conceivable screen direction.

Ultimately it is not only Smith's catalogue of specific techniques that creates the overwhelming sense of kinetic flux and perceptual disequilibrium, but also the generalized compulsive speed with which he executes his metamorphoses. We are really not far from the sensibility of Maya Deren who had formulated the essence of cinema as "not so much concerned with any single instant as with the change from instant to instant."[19]

In #10, the transformations continue in a more representational form: a snowflake becomes a molecule; a hand mutates into a menacing mechanical object. But here the additional technique of Surrealist juxtaposition is introduced: a bird flaunts a skeleton's head; a Buddha figure is apposed to liquor bottles. Most intriguing about the collage film, however, is its creation of a strange and sinister Magritte-like room. It is a chamber with exaggerated depth perspective, and construction panels of continually

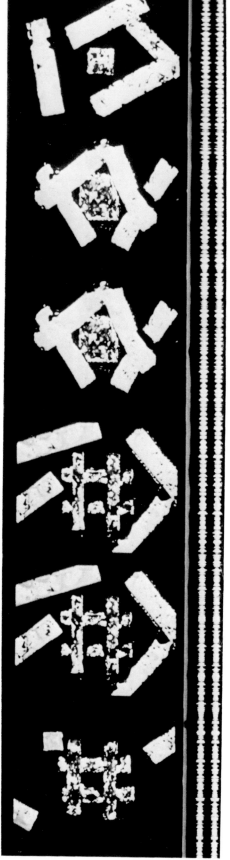

Early Abstractions (#3) by Harry Smith

Early Abstractions (#10) by Harry Smith

changing hue. It houses objects of disproportionate scale, for instance, a huge hand. What seems significant about the room however is not its eccentric formal attributes but rather the way in which it would seem to reconstitute in abstract form the kind of magical space in which the mysteries of *Meshes of the Afternoon, Mother's Day* or *Fireworks* might well have taken place.

It is fitting that we should close with the image of a room, for it was through the metaphor of a chamber becoming a corridor that Deren had articulated the relationships she sensed between her films. However, having now traversed the deeper corridor formed by the collective works of Deren, Maas, Anger, Broughton and Smith, a pattern has emerged. And it is one that seems best formulated in the words of Max Ernst describing the work of the Surrealist generation. He wrote:

> When it is said of the Surrealists that they paint constantly changeable dream reality, this does not mean that they paint a copy of their dreams . . . or that each individual builds his own little world of dream elements . . . but that they freely, bravely and self-confidently move about in the borderland between the internal and external worlds . . . registering what they see and experience there and intervening where, their revolutionary instincts advise them to do so.[20]

—— Lucy Fischer

Footnotes

1. Maya Deren. "Writings of Maya Deren and Ron Rice," *Film Culture No. 39*, Winter 1965, pp. 31–32.

2. The theme of the American avant-garde artist as visionary romantic is the subject of the major text in the field. *Visionary Film* by P. Adams Sitney.

3. René Magritte. *The Surrealists on Art*, Lucy R. Lippard, editor, Englewood, New Jersey: Prentice-Hall, 1970, p. 160. (It should be noted that in *Visionary Film*, P. Adams Sitney compared the works of certain avant-garde filmmakers to other paintings of Magritte.)

4. Deren. *op. cit.*, p. 1.

5. Ibid., p. 11.

6. Ibid., p. 1

7. Ibid., p. 30

8. Ibid., p. 3.

9. Matta in Lippard. *op. cit.*, p. 171

10. Jean Cocteau. "The Testament of Orpheus," in *Two Screenplays*, Baltimore: Penguin Books, 1969, p. 83.

11. P. Adams Sitney. *Visionary Film*, New York: Oxford University Press, 1974, p. 101.

12. Deren. *op. cit.*, p. 1.

13. Sitney. *op. cit.*, p. 97.

14. Ibid., p. 61.

15. André Breton. *Manifestoes of Surrealism*, Ann Arbor: University of Michigan Press, 1972, p. 3.

16. Broughton Issue. *Film Culture No. 61* (To be published in 1976).

17. James Broughton. Note in files of Anthology Film Archives.

18. Harry Smith. Catalogue entry in *Film-Makers' Cooperative Catalogue*, no. 5, New York: Film-Makers' Cooperative, 1971, p. 296.

19. Deren. *op. cit.*, p. 42.

20. Max Ernst in Lippard. *op. cit.*, p. 135.

The Lead Shoes (Sidney Peterson)
Bells of Atlantis (Ian Hugo)
The Wonder Ring (Stan Brakhage)
Bridges-Go-Round (Shirley Clarke)
A Movie (Bruce Conner)
Recreation (Robert Breer)
Anticipation of the Night (Stan Brakhage)

The American independent film of the 1950's stood on the threshold between the isolated initiatives of the 1940's and the explosion of filmmakers and styles which marked the movement's maturity in the 1960's. For many of the filmmakers of the "first wave," it was a period of withdrawal and frustrating retreat. Maya Deren ceased making films for a decade after *Meditation on Violence* (1948) to proselytize for the movement and to pursue her Haitian ethnographic studies. *The Lead Shoes* (1949) was Sidney Peterson's last independent effort before he entered the world of commercial filmmaking. Financial difficulties and personal crises forced James Broughton, Kenneth Anger and Gregory Markopoulos to abandon project after project. All three became expatriates for most of the decade.

The creative achievements of the period exist within the tension of a dual orientation: back toward the formal models of their predecessors, and forward, as they challenged and progressively disburdened themselves of the limiting set of structures and theoretical assumptions that history had made available. The principal casualty of their persistent reevaluation was the long-lived "trance film" drama originated by Cocteau's *Blood of a Poet* (1930) and mediated by Deren's important *Meshes of the Afternoon* (1943). The trance film form whose action is a dream in which the somnambulist protagonist wanders through enigmatic landscapes toward a climactic scene of self-realization[1] was exhausted as a generic option by mid-decade with Stan Brakhage's *The Way to Shadow Garden* (1954-5) and *Reflections on Black* (1955).

The period's best films moved away from dramatic narrative toward freer thematic organization. Two extra-filmic modes which had inspired Deren and Anger—the dance and the dream—were even more radically interpreted to suggest structural alternatives. Oblique glances to the history and practice of Abstract Expressionist painting and contemporary music confirmed the filmmakers in their directions. References to the associative logic of dreams, the visual intensity of ecstatic experience, and the synthetic spatiality of the dance also established the terms for a critical defense of the formal innovations.

In conjunction with the movement away from drama was an emphasis on new modes of image formation which approached thresholds of perception. The heightened editing speeds, the more complex rhythmic relationships, the innovative exploration of color film stock's possibilities, and the variety of image forming techniques including superimposition, optical printing, anamorphosis, and an assault on the celluloid materials themselves highlighted the primary importance of the images and their interrelationships in these films. There was also an expanded creative use of camera and lens ratio ("zoom") movement as well as an exploitation of the disjunctive and synthetic capacities of montage.

The Lead Shoes by Sidney
    Peterson

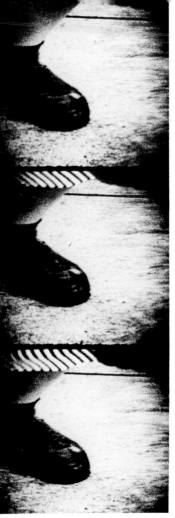

The Lead Shoes by Sidney Peterson

The effect of these creative strategies was the reduction of the illusion of three dimensional space offered by both the construction and the traditional use of the movie camera's optical system. Implicit in the cinematic practice of the period, therefore, is a critique of narrative form through the elimination of that illusionary three dimensional space in which "stories" can take place.[2] With the appearance of *Anticipation of the Night* (1958) and the advent of Brakhage's "lyric" style, narrative space was dissolved into the rhythmic play of color and light.

Attention was thus increasingly drawn to the films' audio-visual compositional modes. In a characteristically "modernist" gesture, filmmakers insisted more vigorously on the aesthetic autonomy of their medium. This novel emphasis usually stopped short of a fully reflexive statement, however. Some of the films under consideration point to the material support or the cinematic processes which subtend their presented fictions (as Conner's *A Movie* and Breer's *Recreation* respectively do). But this affirmation (which constitutes the essential subject of many "structural" films of the mid-1960's) is integrated into and subsumed by a larger extra-filmic thematic statement. Their "modernism" preferred allusive reference to reductive statement, lyric spontaneity to theoretical design. Pragmatic and not prescriptive, the independent cinema of the 1950's accommodated widely divergent styles and themes within an ethic expressed by a political metaphor which remains the movements's fundamental unifying principle and the source of its strength: independence.

The earliest film presented in this program is Sidney Peterson's *The Lead Shoes*. Made on a shoestring budget with his students at the California School of Fine Arts, the film erupts out of the improbable fusion of available props (including a diving suit and a kilt) with a thematic collage derived from ballads and pop culture. *The Lead Shoes* proposes a comic vision that is not at all funny. Extravagant, exhausting, open to the fortuitous and the unintended, its picaresque narrative transforms the dark region of unconscious impulse into an intellectual burlesque. The "story" disintegrates into a warped tissue of allusions and visual puns riddled by ellipses and audio-visual shifts.

Such a structure solicits a constant inventiveness and affords a maximum of formal flexibility. The conflation of the two related ballads ("Edward" and "The Three Ravens"), based on barely concealed unconscious patterns linking incest and death, results in the film's curiously overdetermined iconography. Each object appears as if it were a dream motif. The unwieldy diving suit, for example, refers to the dying knight's armor which figures prominently in "The Three Ravens" as well as to the unseen corpse from "Edward." Later in the film, Peterson's editing on motion across the shot change develops an astonishing series of dream-like substitutions: the "son," pushed off the balcony by his "mother," becomes a loaf of bread which, eaten by the kilted second son (an allusion to the national origin of the ballad), becomes a bone. In the film's associative logic, this transforms the kilted man into a shaggy dog. In Peterson's words, "Narrative succumbs to the comic devices of inconsequence and illogic."

Visually, the consistent use of the anamorphic lens (also used for his prior film, *Mr. Frenhofer and the Minotaur*) distorts the images laterally and vertically, displacing attention from their content to their shape. In a single stroke, Peterson thereby undercuts the illusionary "realism" of the film image most eloquently defended by Maya Deren. His use of the distorting lens signals the assault on the image taken up by vanguard film-

Bells of Atlantis by Ian Hugo

makers of the decade. The use of retarded, accelerated, and reverse motion varies and accents the movement within the shots and also highlights their rhythmic form at the expense of their narrative informativeness.

The most astonishing aspect of the film is its soundtrack. Song titles ("Old Gray Mare"), verses from the ballads, repeated falsetto shouts ("Edward?!"), all sung and spoken at assorted dynamic registers, are suspended over a clanging, untuned patchwork of parodied polkas and New Orleans jazz idioms. The dense sonic texture facilitates an associative interplay with the images. It represents an exceptional example of audio-visual asynchronism based on a Joycean play of word associations used in films as different as Willard Maas' *Geography of the Body* (1943, monologue by George Barker), Breer's *Recreation* (1956, monologue by Noël Burch) and Peterson's own *Mr. Frenhofer and The Minotaur* (1948).

Poetry is the language of multiple dimensions of our inner world.

Anaïs Nin

The great ambition of Ian Hugo's films has been to embody "the language of multiple dimensions of our inner world." More than that of any other filmmaker, his cinema figures dreams and reveries in compositions whose techniques attempt to reflect the metamorphic flow and inexplicable shifts of our subconscious. Most of the formal options available to cinema, particularly superimposition, special printing techniques, and above all, the dissolve, are enlisted to portray this radical subjectivity.

Bells of Atlantis was Hugo's second film and it is related to the trance film genre discussed above. Based on Anaïs Nin's prose poem "The House of Incest," the film explicitly postulates a lyrical self in the narrator's voice (spoken by Nin herself). Her episodic text recites a narrative of the agonizing birth of consciousness from the indistinct fluid realms of Atlantis, the film's metaphor for the subconscious. Louis and Bebe Barron's evocative score, whose meandering tones bent by an electronic synthesizer sound as if they too emerged from under the sea, restates in a different mode the film's primary image: water.

The visual track of *Bells of Atlantis* presents the alien but strangely familiar visionary realm "beyond the reach of human eyes and ears." The camera sways gently in contrasting directions over each of the three layers of superimposed images that are usually present. Hugo uses inner-cutting, slowly changing one layer of imagery (usually by dissolves, fades, and plastic cutting on black), while the other layers remain constant. The ebb and flow effects thus produced convey the rhythms and even the visual textures of water. The movements of the narrator (performed by Anaïs Nin) can be glimpsed through the "aquatic" space.

Hugo concentrates on shooting highly contrasted reflections off water whose colors are further intensified by various printing techniques which exploit masking and combined negative and positive imagery. (Hugo was assisted by Len Lye, pioneer avant-garde filmmaker whose experiments with painting and stenciling directly on film in *Color Box* (1935) and *Kaleidoscope* (1936) anticipated many formal initiatives of the 1950's). One of the great colorists of the independent cinema, Hugo uses color symbolically. Blues and greens, occasionally accented by more intense contrasting orange-red hues, represent the erotic subconscious which is night-filled Atlantis. As the narrative progresses, reds and pinks symbolizing flesh, daylight and terror come to dominate the color scheme. The washes of subtly related colors flow across the screen in rhythmic waves through-

The Wonder Ring by Stan Brakhage

Bridges-Go-Round by Shirley Clarke

The Wonder Ring by Stan Brakhage

out the film, evoking those "colors running into each other without frontiers," announced in the monologue, as the space where one finds "no currents of thoughts, only the caress and flow of desire." This realm, articulated by the veils of color and flow of hypnagogic imagery (evanescent images preceding sleep), becomes the matrix for the presentation of the inner self, a lyrical theme adapted and greatly modified by Stan Brakhage.

Because of the extraordinary quality and variety of his prolific *oeuvre,* Stan Brakhage has come to be the exemplary figure of the American independent cinema. His films, made over a quarter century, encompass most of the major modes that have been developed and contain much of what has been and will be of enduring value in the history of American film art.

His early films were shaped by the formal and thematic preoccupations of the trance film genre. *The Wonder Ring,* made on a commission from Joseph Cornell, began his long apprenticeship to the modalities of visionary experience which would become his principal theme. The film's visual complexity emerges from an intensive examination of the soon-to-be-destroyed platforms and train cars of New York City's Third Avenue elevated subway. The multi-colored virtual spaces of glass reflections, the saccadic movement of light through the train, the web of girder silhouettes, and the rippling distortions of window panes that Brakhage records and edits into a rhythmic form that recapitulates the jerking movement of a subway ride, reveal the wealth of visual stimulation available to an attentive eye. More than that, Brakhage finds in the train's movements through the urban landscape a "natural" repertory of cinematic strategies—superimposition, distortion through special lenses, etc.—which are the tools of his art, and eventually form the essential vocabulary of his "lyric" style.

In a letter to P. Adams Sitney in 1963 (published as part of *Metaphors on Vision,* Brakhage's meditation on film and language), Brakhage wrote:

> My sensibilities are art-oriented to the extent that revelation takes place, naturally, within the given historical context of specifically Western aesthetics . . . most of what is revealed, thru my given sensibilities, clarifies itself in relationship to previous (and future, possible) works of art . . .

Perhaps more than any other of Brakhage's films, *The Wonder Ring* situates itself in the history of the twentieth century visual arts. Numerous "pictures" in the styles of Expressionism, Cubism, and Abstract Expressionism, the main stages of the moderns' critique of Renaissance pictorial space, virtually constitute a museum without walls within the film. These fleeting allusions are incorporated "naturally" within the shallow space of action characteristic of Brakhage's "lyric" style. Their inclusion also introduces an important problem later explored analytically and didactically by Ken Jacobs in *Tom, Tom, the Piper's Son* (1969): the relation of filmic spatiality to the catalogue of pictorial spaces proposed by the Western tradition in painting.

Bridges, especially those of New York City, have been central icons of modern American poetry and painting. Joseph Stella's "Brooklyn Bridge" canvases and Hart Crane's *The Bridge* come immediately to mind. A stanza from Crane's prefatory *To Brooklyn Bridge* might, in fact, serve as an invocation to the dancing bridges in Shirley Clarke's *Bridge-Go-Round.*

And Thee, across the harbor, silver paced
As though the sun took step of thee, yet left
Some motion ever unspent in thy stride,—
Implicitly thy freedom staying thee![3]

That Clarke's bridges should seem to dance is not surprising: she was
trained as a dancer before she began to make films. Her earliest works such
as *Dance in the Sun* (1953), *Bullfight* (1955), and *A Moment in Love*
(1957, choreographed with Anna Sokolow) belong to a lyrical dance film
form pioneered by Maya Deren's *A Study in Choreography for Camera*
(1945). This genre's synthesizing of diverse spaces by cutting on the
dancer's leap and matching shots along his implied trajectory is carried
over to the immobile subjects of *Bridges-Go-Round*.

The film's formal strategies make the massive structures seem to float
in a flowing, gravity-less space. "Sandwiching" and "inner-cutting," techniques which suspend the spatio-temporal coordinates by which gravity
can be measured, are the principal means used. In a note written for the
1958 Knokke-Le-Zoute festival catalogue, Clarke described their effect:

> "Sandwiching" [printing two or more image layers laid directly on top
> of each other] as opposed to superimposition, does not create a dark
> and a light (ghost) image but permits colors and shapes to have equal
> density in both images. . . . Red and blue in sandwiching make
> purple, whereas in superimposition only one of the colors, either red
> or blue is seen. . . ."Inner-cutting" means cutting during the course of
> the sandwiched shot, not at the beginning or end of it, but within the
> shot itself. This is a form of overlapping that produces the sensation
> of perpetual motion and flow which I have always sought to attain in
> my films. . . .

Though she did not originate these techniques, Clarke exploits them
elegantly in a film which almost consistently avoids the disjunctive breaks
of the simple cut.

Clarke's use of camera angles, highly contrasted images and compound
camera-zoom movements dematerialize the bridge forms and help to induce the sense of weightlessness. The generally low angles and high backlighting transforms the three dimensional shapes into two dimensional
abstract patterns. She often holds these visual shapes constant while
changing the image's tint, or makes sandwiched shapes meld into a new
graphic form. Most original, however, is her use of the zoom lens which
creates the illusion of motion through a change in lens ratios. Fixing on
a point of the bridge, she zooms in or out while continuing to move around
or through its structure. The bridge appears to rise from its foundation
and leap across the water separating it from the totemic sky-line of New
York City distantly sighted at the film's beginning and approached at its
conclusion.

A Movie's unassuming title masks the scope of its ambition. Conner's
first effort in the medium, it was originally exhibited in a show of his
collage sculptures which juxtaposed diverse objects with ambiguous
emotional charges to produce humorous effects. *A Movie* widens the
implications of these procedures. The twelve minute film aspires to be
more than a mere example, a film like any other; it elaborates an exem-

plary myth in a paradigmatic form. *A Movie* filters the abstracted energy of a Keystone cops short through forty years of cinema history to synthesize from the magnificent heterogeneity of the chasers and the chased, the bizarre and the traumatic, a persuasive comic vision of American catastrophe.

A Movie's formal structure is governed by the twin notions of collage and montage. Scrap film leader and movie scenes culled from a variety of genres (fictional narrative, documentary, military, etc.) are Conner's compositional materials. He fuses the diverse excerpts with a tongue-in-cheek academic montage which cuts on the movement of objects and subtly varies the direction of motion within the frame. These formal principles are further extended to the musical accompaniment. Odd fragments of popular classical and "mood" music parallel or contrast comically with the rhythm of visual events.

In a new demonstration of the famous "Kuleshov effect,"[4] the film's editing exploits the power of consecutive shots to suggest a continuity, even a causality, where none can plausibly exist. Teddy Roosevelt speaks and a bridge sways violently in the wind. A king is crowned and a volcano erupts. Or, in a remarkable sequence, a submarine captain is made to spy on an alluring woman-siren. The following shot of the firing of a torpedo shifts in meaning to become a sexual metaphor. A white mushroom cloud then explodes into a black-comic image of the orgasm. This supreme figure of annihilation is quickly reintegrated, however, into the ongoing action: the tidal waves it "causes" seem to "wipe-out" a surfer. And so on.

Conner's comic vision thus depends on hyperbolic extension of the action, anachronism, and shifts in the semantic structure of the images. Each strategy threatens to break apart the series of oxymoronic phrases fused by the montage. The film embodies these centrifugal energies in its own formal structure. Image sequences are repeatedly jolted by interruptions of black leader or puzzling reiterations of the film's title and filmmaker's credit. *A Movie* remains marvelously perched at the unstable juncture of these multiple formal and thematic tensions.

Robert Breer's first films, elaborated in a series titled *Form Phases*, grew out of his work as a painter committed to the geometric idioms of European neo-plasticism (Mondrian and Kandisky). This tradition's abstract formal vocabulary—flat color planes, clear ruled lines—were initially carried over into his films. Phases of abstract shapes or elements of drawing were photographed a single frame at a time (essentially the technique of cinematic animation). When the film was projected, the form appeared to develop continuously—a painting in motion. As Breer noted later, various abstract animated films from the 1920's, particularly those of Hans Richter, were important influences on his initial experiments.

The new medium was soon perceived to offer wide possibilities for invention and discovery. In Breer's words:

> Films were very liberating. . . . I wanted to see some things I'd never seen before. . . . For me, film was another medium that permitted mixing of all this extraneous stuff, ideas and words and configurative elements that I couldn't justify putting in paintings anymore.

Two important consequences thus resulted from Breer's extended encounter with film. First, he expanded his compositional materials to include collage elements, three-dimensional objects and figure drawings.

Recreation by Robert Breer

Secondly and more importantly, Breer began to investigate a problem which was to inform his best work for nearly a decade: isolating the "threshold" between cinematic and "normal" perception.

As its title connotes, *Recreation* emerged from playing with the film medium to invent a personal cinema based on speed and rooted in wonderment, which was to last through the early 1960's. In barely three minutes, an astonishing variety of two and three-dimensional objects— essentially the detritus littering an artist's studio which has invaded modern iconography since the Cubists—flash across the screen in static single-frame bursts. Even a partial list of the objects Breer used will convey their diversity: newspapers, Christmas cards, burlap, balls, photographs, film reels, colored shapes, crumpled paper, an orange peel, a leg, coiled rope, three-dimensional cartoons, contact sheets, a knife, and a mechanical mouse. Some images initially seen right side up reappear inverted or rotated ninety degrees to become entirely new perceptual units. Most of the images appear on screen for a mere $1/24$th of a second, the duration of one cinematic frame projected at normal sound speed. Because of their extraordinarily short duration on screen, the highly contrasted shapes and colors fuse into an optical blur of afterimages.

Recreation's speed and the heterogeneity of its images subvert the psychological bases—the so-called "persistence of vision" and "phi-phenomenon"—upon which our perception of moving objects in an illusionistically real space depends. The longer images—the longest lasts approximately three seconds—thus function both compositionally and theoretically. Visually, these static camera images punctuate the blur with a rhythmic ritard. Attention is drawn to the content of the shot— the little mechanical mouse crossing the screen space or a cartooned figure in motion—and away from the fact that such movements are composed of the integrated static phases (frames) of an action. The illusion of three-dimensional space and the ability to recognize objects are thus determined by the rate of image change and the degree to which the shapes in consecutive frames are integrated or disjunctive. These basic parameters define a threshold between recognizing an object that has been filmed and perceiving the film as an object composed of the rapid montage of static frames.

Heard over the image stream is an elaborately constructed run-on sentence spoken in French (composed and recited by Noël Burch) describing a fragmented chain of verbal reactions to the film (" . . . suddenly . . . this mysterious object . . . fortuitous convergence . . . popular images . . . mouse—or a smile—at the end.") The narrator's breathless struggle to keep pace with the images quickly becomes a witty joke.

The lyrical form which Brakhage pioneered posits a fictive self as the source for the images seen on screen. In the first masterpiece of this style, *Anticipation of the Night,* a nervously pacing "shadow man" seen at the beginning becomes the mediator—a thinly disguised replacement for Brakhage himself. (The two are joined in the hanged man at the film's conclusion.) The long central section figures his contemplation of suicide. His memories, hopes, speculations and desperate fascination for the light are fused by Brakhage's plastic cutting on dark or unfocused images, and his use of continuous camera movements across the shot changes. Each motif of his meditation is articulated as a rhythmic-textural unit of related image clusters (the pacing man, the child on the grass, the amusement park, the temple structure, the sleeping children) which, from its first

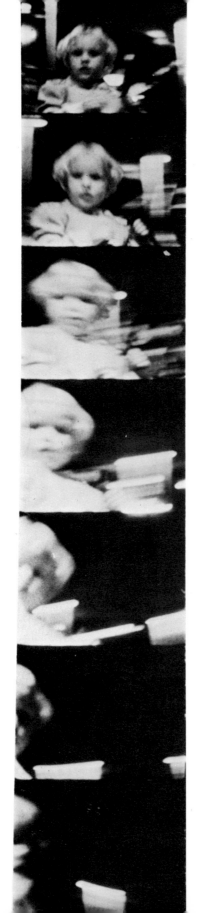

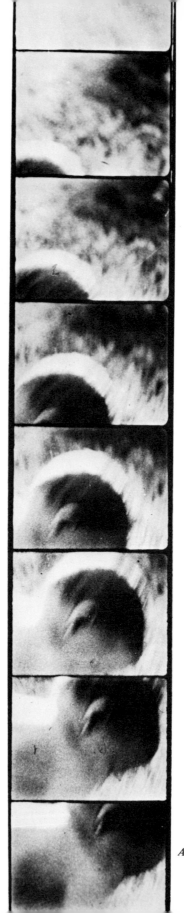

Anticipation of the Night
Stan Brakhage

brief appearance, gradually assumes dominance as the previous motif recedes to become a punctuating interlude.

The conventional uses of film techniques are deliberately violated as Brakhage translates all aural and tactile sensations into modes of visual experience. The rapid camera movements behind which can be sensed the filmmaker's violent gestures swing freely through space, transforming objects into streaks of light on an ambiguously deep ground and unifying discontinuous spaces.

By contrast, the earlier work, *The Wonder Ring*'s smooth slow movements follow the horizontal and vertical directions of the traditional pan and tilt and respect the spatial *données*. The speed and complexity of *Anticipation*'s editing undermines the coherent spatial and temporal order of conventional narrative exposition. Inverted images, accelerated motion, varying degrees of exposure and focus, the inclusion of film leader and end flares are all employed to weld disparate objects and spaces into a chain of metaphoric transformations which forms *Anticipation*'s poetic argument. Condensing time and space into a perpetual present,[5] the film's formal structure ultimately embodies Brakhage's great project: the representation of the movements of consciousness itself.

—Stuart Liebman

Footnotes

1. P. Adams Sitney. *Visionary Film,* New York: Oxford University Press, 1974, p. 21.

2. Annette Michelson, "Camera Lucida/Camera Obscura," *Artforum,* Vol. XI, No. 5, January 1973, p. 37.

3. Hart Crane. *The Complete Poems and Selected Letters and Prose of Hart Crane,* edited by Brom Weber, New York: Anchor Books, 1966, p. 45.

4. Named after the pioneer Russian director and theorist, Lev Kuleshov, the Kuleshov effect (also occasionally referred to as the "Mozhukin experiment") emerged from an experiment conducted with filmed images of the matinee idol, Mozhukin, intercut with three unrelated shots (a bowl of soup, a child at play, a woman in a coffin). Though the same image of the expressionless actor was used in each sequence, viewers interpreted his mood respectively, as hungry, happy and sad. Kuleshov thereby "proved" that an individual shot was "neutral" in meaning and that it acquired significance only when linked in a sequence with other images.

5. Michelson. *op. cit.,* p. 37.

Science Friction (Stan Vanderbeek)
Prelude, Dog Star Man (Stan Brakhage)
Notebook (Marie Menken)
Little Stabs at Happiness (Ken Jacobs)
Mass for the Dakota Sioux (Bruce Baillie)

Imagine an eye unruled by man-made laws of perspective, an eye un-prejudiced by compositional logic, an eye which does not respond to the name of everything but which must know each object encountered in life through an adventure of perception.

–Stan Brakhage, from the beginning of
Metaphors on Vision

. . . I just look at the pictures in the articles, it doesn't matter what they say about me; I just read the textures of the words. I see everything that way, the surface of things, a kind of mental Braille. I just pass my hands over the surface of things.

–Andy Warhol, from an interview

In 1964, two rather distinct and often contradictory modes of filmic structure were evident in the foreground of New American filmmaking. Neither approach was organized or consistently applied—in the manner of a School—and neither derived from a single impulse or set of sources. A number of artists worked with only marginal participation in or totally divorced from the prerogatives of either approach. And by the mid-sixties, one style had achieved its apogee—serving primarily as a negative model for subsequent filmmaking—while the other was in a state of growth and transformation, evolving as the dominant mode of the late sixties.

In articulating the genesis of the former, the mature style, P. Adams Sitney has stated:

What took place between 1950 and 1960 was the growth of a form which could contain many simultaneous characters, episodes, and fantastic changes of space: a comparative cinema, with symphonic organization of parts into a grand mythopoeic whole. I've called this elsewhere the exchange from a cinema of conjunction to a cinema of metaphor.[1]

This cinema of metaphor generally displays a tight, highly conscious organization suffused by a density of formal and thematic image correlations. Editing is the principal means of generating comparison (superimposition can also serve this function) and the temporality in these films is most often multi-valent and achronological. Stan Brakhage, Bruce Baillie, Kenneth Anger, and Harry Smith have all produced major films containing these qualities.

The other tendency might be termed a cinema of "informal structure" in its suppression of the rigid bonds of color, shape, texture, and verbal association which solidify the "mythopoeic" films. There is a marked de-emphasis on analytical montage—implicit in the use of extended takes—

and a tendency to identify cinematic time with the viewer's sphere of temporality. This group of films often retains a parodic attachment to the Hollywood narrative, an attachment consistent with its higher degree of photographic illusionism (temporal as well as spatial). Spontaneity, improvisation, and chance correspondence—framed by quasi-narrative situations—establishes an ambiance very much at odds with the concentrated bursts of associative material found in the films of Brakhage or Anger. In its distension of the cinematic moment, its obsessive attention to "posing" and "acting," and its engendering of a heightened awareness of the camera as observer and mediator of action, the "informal structure" invites a reconsideration of cinematic construction devoid of internal metaphor or complex balancing of parts. Certain films by Andy Warhol, Ken Jacobs, and Jack Smith exemplify this form.

Despite their apposite approaches, both forms share the aspiration of creating a dialogue between the illusionistic and expressive capacities of the film medium and its material bases and working processes—a dialogue that was at least partially resolved by the procedures of the later "structural" cinema. In Brakhage's *Prelude,* the formation of metaphor is subtended by an awareness of the film's material surface. In Jacob's *Little Stabs at Happiness*, the employment of a deep illusionistic space is countered by a variety of techniques which obscure the lens and cancel depth. A central issue, then, for both forms is the problem of representation: how to continue to use human subject matter (particularly the human body) by transforming or endistancing it from a naturalistic context and, at the same time, affirming various "objective" qualities of the medium. This dialogue is inscribed in the spectrum of formal and thematic concerns defined by the films on this program.

If the presence of explicit political commentary in Stan Vanderbeek's *Science Friction* and Bruce Baillie's *Mass* separates these films somewhat from the dominant thematic context of the mythopoeic film (creation, self-identity, "death, judgement, heaven and hell"), the structures of both works rely on a condensing of disparate associative material into metaphoric clusters. Vanderbeek was an early experimenter and propagandist for a wide range of technological options: multiple-screen projection, film loops, computer-generated images, and film/video synthesis. He is best known, however, for his collage animations on topical issues, films which he refers to as "Poetic-satires." *Science Friction* uses a variety of techniques—live-action footage, object animation and graphic cut-outs, the direct application of paint—to underline a theme of "the insidious folly of competitive suicide (by way of rockets.)"[2] In the course of the film, popular media (television, newspapers, and movies) are implicated along with political figures in the propounding of "Space Race" ideology.

The film begins with scientists peering through a microscope at a multi-limbed muscleman whose internal organs are revealed as a concoction of television advertisements. This "modern" man becomes a Frankenstein head, bursting from its confinement, initiating a rocket blast toward the moon, and obliterating the scientists in a deluge of paint. The reference to Frankenstein is soon bolstered by a live-action sequence of a mad experimenter (played by Vanderbeek) mixing some colored potions in a laboratory. A T.V. screen emerges, flashing a collage of commercials and dramatic scenes; then the finger which had animated the set shuts it off. A rocket shatters the screen, pierces the finger and finally comes to rest in the target of Nikita Kruschev's bald head. This begins a flurry of "take-offs" constituting the central portion of the film. A newspaper folds itself into the shape of a rocket and rises out of the frame. As Eisenhower and Kruschev observe through telescopes, a cigar, a teapot, a fountain-pen, an ice-cream sundae, and other objects are projected into orbit. At one point, a rocket crashes through the house of an unsuspecting consumer and impales him.

A brief newsphoto survey of architectural monuments—East and West—is followed by the ignition and assumption of the Empire State Building, Eiffel Tower, Kremlin, and Washington Monument, among other buildings. The world is revealed as a place of potential rockets and potential targets. The heads of the two Cold War leaders emerge through the ends of their telescopes in time to set off a montage of a single-frame images and sections of blank leader figuring an imminent nuclear holocaust, ending—quite literally—with an image of the earth as a fried egg.

The pun in the film's title makes reference to a Hollywood genre whose popularity in the fifties was due in part to its thinly-allegorical rendering of Cold War conflicts (Don Siegal's *Invasion of the Body Snatchers* is a good example). Vanderbeek's film seems to implicate—in a playful manner—the technologized vision of *science fiction* as contributing to the cult of missile hardware. The soundtrack of machine noise and electronic tones, the intermittent cutting to patterns of revolving concentric circles (reminiscent of Duchamp's *Anemic Cinema*), and the stuttering movement of the animated cutouts, suggests *Science Friction* as a kind of self-destructing machine whose collage images pull apart and vacate the frame. Each successive composition is subject to a reverse gravitational force that destroys its stability.

The relation of television to political attitudes is again a theme in Bruce Baillie's *Mass,* although here the filmmaker's questioning of his own status within a deteriorating environment results in a highly complex and ambivalent statement. In his notes for the film, Baillie identifies an emphatic ritual structure:

Introit: A long, lightly exposed section composed in the camera.
Kyrie: A motorcyclist crossing the San Francisco Bay Bridge accompanied by the sound of the Gregorian chant.
The *Epistle* is in several sections. In this central part, the film becomes gradually more outrageous, the material being either television or the movies, photographed directly from the screen. The sounds of the "mass" rise and fall throughout the *Epistle.*
Gloria: The sound of a siren and a short sequence with a '33 Cadillac proceeding over the Bay Bridge and disappearing into a tunnel.
The final section of the *Communion* begins with the *Offertory* in a procession of lights and figures in the second chant. The anonymous figure from the introduction is discovered again, dead on the pavement. The touring car arrives, with the celebrants; the body is consecrated and taken away past an indifferent, isolated people accompanied by the final chant.[3]

Although several distinct sections are evident, the global form retains an ambiguity—in point-of-view and narrative evolution—not suggested by Baillie's account. The dedication—"For the Dakota Sioux"—indicates a thematic element that, of necessity, is articulated indirectly. As Baillie writes: "The dedication is to the religious people who were destroyed by

Science Friction by Stan Vanderbeek

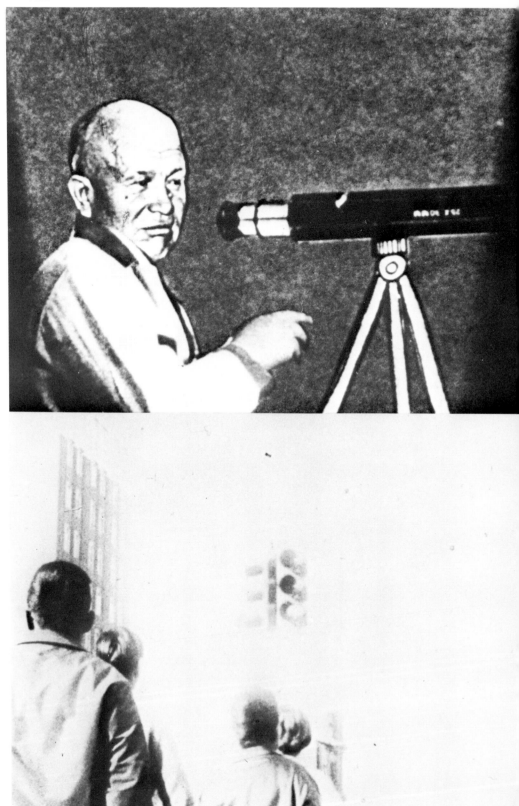

Mass for the Dakota Sioux by
Bruce Baillie

the civilization which evolved the Mass."[4] The title itself can be read on
at least two other levels: as a reference to the density and weight of both
the image and sound tracks, and as a description of the nameless, ghostlike
faces that populate the film's urban landscape. That the human figures
command an expressive physical presence within a context of dimly and
brightly exposed images, layers of superimposition, and shots in negative,
confirms the filmmaker's extraordinary sensitivity to his unposed subjects.

After an epigraph by Sitting Bull ("No chance for me to live
mother/You might as well mourn"), the first image is a close-up of clapping hands—a framing device that recurs following the central section. On
a dark sidewalk we see a man crawling just beyond a square of light. He
appears to be drunk or seriously ill.

After this introduction is a section—much of it superimposed—of city
shapes and movements. Smokestacks, telephone lines, a busy street
corner, an automobile harboring a face in the window, drift through the
frame articulated by slow panning shots and dissolves. The filmmaker is
glimpsed for a moment through a luminous haze that surrounds much of
the footage. In this section, Baillie sets up a cross-directionality of screen
movements—with specific images seeming to advance or recede through
layers of texture—that conveys both a sense of weariness and ritual motion
and has a precise parallel in the soundtrack. Street noises intermingle with
the Gregorian chant, one element then the other assuming audial
dominance. As the voices of the chant rise and fall in pitch, the patterns
of imagery shift in direction or velocity through matched editing.

In the second section of the film, a long travelling shot precedes a
clear image of the cyclist, possibly the protagonist and mediator of the
urban vision. A long pan across rooftops is connected to a shot of rows of
suburban houses squeezed together on an incline. A title appears: "Behold,
a good nation walking in a sacred manner in a good land." The resemblance
of the peaked roofs to Indian tepees underscores the bitter irony of a displaced people.

This signals the start of the central and most intense portion of the
film, elaborated by increasingly ironic and politicized juxtapositions. A
frieze of the Virgin is enjambed with the face of a church gargoyle. A
montage of television images—Boris Karloff, commercials, a marching
band—develops a theme of spectatorship and mass destruction. In one
sequence, a shot of a street derelict cuts to a woman's face in an advertise-
ment: "Doctor, I've been having these terrible muscle spasms in my arm."
The next shot is of a field cannon spasming as it discharges its shell. The
implication that media—and the culture in general—trivializes pain and
death thereby fostering an acceptability of human and ecological disaster
is extended through a series of violent match-cuts.

At the end of this section, three men and a boy are seen against a
window clapping enthusiastically. This highly problematic shot simultaneously offers a climax to the preceding sequence and acts as an un-
comfortable distancing device to the film's structure. The opening shot of
the crawling man and the closing sequence described in the notes are obviously acted and extremely artificial in nature. The clapping audience
calls attention to and makes suspect these heavily dramatic scenes and
also the editing tour-de-force just witnessed.

In the midst of the rapid montage—and later at the close of the film—
an image of waves breaking onto a beach tries to insert itself through the
welter of urban violence. But this invocation of the "natural," the peace-
ful, is finally unattainable. The ocean is filled with battleships or, in the

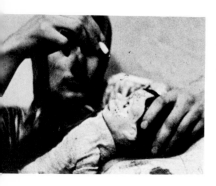

second to last shot, is screened by a bright haze with the silhouette of a solitary figure poised at its edge. The exploration of what Sitney calls the "heroic" in Baillie's films has its locus in the condition of the "outsider," one incapable of sustaining meaningful contact with either the victims of a culture he condemns or with his nostalgic intimation of a pastoral existence. This is one of the supreme tensions underlying all of Baillie's work, finding its most poignant expression in *Valentin de las Sierras* (1967) and its tentative resolution in *Quick Billy* (1971).

In Ken Jacobs' *Little Stabs at Happiness,* the alienated human presence is relaxed from the confines of social and political realities—and from a formalized structure—in order to indulge and be indulged by the casual, if insistent, gaze of a mediated camera eye. Jacobs, who later produced the rigorously analytic *Tom, Tom, the Piper's Son* (1969), here constructs a form whose episodes—based on the flimsiest of narrative situations—never coalesce into a temporal, spatial, or thematic continuum. *Little Stabs* is comprised of six sections of differing lengths assembled more-or-less as they emerged from the camera: four sections have titles ("In the Room," "They Stopped to Think," "It Began to Drizzle," "The Spirit of Listlessness"); four have sound attached (three musical interludes and a spoken monologue), two contain Jack Smith. Just as each episode is subverted visually or aurally or in terms of duration by the one that follows it, each episode contains numerous internal disruptions induced through editing, composition, or camera movement.

A rough breakdown of the first section will indicate Jacobs' method. After a title card, "In the Room," the sound of surface scratches on a presumably old 78rpm record is heard. The underlining of the source and age of the sound accompaniment is expanded in the monologue of the second section to include ellipses, asides, and direct, personal references to people on the screen. A light flare (signifying the start of a roll) initiates a tilt-down and pan right over the top of a head. There is a cut to a medium close-up of a hand flicking ashes into a paper flower. Roll perforations intrude, denoting the source and material basis of the projected image. A pan to the left from a woman in a bathtub discovers Smith, who acknowledges the camera with an animated expression and begins to puff furiously on a cigarette. This cuts to Smith in medium shot jabbing a cigarette into the eye of a doll, then to several takes of the woman lifting the cigarette from the eye. Christmas ornaments are dangled in front of the camera lens obscuring the field, and this is followed by several shots of a light bulb, a clay-like form, then a soft-focus extreme close-up of Smith gnawing at the crotch of a doll. The background music is a rendition of "Bubble Your Troubles Away." A shot near the end of the section displays a crowded, heavily textured and gaudily colored composition—recalling, perhaps, Joseph von Sternberg—involving the two actors and various objects.

The alternation of distracted, unfinished-looking compositions with carefully mapped, quasi-aesthetic views is a strategy reiterated in several interludes. Its exposure and assault on conventional notions of pictorial "beauty" are paralleled by seemingly arbitrary intercuts (the shot of the pigeon in the fourth section) and the replacement of stable camera setups by manically hand-held movements. Further, any expectation of narrative or dramatic development is dispelled by a rupture in the visual style or, simply, by the ending of a roll. The episode entitled "It Began To Drizzle" suggests a potential incident: the arrangement of the male and female players, the "decor" and studied compositions anticipate a liaison, a seduction. Yet nothing happens between them. Eventually, a car enters the

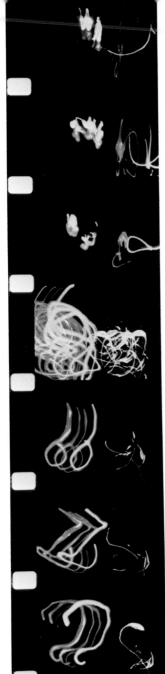

scene and they proceed to exit. In the film as a whole, what is perceived initially as spontaneous clowning emerges as a carefully executed system of disruptions of continuity—a revision of the Surrealist aesthetic operating in Buñuel's *L'Age d'Or* and filtered through a previous generation of American experimental film.

Although the shooting was completed for Jacobs' film in 1960, it was assembled and a soundtrack was added sometime after the first screening of Marie Menken's *Notebook* in 1962. Constructed from fragments of footage stored since the late 1940's, the casual unfolding of *Notebook* belies a number of formal correspondences cementing the nine sketch-like segments. Several commentators have remarked that the only way to fully appreciate the film is to view it as an unprojected strip since it was edited for visual qualities contained in lengths of film, rather than individual frames. The most obvious example of this is the hand-painted sketch "Copycat" in which diagonal bands and blocks of color transcend the boundaries of the inscribed frame to form diamond shapes and trapazoids. The segments "Lights" and "Moonplay" also share a sense of shape as defined by the graphic flow of successive images.

Each section of the film is introduced by a title appearing on a background of clear leader. The transparency of these shots performs the function of voiding the material of the concluding section and easing transitions between color shape. There is a progression from black and white in the opening sections to gradually saturated color in the middle parts, and a similar movement from static camerawork in "Raindrops" to frenzied swish-panning in "Nightwriting." A structural tension between prominent round forms (particularly in "Raindrops," "Moonplay," and "Lights") and linear configurations (in "Copycat," "Nightwriting" and "Etc. Etc. Etc.") is also present.

Several persistent formal concerns are in evidence. In the first two sections, internal shapes and movements of objects within the frame are explored. In "Moonplay," "Lights," and "Nightwriting," the external movement of the camera—at times amplified by pixillation—transforms objects and light sources, creating its own synthetic shapes. In "Copycat" and "Paper Cuts," movement and shape are functions of graphic manipulation. In the last section, "Etc. Etc. Etc." Menken combines camera movement and object movement, with the recording speed controlling velocity and rhythm.

Notebook is a work which bridges the options of both the "informal" and "metaphoric" approaches. Its ostensibly simple abuttment of discontinuous sections reflects a loosening of global schemata. And Sitney, in *Visionary Film*, identifies a series of procedures used by Menken that are found in Brakhage's output of the late 1950's and early 1960's.[5] The maker of *Prelude* confirms this observation in the following tribute: "It is the ideology, if you can call it that, of Marie's working processes which have influenced my work. She made me aware that I was freer than I knew."[6] Brakhage goes on to state that her use of the hand-held camera and orientation to the film-strip (rather than the screen) provided him with important insights into the possibilities of filmic structure.

Prelude is the first section of the five-part *Dog Star Man*, begun in 1960 and completed at the end of 1964. It is a film of monumental scope and achievement and its prelude—the most independently structured of the five parts—can be fully comprehended, only in relation to its subsequent development.

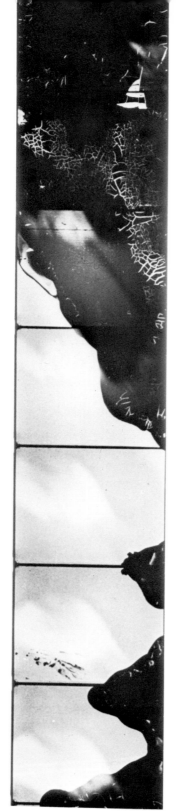

Prelude, Dog Star Man by Stan Brakhage

In an account of *Dog Star Man*'s structure and narrative evolution, Brakhage provides this brief synopsis:

> The man climbs the mountain out of winter and night into the dawn, up through spring and early morning to midsummer and high noon, to where he chops down the tree . . . There's a Fall—and a fall back to somewhere, midwinter.[7]

Brakhage says of this first section that he "wanted *Prelude* to be a created dream for the work that follows rather than Surrealism which takes its inspiration from dream."[6] This "created dream" is composed of two superimposed layers of imagery (at times various techniques appear to multiply the layers); the first is a "chaos" roll assembled by chance operations from the totality of the film's footage and later re-edited to integrate with the second, consciously ordered roll. The superimposition—which can take many forms[8]—conflates with techniques such as anamorphic photography, scratching or painting on the film surface, rapid camera movement, and dimly or brightly exposed images in producing a consistently flattened depth. Moreover, the cutting between layers of superimposition generally obfuscates clear shot transitions, rendering the illusion of a continuous flow of rapidly changing shape, texture, and subject.

Prelude begins with a minute or so of darkness. As the viewer's eye becomes adjusted to the field, two dim emanations of light—one diagonal, the other circular—penetrate the visual stillness. A bright flash precedes another dim light that appears to advance from the depth and pass over the camera. Darkness returns, then an uncovering of a blank, lighted surface. Fingers, perhaps a face, are vaguely discerned. Images of ice, the lights of a city at night, a flame, materialize. Fred Camper has said of this opening: "It is the beginning of the film, the beginning of the dreamer's . . . dream and perception: it is the beginning of the universe."[9] One could add that it is also the genesis of the photographic image—the first seepage of light onto the *tabula rasa* of the emulsion. In the multiple comparisons between human, natural, microscopic, and telescopic elements, a constant implicit element is the structure and processes of film image formation. For example, in the linkage of capillary action within the body and a solar eruption, a secondary association with the rhythm of the filmstrip arises. The "universe" invoked in *Prelude* is anchored by the twin presence of the dreamer and shaper of filmic artifice.

Some of the methods by which Brakhage articulates comparison of diverse material are verbal association, color, texture, shape, camera movement, internal motion, placement in the frame. Metaphors are often generated by manifold elements; a woman's breast and the moon may be connected by verbal association, tonality and placement as well as shape. Images may be yoked in superimposition or compared across a cluster of shots. And elements once joined are later compared separately with apposite elements (women's bodies are conjoined with the sun, a flame, the moon, a tree trunk in different sections).

Also, sets of opposing elements which are dominant in one portion of the film become recessive in another: the fire/water opposition at the beginning gives way to sun/moon juxtapositions which in turn develop into male/female comparisons. It is also the case that the moon is more evident in the first half and the sun more evident in the second. There are elements—such as the wooded landscape—that are excavated gradually to assume a central position and other elements which make relatively few appearances (the beating heart). Non-photographic elements—painting and

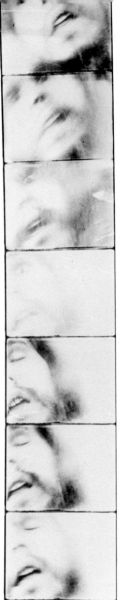

Prelude, Dog Star Man by Stan
Brakhage

scratching—acquire symbolic portent in proximity with photographed images or, as is the case with dark and black leader, serve as visual silences.

A tentative progression from darkness to subdued color to fully saturated tones and back to an understated palette is balanced by a prominence of blue and red in one section and an accenting of yellow and orange in another. A pattern of evolution from round or amorphous forms to a prevalence of vertical or linear figures presages the central narrative episode in the film: the Dog Star Man's struggle with the tree.

An asynchronous doubling of action on both layers of superimposition, the use of rapid zooms into and out of the man's almost sexual embracing of the tree, and a heightened employment of negative images and reverse motion set this sequence apart from the rest of the work. In this confrontation, the tree is associated with female genitals, seasonal indications fuse, solar and lunar references are merged. The Dog Star Man and a woman are seen kissing, then images of a baby breast-feeding and being held aloft by the protagonist are conjoined with scratches, solar explosions, and capillary flow.

The intensity of montage subsides into shots of a dark landscape with clouds passing in fast motion. After several more clusters—reiterating the moon and woman—separated by two dark pauses, the film ends on a landscape. This is the landscape into which the man will be thrust upon awakening. The flare-out at the end of *Prelude* suggests this awakening, but it will fall to the following four sections to develop and apotheosise this central theme.

—Paul S. Arthur

Footnotes

1. P. Adams Sitney. "The Idea of Morphology," *Film Culture, No. 53-54-55,* Spring 1972, p. 18.

2. Stan Vanderbeek. "On *Science Friction,*" *Film Culture No. 22-23,* Summer 1961, p. 168.

3. *Canyon Cinema Cooperative Catalogue,* 3, Sausalito, 1972, p. 19.

4. *Film-Makers' Cooperative Catalogue,* No. 4, New York, 1967, p. 13.

5. P. Adams Sitney. *Visionary Film,* New York: Oxford University Press, 1974.

6. Stan Brakhage, *Metaphors on Vision,* New York: Film-Maker's Cooperative, 1963.

7. Ibid.

8. Sitney. *Visionary Film, op. cit.,* p. 218.

9. Fred Camper. "*The Art of Vision,* A Film by Stan Brakhage," *Film Culture No. 46,* Autumn 1967, p. 40.

Scorpio Rising (Kenneth Anger)
Fire of Waters (Stan Brakhage)
Window (Ken Jacobs)
The Flicker (Tony Conrad)

Kenneth Anger's *Scorpio Rising* (1963) and Tony Conrad's *The Flicker* (1966) define a spectrum of film form and sense along with the work of other filmmakers of the sixties such as *Fire of Waters* (1965) by Stan Brakhage and *Window* (1964) by Ken Jacobs can be situated. On the one hand, evident in the latest film in this program, is Conrad's interest in the most basic, abstract units of film construction: light and shadow condensed into solid frame units, mathematically distributed along the film strip's space-time continuum and projected to produce an hypnotic, changing, and surprisingly unmeasurable experience of pulse and flux. As if searching out possible natural sources of such light and shadow play, Brakhage studies the black and white flashes and stillness of what appear at first to be the lightning apparitions of a thunderstorm; but these are soon discovered to be the equally synthetic manipulations of exposure, film stock, and single-frame pixillation which hint at and then reveal actual spaces, objects, and strange and fleeting fragments of sound. Jacobs captures similarly ephemeral shadows of forms and structures in a city scape as they are endowed with rhythmic and choreographed movements of a lyrical, gesturing camera. Anger in *Scorpio Rising* also exploits the unifying and graceful properties of camera movement, sharp colors, forms, and lighted surfaces, uses irony in the form of sound-image and editorial juxtapositions to create a ritual documentary of an era's cult and its magic.

Of the four films, *Scorpio Rising* is the most elaborate and seductive, with its intriguing mixture of sensuous surfaces caressed by a smooth moving camera and rock songs with pleasingly familiar, now nostalgic, tunes and lyrics. The combination is more perverse and explosive than one at first suspects. The thirteen songs, played for the most part in their entirety, provide the primary subdivisions of the film and tend to undermine or comment on the visual material. "Fools rush in, where wise men fear to tread" accompanies the first bike polishing and fitting rile. "My boyfriends' back and he's comin' after you-oo" greets a biker as he carefully prepares a ritual toilette and introduces the latent and blatant, largely homosexual, eroticism which dominates the film. "She wore blue velvet" comically contrasts with the zipping up of blue jeans, mimicked by a vertical camera tilt, while red flashes and "Heat Wave" reproduce on aural and visual levels a "high," as the biker snorts cocaine. "I will follow him, whereever he may go" equates the cyclists' allegiance with Christ's disciples and Hitler's troops, a comparison underlined by match cuts joining similar lines of movement and actions in the Hollywood Christ film footage and a Hell's Angels' initiation "party." The songs, often mixed with loud bike noises, and camera movements carry over the enormous number of cuts which join a large inventory of diverse materials: shiny fenders, studded belts and jackets, James Dean memorabilia, comic strips, muscle-bound bodies, flashes of color and lights, scorpion insignias, video-

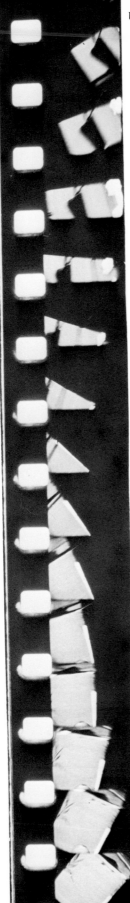

textured movie footage, Nazi emblems and checkers, and stock shots of Hitler and army ranks.

More so than any of the other films, *Scorpio Rising* follows a procession of events which do not constitute a linear narrative as such, but do suggest a ritualistic progression from arising and dressing in preparation for a "party" cyclist (the initiation and convocation) and bike race (the apocalypse and sacrifice) which ends in an actual "wipe-out" death for one and a metaphorical death for all. Individual bikers are seen in full figure in deep spaces as they perform their polishing and dressing rites. These deep, narrative spaces and actions are then, however, systematically undercut with materials in flatter spaces which are tangentially or metaphorically related to those activities. The hand-held camera which circulates around the party sequence is the furthest removed element from the formal control which unifies and stylizes much of the other action footage. The intercutting, for example, of a mustard-plastered crotch and wagging penises with shots of an indignant Jesus Christ sets up still another synthetic framework to reorient and comment on this quasi-documentary footage.

Beneath the often comic action and ironic commentary of these moments is a sense of violence accentuated by abrupt contrasts of light and shadow, flat and deep spaces, and noise and song. The erotic and sado-masochistic anointment of mustard, the tough leathers, the screeching of cycles, the tyrannic leader's defamation of an altar and his gun waving, and the final montage evocation of a biker's death double the irony of "Hit the road, Jack, and don't you come back no more, no more, no more . . ." And, the film occasionally parodies and marvelously invokes the concerns of all of Anger's film work: demons, the occult, sexual rites, Magick, myths, fire, and death.

More quiet and abstract is *Window*, Jacobs' study of the lines, frames, shadows, and recesses of a window space animated by a constantly moving camera. Jacobs describes his method:

> About four years of studying the window-complex preceded the afternoon of actual shooting (a true instance of cinematic action-painting). The film exists as it came out of the camera, barring one mechanically necessary, mid-reel splice.[1]

The careful relationships of planes, textures, and lighting would not lead one to expect such a spontaneous method were it not for the marvellously fluid, active "choreography for camera." Jacobs continually manipulates focal distance, lighting, and lenses to endow one, static space with hundreds of new aspects and directions and speeds of motion.

Major contrasts, imperceptible in the flow of a continuous viewing, can be seen on closer scrutiny of the film on an analytic projector: contrasts between flat, screen-surface planes and a deeper, textured, more recognizable geography; between geometrically shaped areas of solid black and white and grainier, colored, reflecting or textured surfaces; between objects which occupy space, such as a water-beaded horizontal sheet of tar paper, a man and woman, a hanging globe, and a statuette and again more abstract, graphic spaces from which shapes often seem cut out; between spaces on a firm, horizontal/vertical axis and those which rotate in and around that axis; and finally between movement and frozen stillness.

Devices and materials which create the smooth, invisible transitions from shot to shot and space to space are fades done in the camera, changes in focus, backlighting modulating to frontal lighting, a window shutter which opens a slit of light in the shadow before it, and camera

Window by Ken Jacobs

Fire of Waters by Stan Brakhage

movement continuing over the cut. Nearer the end, superimpositions juxtapose in the space of one shot two spaces and times which overlap and define the distance between them. The film presents a few moments of visual beauty in the shifting network of a multitude of frames. Transforming the inert into the moving, Jacobs' camera travels from form to form with delicacy and grace.

Although Brakhage, in earlier films, pioneered the art of gesturing camera and lyrical combinations of refracted planes and light, in *Fire of Waters* he reduces more rigorously than Jacobs the area and units of his visual concerns and derives from shadow, light and mysterious spaces a remarkably subtle evocation of forms and their dissolution in cinematic time. Far removed from the epic dimensions of *Dog Star Man,* Brakhage presages the intimacy of the *Songs* in *Fire of Waters*'s quiet, vanishing windows and lights. And, in addition, the film explores and exploits momentarily the mysteries of film illusionism: frame, grain, light, dark, sprocket holes, sound, silence, and motion.

On first viewing, one perhaps assumes that Brakhage has captured the momentary flashes of light and long periods of darkness with which lightning reveals the silhouette of a house and then engulfs it. Yet the strangely minimal sound track, the presence of "defects" in the film stock and frame alignment, and above all the nearly comical moving around of people in a real, deep landscape suggest that still another level of magic is at work. To quote the seer of *Blue Moses*, the lightning is like "An eclipse—manufactured, but not yet patented . . . for your pleasure."[2]

Paul Arthur, in his analysis of four Brakhage films in *Artforum,* suggests that the film is a product of systematic single frame exposure and underexposure, as close examination of the film strip confirms.[3] The lightning flashes seem to be the result of severely overexposing one frame and underexposing the others, all during daylight hours. The flickering on the house at full exposure further suggests that changes are synthetically created. The propelling of a figure down the sidewalk is even clearer evidence of single-frame construction. Passages of pure flickering light on film stock are another synthetic occurrence.

Until this daylight section at the end, the film seems to be a piercing of a dark ground by lit-up shapes and silhouettes at unexpected intervals: a circular light source on the far left of the frame, two window frames or one window frame, or a cloud-covered moon. The carving out of that black field in turn suggests a deeper, "real" space slightly behind. Horizon lines and house frames horizontally divide the field into light top, dark bottom, forms which quickly recede into that field again. These shots appear to be a series of continuous, static takes of horizons or houses which lightning illuminates from behind.

Still another surface seems to hover in front of this plane of houses and the space behind it, defined by the very grainy, gray field, slashes of white on black leader, water spots or emulsion defects appearing over the dark field or lightning images, and areas of light in the shape of sprocket holes on the upper and lower edges of some frames. At one point, in a bright section, what seems like a liquid bleeding in of white from the edges into areas of grainy emulsion defines a very slightly more sculptural surface.

The most enigmatic part of Brakhage's "last sound film" until 1975 is the highly fragmented track consisting of three intervals of "sound,"

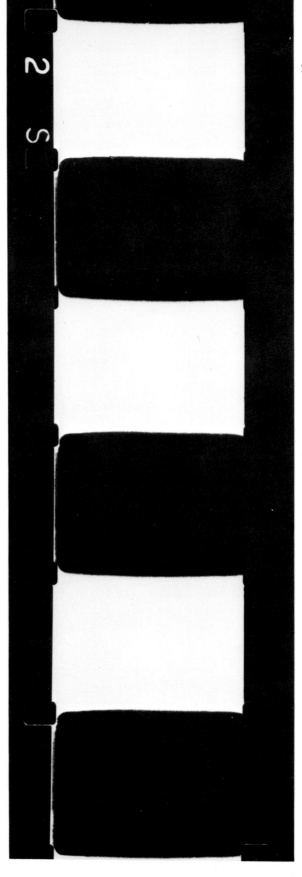

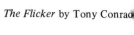
The Flicker by Tony Conrad

and of the crackles and clicks produced by the blank portions of the track passing over the sound drum in the projector. Again, close examination of the film strip shows zig-zags in the soundtrack area through only a few feet of the film; the rest is clear celluloid. The first section of the track accompanies the titles and sounds like the clatter of hooves or guns firing in a Western on a TV at a distance from the sound recorder. This seems to me to be Brakhage's ironic and even funny comment on synchronous sound and narrative modes which are rejected in this film and nearly all others.

The sound in this first section stops abruptly. Several minutes later we are reminded that this is a sound film by the rather pitiful scratching out of three descending notes repeated three times on a cello on what sounds like a very worn out record surface with louder, more defined cracklings than just the blank parts of the soundtrack provide. Accompanying the dark, imageless screen, the strains of music seems to parody the emotional accents which music has traditionally provided for narrative films. The final squeaky, shrill noise, possibly the persistent yelp of a dog seems again to be a comic accompaniment for the fast-motion, pixillated movement of cars and pedestrians forward along the street by the house which is now fully and therefore potentially "narratively" visible. The sound track then also confirms reports that Brakhage is up to magical appearances and disappearances, an abstracted inheritance from Méliès.

It is unfortunate that audiences of a film like Conrad's *The Flicker* cannot be given a print of a few feet of the film to hand around and examine after its projection for there really are two very different experiences of the film: the first, a bewildering play of flickering light and shadow, with appearing and disappearing, always imagined forms and even colors, which radically flood and darken the screening room; the second is the revelation that all these effects and illusions are produced simply by the metrical alternation of black and clear frames of celluloid in seemingly endless permutations and combinations which can be counted and even reproduced on another celluloid strip, if one had the enormous patience which the film's construction must have required.

The projected experience of the film begins with what seems a sarcastic suggestion on a title card that the film can induce nausea, migraine headaches, and epileptic seizures, and therefore requires a physician in attendance. Actually, such optical stimulation *can* cause serious physical responses quite different from the aesthetic, as literature on stroboscopic effects distributed by societies for the treatment of epilepsy warns.[4] The accompanying sound tape (separate from the film and to be synchronized during projection) begins with old grammaphone music and calls into question the seriousness of this long-held message which it accompanies. A one-frame, graphically compact card reads "Conrad presents" and dissolves to another black and white graphic composition of the film title. Finally "1966 Conrad," scratched into the emulsion, gives way to the flickering light from which the title is derived.

The film itself is so fluid in appearance that it is difficult to subdivide it. At the beginning, there seems to be a faster and faster pulse which is vaguely perceived as the throbbing of a white field. With no subject matter to enforce one's attention, one's eye tends to wander around the frame and room to gather in the full and wild impact of the film. Depending on the projection conditions, dust around the frame edge and particles and scratches in the field, often moving by quickly, can be noticed. Also, the frame line at the top or bottom appears to vibrate up and down a bit, giving another sense of rhythm or periodicity to one's viewing.

The light vibrations of the flicker bring optical illusions into play, which vary with different viewers and viewing situations. Patterns of light, colors, and even shadows of seemingly hidden forms appear as the film continues. At times there seems to be a swirling movement hovering around the center of the frame; at other times yellow and/or green and purple seem to vibrate in and tint the field. The surface of the screen seems radiant and brilliant as the light strikes forward into the space before the screen and assaults the viewer.

Later on, the light and dark interchange seems to thrust in and out in an even deeper space and seems to speed up again toward the end. Meanwhile, the taped sound of white noise also varies in volume and quality, fading in and out, speeding up and slowing down, sometimes in coordination with the flicker, sometimes more independently. It is a clicking machine noise, reminiscent of the non-existent sections of the sound track of *Fire of Waters*. Strained to the limits of the persistence of vision which makes the actual units of the film illegible, the eye comes to a rest at last; the stare is cut off and dissolved into conversation and questions.

What is the film, anyway? According to Conrad, a musician as well as a filmmaker:

Each pattern is then seen to suggest a "chord" related to the "tonic". The patterns used were, in fact, constructed in such a way that each one contains visible components contributed by up to three related frequencies. These flicker triads represent, to my knowledge, the first meaningful extension of harmonic principles to the visual sense.[5]

Examination of the strip does not make a triadic principle any clearer. Approximately the first half of the film is constructed on a certain ratio of clear leader frames to one black frame which separates each grouping of clear leader frames. In other words, the light frames dominate any series. For example, a group of twenty-three clear frames and one black frame is repeated twenty-five times at the beginning, a series exactly one second or 24 fps in duration. Then a gradual decrease in the number of clear frames per black frame from 11 clear frames per 1 black to 5 clear frames per one black is executed. From then on, the patterns are for the most part more complicated and require very careful counting. Sometimes there will be an alternating pattern (5 clear, 1 black, 4 clear, 1 black, 5 clear, 1 black, etc.) and then a continuation of the series' reduction (4 clear, 1 black, 4 clear, 1 black, etc.). Finally the number of clear and black frames is equal in a pattern of exact alternation (1 black, 1 clear, 1 black, 1 clear, etc.)

At one point it appears that the number of black frames will increase regularly in proportion to the number of alternating clear frames, but this pattern is not as simple as that of the first section. The mixture of patterns of black and clear frames becomes very complex, for example, 2 black, 1 clear, 2 black, 2 clear, etc. There are tricky deviations from the main patterns, even within a series, which force the frame counter never to assume that a series is entirely regular. At the end, the pattern of the beginning is reversed with 5, 6, 7, 8, 9, 11, and then 23 clear frames interspersed with one black frame. The startling transformations of the film during projection belie the systematic means by which it was created.

Many of the filmmakers of the avant-garde of the sixties have explored what P. Adams Sitney has termed the "structural film." Its methods seem more closely related to serial music's mathematical patterning of musical tones, although the analogy applies only partially. What is amazing is how diluted the mathematics of such structures become in the final viewing, how the clear frame or empty screen seems to dominate, with dark shadows pulsing behind and apparitions forming above and beyond the simple alternating of black and white.

—Lindley Page Hanlon

Footnotes

1. Ken Jacobs. As quoted in *Film-Makers' Cooperative Catlogue No. 6,* New York: Film-Makers' Cooperative, 1975, p. 131.

2. Stan Brakhage. "Respond Dance," from "Metaphors on Vision," *Film Cuture No. 30,* Fall 1963.

3. Paul Arthur. "Four Brakhage Films," *Artforum,* January 1973, pp. 44–45.

4. See letters and articles in the Tony Conrad File at Anthology Film Archives, 80 Wooster Street, New York, New York.

5. Tony Conrad. "The Flicker," 1967. A piece distributed at screenings of the film, which can be read at Anthology Film Archives.

6. P. Adams Sitney. *Visionary Film,* New York: Oxford University Press, 1974, pp. 407–435.

5

Samadhi (Jordan Belson)
***Film in Which There Appear Sprocket Holes, Edge Lettering,
    Dirt Particles, Etc.*** (George Landow)
Castro Street (Bruce Baillie)
Notes on the Circus (Jonas Mekas)
Lapis (James Whitney)
Wavelength (Michael Snow)

The ability of the motion-picture camera to photograph events with some fidelity to our common seeing has been used in many films to create a reference between objects on the screen and similar or identical objects in the "real" world. But the same photographic system which can represent so precisely can also alter with equal precision, and other kinds of films do alter their subject matter to transform it into the material of a more interior expression. In fact, a major achievement of the New American Cinema has been the creation of a series of films which do not seek to represent the shared seeing and knowledge we have of objects and events, but rather to present those things only as the filmmaker reacts to them. Instead of the apparently realist conventions of the documentary or some Hollywood films, we find in the avant-garde cinema a series of techniques which manipulate and alter the recorded image: camera movements which seem a direct expression of the filmmaker's physiology, images that are altered photographically or by lab-work, and editing which fragments that which we might normally see continuously.

Notes on the Circus and *Castro Street* are both films which take relatively commonplace subjects, the circus and a street, and remake them into something unique. Both break up the subject matter with complex editing patterns; the editing does not simply fragment but works throughout the films to create a new and less familiar unity. However, the methods each film uses differ greatly, and the final effect of each is as unique as the personal vision that each constitutes.

Jonas Mekas' *Notes on the Circus* is both a separate film and a part of his much longer *Diaries, Notes and Sketches*. As in the rest of *Diaries*, Mekas has edited *Notes* in the camera. During the filming of the circus, he continually stopped and restarted his camera in reaction to what he saw, with an editor's awareness for each of the cuts that the restarting creates. This method contrasts with the more usual treatment of footage shot as "raw" material to be totally reordered and thus reformed by post-filming editing, and gives *Notes on the Circus* a spontaneous, even nervous intensity that requires each of its moments to be experienced with an immediacy that would not be possible with a more obviously structured and balanced edited form.

The film's sense of immediacy also results from the kinds of in-camera cuts Mekas uses and the speed with which they occur. The eye is continually jarred and unsettled, prevented from perceiving the "scene" in any continuous way and forced to continually re-see it through each new image. The subject, denied any existence for the viewer outside of each shot, is thus presented to him solely through Mekas' personalized rendering of it. Three things are thus at work here: the interiorization of subject matter; the modernist assertion that subject has no transcendent existence outside of its presentation in a work (an assertion shared by many New

Notes on the Circus by Jonas Mekas

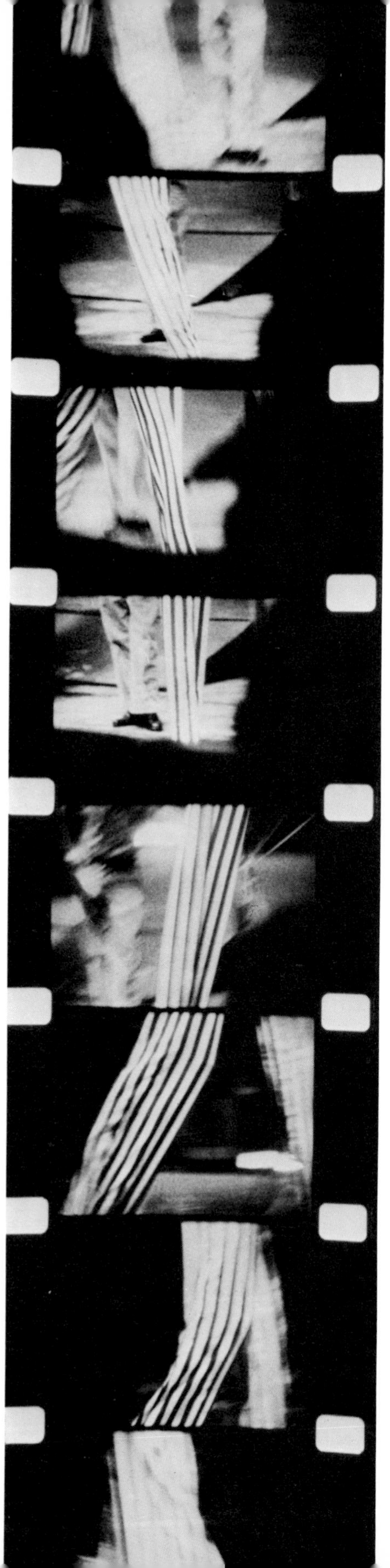

Notes on the Circus by Jonas Mekas

American films); and Mekas' own particular attempt to intensify and make immediate.

Various techniques help achieve these ends. One kind of cut used repeatedly involves no change of subject matter or camera angle, just a transition to a slightly later time. A series of these brief ellipses makes the action seem speeded-up, but more importantly, forces the eye to continually jump with the editing to re-see the subject. This has an analogue in a kind of camera movement used: jittery, rapidly vibrating movements separated by brief pauses in which the subject is seen more clearly. Other kinds of cuts involve shifting to a different camera or lens framing of the same subject matter, cutting to a completely different part of the same subject, and cutting to completely different subjects. As well, Mekas cuts between out-of-focus and in-focus shots, often of the same subject. Finally, brief superimpositions are used at unexpected moments, adding an extra layer of object, color, and movement, and creating another kind of cut: between single image and superimposition.

It should be noted that these techniques combine quite remarkably in the whole film, so that, for instance, the viewer does not sense an enormous difference between certain jittery camera movements and certain cuts, and senses instead that each technique is analogous to the others.

These techniques combine to deny the subject any continuity outside the film and force it to be seen as something which occurs, and occurs differently, in each image, each frame. Further, Mekas as film-maker seems ever present, and thus making the subject "his," through the techniques described. But the particular attitude that Mekas takes toward his subject, and the particular kind of immediacy he achieves, needs further discussion.

It must first be said that even more than most films *Notes on the Circus* both demands and depends on a very particular mode of watching it. It is only out of an attempt to see the film clearly that one can understand its statement. Consider first the circus itself. A "normal" trip to the circus occasions a continuous viewing of its acts; that is the usual purpose of going. The spotlighting of specific acts encourages this. This lighting is accepted by Mekas in his film, so that in most images the background is all or mostly black and the bright colors of the performers are highlighted. Thus the eye is encouraged to focus its continuous attention on them. Mekas' continual disruption of that attention causes a kind of struggle: the eye is continually refocusing itself after each cut, trying once again to "see" the subject. This effect is especially strong when Mekas cuts between slightly different framings of the same subject: the process of seeing a common subject through two slightly different and briefly sustained angles which are intercut involves a struggle of the eye to stay on that subject across the cutting; this struggle startles the eye out of its everyday complacency and asks it to look with an energy as great as the energy of the rapid movements themselves. The same might be said of transitions between out-of-focus and in-focus images of the same subject, or of the rapid camera movement, or, in a way that involves a total readjustment, of the cuts to new material. The viewer is engaged in a rapid and continual process of trying to see; the degree to which he has to use his eyes greatly intensifies that seeing. Specifically, the continual refocusing seems to involve the eyes' very muscles; the eye energy called upon produces heightened seeing of each thing. Passive acceptance of subject matter is destroyed; each bit of subject seems to be seen only at its moment of coming into being; in this sense, the film can be seen as denying any transcendent subject by asserting that subject is only a product of the instant.

The result is to locate the subject solely in the viewer's instantaneous process of perceiving it. Each image bursts suddenly on the viewer's eye and mind, as if it had no prior existence, implied or otherwise, in the film or in the viewer's experience. By contrast, many films in both narrative and non-narrative traditions use editing which obeys more classical unities, locating every shot in relation to every other shot, so that it is only in the context of the whole that each shot can be understood. In these, each image's place in the film depends on what has preceeded and on what will follow; the images have a past and a future in a way that those of *Notes on the Circus* do not. *Notes* does, of course, create optical afterimages, but in so doing, it is still really locating its effects in momentary perception; the film develops with a remarkable linearity rather than working towards an architectural whole.

P. Adams Sitney's description of *Castro Street* suggests it is less obviously personalized than *Notes on the Circus:*

> [it pushes] toward cinematic visions of impersonal or unqualified consciousness . . . succeed[s] in momentarily disengaging the self from vision.[1]

On one hand, this can be seen in the film's absence of any direct reference to the physiology of seeing, and in the way it avoids the implied assertion of *Notes on the Circus* that the film is an individual's reaction to events seen. At the same time, it is a highly constructed and manipulated film of a single street. But the effects of this manipulation are not as immediately personal as they are in *Notes on the Circus*. To understand this, we need to look at the details of the film's form.

While the editing devices of *Notes* may imply an individual behind the camera, literally "making" the film in the order which we see it, *Castro Street* uses a far wider array of image and editing forms, and further combines several of them at once in a highly structured simultaneity. Baillie mixes positive and negative black and white with color footage; frames are partially masked, so that only part of the frame is visible, and various shapes of masking are used; an intentionally wrongly-threaded camera blurrs some images vertically; distorting lenses blur the image in various other ways. All of these kinds of images are combined throughout the film in multiple superimposition. The combinations appear to be non-systematic; as many different types of combinations as are possible seem to be used. Clearly, this film could not have been made within the camera; further, it cannot be seen as a linearly-ordered set of personal reactions. Baillie's reaction to his subject is to represent it in a nearly disorienting variety of different ways. While the film's final effect is that of a specific and singular consciousness interacting with a subject, that consciousness seems to be continually expanding upon itself.

One effect of the variety of combinations is to reveal every form that the image takes, and ultimately its content as well, as a photographic artifice. This is even true of those shots which appear clear, in color and not superimposed; they are only a few in the context of a highly manipulated whole, and even in these, the colors have an almost-too-rich artificial quality, only possible with color *film*, and which may thus implicitly refer to that film. But this is not a deeply reflexive work: the image-as-artifice works to open it out, to deny it a firm ground, to suggest that everything seen is created. Over one kind of image a different type

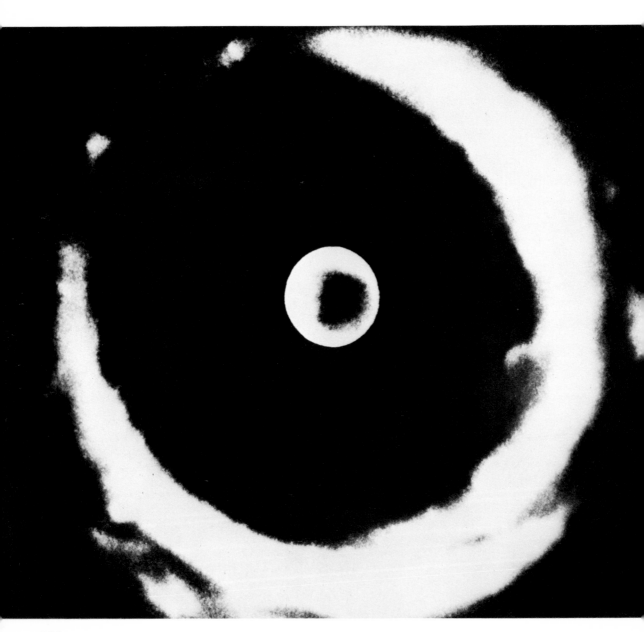

is superimposed; whole sections are composed based on sets of such transitions; they appear to be continually expanding on, or out of, themselves. Nominally a portrait of a street, the film does not build to a view of the "whole street," but really does the opposite, destroying not only geographical fixity but the permanence of everything seen. In many images, darkness fills much of the frame, seeming to lie behind the shifting fragments of visible objects. This is a visual materialization of the film's deepest idea: if all is artificial and impermanent, then behind lies darkness, silence, nothing. Baillie himself has articulated his goals:

> I always felt that I brought as much truth out of the environment as
> I could, but I'm tired of coming *out of.* It's like being comfortable . . .
> It's home . . . But I want everybody really lost, and I want us all to
> be at home there . . . I have to say finally what I *am* interested,
> like Socrates: peace . . . rest . . . nothing . . .[2]

Bruce Baillie's acquaintance with Eastern philosophy has informed his filmmaking. Jordan Belson, like Baillie, is a California filmmaker, and *Samadhi* goes much farther than *Castro Street* in its dependence on Eastern religious thought, in the extreme instability of its image, and in the degree to which the filmmaker, viewer and screen are united. A film like *Notes on the Circus* partially separates the camera's recording function, the filmmaker's manipulations through movement, focus and editing, and the viewer's perceptual reactions to them; questions can then be asked about the relationship between content, artist, and viewer; such relationships are forms of the subject/object split that the experience of *Samadhi* seeks to close. Belson's images are to be seen whole, and do not invite questions about how they were created; for him, they are not images at all, but forms of consciousness.

The film begins with shifting light and color over indistinct repeated patterns. Circular shapes are seen in continuous transformation; circles here act as planetary or celestial references, and as representatives of a unity of inner consciousness; P. Adams Sitney has pointed out the relation here to Emerson's notion of circles as extending from the eye throughout nature, and found metaphorically in various aspects of human life and civilization.[3] This connection is apt; not only do the circular shapes of the film continually reform themselves into different patterns, but no single image is allowed to stand for any one thing: its associations may be several, but more importantly, it also seems not to stand for, but literally, to be a state of consciousness of which it is a complete description. The film's continuous transformations create an extreme mutability in each of its frames; while in *Castro Street,* the instability that results from a comparison of several different kinds of images leads to a sense of the emptiness between them, *Samadhi* has no such separations; its instability cannot suggest itself as a subjective statement any more than its individual images beg specific interpretations: the film is very much of a single piece.

Samadhi has a soundtrack which is integrally connected with its imagery: mostly electronic sounds blend into one another in a complex way. The sound has a kind of absolute presence which also matches the images: it does not seem created, but simply present. But sound in abstract filmmaking is often in danger of degenerating into a redundant accompaniment that imposes an alien rhythm on and makes it difficult to

Lapis by James Whitney

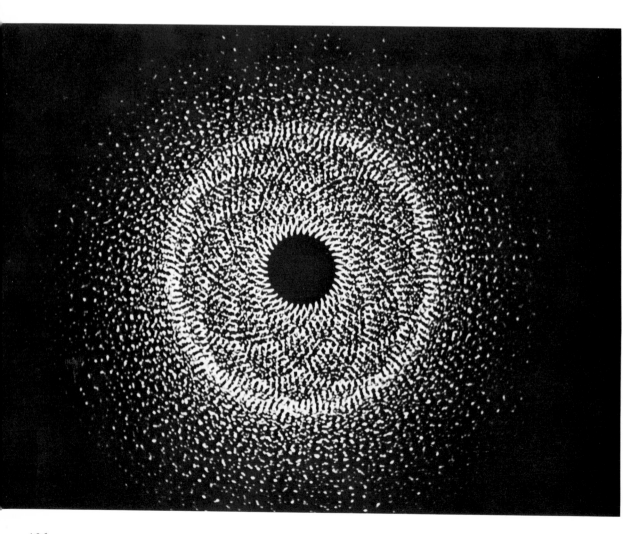

Wavelength by Michael Snow

see the images' complexities. Opinions differ on the sound of *Lapis*; if the viewer finds it reductive he can try concentrating on the images alone. If he can do so he will find elaborate shifting patterns created with computer animation; shapes made of hundreds of parts are organized through the use of geometry and repetitions of detail. The film pauses briefly on some of its more complex images, involving geometrical arrangements of myriad tiny dots. Pauses are appropriate, for these patterns are complex enough for the eye to want to move around in them; this eye-motion, plus the sense that the changes are always about to resume, make it a film without any truly static moment.

P. Adams Sitney has compared Brakhage's humanized camera with Michael Snow's camera and found in Snow a "disembodied viewpoint" which he also sees in Belson's films; he identifies Snow as differing from Belson in his concern with cinematic illusionism.[4] In *Lapis* and *Samadhi*, the fact that the mediating action of the filmmaker is not directly visible—as it is in Mekas or Brakhage—gives the images a more absolute status: they *are*; the viewer is *in* them. *Wavelength* raises more questions than these two films; consciousness of film and the film-making process is strongly suggested, but ultimately its zoom has an absolute quality.

Wavelength is most simply described as a 45 minute film consisting of a single zoom which proceeds from a view of a large loft to a shot filled with a single still photograph of waves hanging on its wall. As such, it explores different aspects of the loft's space; simultaneously, and it is important that these are not clearly separated, it explores the nature of film space. Specifically, a zoom not only changes the camera's field of view; it changes the amount of depth in the frame as well. Further, the zoom creates various expectations, which themselves are constantly shifting: it is only after some minutes that we begin to see the zoom and suspect that it will constitute the whole film; we then wonder where it leads; it is only much later that we first surmise and then know it will end on the photo. Annette Michelson has stated that

> "The camera, in the movement of its zoom, installs within the viewer a threshold of tension, of expectation . . . [this] creates . . . that regard for the future which forms an horizon of expectation. We are proceeding from uncertainty to certainty, as our camera narrows its field, arousing and then resolving our tension of puzzlement as to its ultimate destination, describing, in the splendid purity of its one, slow movement, the notion of the 'horizon' characteristic of every subjective process and fundamental as a trait of intentionality."[5]

The film is in fact much less easily unified than *Samadhi* or *Lapis*, for it contains within the zoom a series of comparisons and disjunctions. Snow breaks up the zoom by changing the color of the image, by cutting to negative, by altering the film stock used; other cuts change the time of day visible through the windows. The "purity" of the single movement across an empty space is disrupted by people at several instances: a radio is played, someone appears to die; these narrative elements call for a different mode of apprehension than that involved in the seeing of the slow zoom. Finally, there is a paradox involved in the progress of the zoom itself. Snow identifies a space "natural to film" as "maybe conical, but flattened;"[6] he is of course describing the space suggested by the progression of his zoom; this also is another way the zoom relates to film space. When it concludes on the sea photograph, one might expect to have an affirmation of the flatness and photographic nature of film itself; instead, the image seems to open out into "limitless space."[7] These contrasts involve a questioning process. Partly they refer the nature of film: the shifts in film color and stock, for instance, contrast different emulsion and filter characteristics with the still-present continuity of the zoom; perceiving the zoom and the narrative elements together causes the viewer to question and compare the nature of each, since they seem so different; certain narrative events heighten the contrast by occurring offscreen after the zoom has passed their location in the loft. The film is unified by the fact that all these questions are related and form a system of similar kinds of questions, and by the fact that all are encompassed within the single zoom.

Wavelength sometimes troubles viewers relatively new to its kind of cinema by the apparent sparseness of "events" within its length. But one thing Snow is doing is creating a new sense of film time, one which is defined and determined by the slow movement of the zoom. To appreciate this, however one finally evaluates the film, is to suspend any other expectations one may have about film time, whether derived from the attention-getting density of narrative events in a Hollywood film, the visual density of Brakhage, the rapid cutting of Mekas or the subsuming of linear time into a continuous flow in *Castro Street* or *Samadhi*. It is important to understand that any film can define its own sense of time.

These considerations might well be applied to George Landow's *Film in Which There Appear Sprocket Holes, Edge Lettering, Dirt Particles, Etc.*, which may at first glance seem even "slower" than *Wavelength*, although it is in fact only four minutes long. Landow's image material is a frame which contains within it two whole and two parts of film frames of a woman's face, together with the items listed in the title: edge letters go by, dirt particles appear and reappear. In the fragmented frames on the right, but not in the whole frames on the left, the woman blinks regularly. The edge letters and dust patterns seem to recur regularly; in fact, the film's material is a strip only a little more than a second long, which is continually repeated, occasionally shortened by a few frames.

This is one of a number of films that have been called "minimal," both as a description of the minimum of subject-matter and with reference to "minimal art." In fact, if you really *watch* the film, you will become aware of a great variety of experiences within it: of the regular fascination of the blinking, which, as Landow says, also "forces all the attention of spectator to the edge of the screen;"[8] of the rapid patterns of edge letters; and finally of the complex repeating patterns of dust particles. Many, on first viewing, find this film too long. But for me, on a purely optical level, this film hardly runs long enough for all that is contained within it to be seen.

If Mekas' and Baillie's films can be called non-objective documentaries of places, and Snow's a zoom-record of a room space, *Film In Which . . .* can be seen as a documentary of film itself. Not only is its image material taken from some Kodak test footage, but Landow re-printed it in a way which made film's usually invisible frame-lines, sprocket holes and edge letters part of his image. In documenting film itself, however, Landow has made a very different kind of film than one which documents a subject external to film. Further, the entire approach that the film embodies, and hence the mode of perception it asks its viewers to bring to it, sharply differentiates it from all the other films on this program.

Film in Which There Appear
Sprocket Holes, Edge Letter-
ing, Dirt Particles, Etc. by
George Landow

This film is, in fact, a polar opposite to those of Mekas, Baillie, or Brakhage, whose films' internal structures use image, editing, color and movement to express their makers' selves to the viewer. Rather than making a film which explicitly materializes his personalized reactions to a subject, Landow has made a film which is about the viewer's process of perceiving it.[9] *Film in Which* . . . is, first of all, an object to be looked at, but its statement emerges out of the processes of one's looking at it rather than being embodied in its internal structure.

Each of the film's important aspects can in fact be shown to lead to this. Its "unusual" use of film time immediately surprises the viewer, causing him to question his mode of watching it. Its unusual subject matter similarly startles the eye; like *Wavelength*, it contains complex contrasts, though not actual opposites. Looking at the whole woman's face on the left is quite different from looking at the fragment on the right; watching her blink is different from watching her unblinking face; watching the sprocket holes is much more static than watching the single-frame edge letters; watching the dust is different as well. The dust, for instance, is multiple, and each particle lasts only a frame; to watch it, the eye must continually shift. The face, by contrast, is far more static. The edge letters change a frame at a time, but, unlike the dust, are always seen in the same part of the screen. Looking at each of these elements involves a totally different type of attention. The extreme shifts that the viewer goes through as he looks at different parts of the film cause him to notice his own watching-processes, which is what the film is in fact reflecting on.

Finally, the very fact that the image, and certainly the dust, are "found" objects, suggest each as something to be looked at, rather than as an element making a personalized statement. Landow's alterations—for instance, getting the sprocket holes to appear in the middle—simply heighten the internal paradoxes which refer back to the viewer.

The film's length seems to me to be the absolute minimum required to exhaust its material.[10] The brief strip is repeated several hundred times, but the many possible ways of looking at it seem to require at least so many repetitions. The effect that the film finally achieves goes far beyond simply making one aware of one's perceptions of it; rather that awareness involves a process of double perception—watching the film, watching oneself watching the film—that becomes an aesthetic statement and places the work profoundly outside the tradition of directly expressive art.

—Fred Camper

Footnotes

1. P. Adams Sitney. *Visionary Film*, New York: Oxford University Press, 1974, p. 210.

2. "Bruce Baillie: An Interview," *Film Comment*, Vol. 7, no. 1, Spring 1971, p. 31.

3. Sitney. *op. cit.*, p. 307.

4. Ibid., p. 413.

5. Annette Michelson. "Toward Snow," *Artforum*, Vol. 9, no. 10, June 1971, p. 31.

6. *Film Culture No. 46*, Autumn 1967, p. 3.

7. Michelson. *op. cit.*, p. 32.

8. George Landow, "Letter to Sheldon Renan," *Film Culture No. 44*, 1967, back envelope.

9. In Landow's *Remedial Reading Comprehension*, the words "THIS IS A FILM ABOUT YOU NOT ABOUT ITS MAKER" appear printed on the screen.

10. There is also a longer two-screen version of this film; see filmography.

T,O,U,C,H,I,N,G (Paul Sharits)
Runaway (Standish D. Lawder)
69 (Robert Breer)
Diploteratology or Bardo Folly (George Landow)
Our Lady of the Sphere (Larry Jordan)
Bleu Shut (Robert Nelson)

> The object itself has not become less important. It has merely become less *self-important.*
>
> Robert Morris ("Notes on Sculpture", 1966)

The period 1967–1970 was marked by a pervasive restlessness and tension within American society unequaled, perhaps, since the start of the Depression. The sources of this tension, while far from monolithic, produced a succession of "movements" and behavioral models that bordered on the chaotic in their attacks on the prescribed order of social functioning. These four years witnessed the prominence and decline of hippie/drug culture, the apogee of organized resistance to the Vietnam War, the first stirrings of the Women's Movement, the end of the Black Panther Party as a national entity.

The situation in painting and sculpture during this time appears only slightly less acephalous. The sheer number of styles and modes of presentation (it is difficult to call such a manifestation as *earthworks* a style) that shared critical as well as economic currency suggests a potential commonality with the scope of "life styles" present in the culture at large. Despite the fact that very little of the art being made directly reflected political or social issues (although sensibilities as apposite as those of Claes Oldenburg and Les Levine included overt social commentary in certain pieces), one can posit a common thread of motivation among Op, Minimalist, Conceptual and Systems art and performance-oriented works in their attempts to redefine the relations between art object and its audience. The reconsideration of how, where, and when we perceive a specific art product was elaborated through a diversity of strategies entailing scale, material, situation, required duration of viewing, and required participation (by physical, deductive, or inferential activities).

In describing one aspect of the altered relationship between (his) sculpture and its viewer, Robert Morris concluded that " . . . the major aesthetic terms are not in but dependent upon this autonomous object and exist as unfixed variables that find their specific definition in the particular space and light and physical viewpoint of the spectator . . ."[1] The thrust of such a situation is against the sacrosanct nature of the object, its commodity value and attendant notions of "quality" and "privileged viewing." The experience of an art work thus became paradoxically governed by its spatio-temporal context, with self-consciousness the inherent attitude of perception.

The situation in filmmaking was necessarily of a different order. First, independent filmmakers remained even more distanced in their work from pressing social and political controversy. Second, since both the constituencies of artists and audience for New American Cinema are appreciably smaller than those for painting and sculpture, the reconsideration of prescribed methods of production and distribution and their connections with the commercial market was undertaken—was indeed required—at an early point in the movement's history.

From 1967-1970, there were attempts to expand the context of film viewing through the employment of multiple screens or incorporation of live performance elements with film projection (Paul Sharits, among others, has worked in both areas), but most filmmakers accepted the mechanically determined requisites of the single flat screen and projected image. Within these requisites, filmmakers explored a number of issues parallel to those in painting and sculpture in this period. And although the six films on this program present a multiplicity of styles and elicit myriad responses, one can isolate certain general shared concerns, the most important being the formulation of new structural modalities that redefine perceptual and cognitive relations between film image and viewer (*Our Lady of the Sphere* participates in this process only minimally).

One characteristic element is the attention to materiality, either of the film strip and screen itself or latent in the manipulation of "found" images. All six films make use of images not constructed by or not originally photographed by the filmmaker (*69* and *T,O,U,C,H,I,N,G,* use these materials only peripherally). The displacement of images from their original contexts and their repetition (*Runaway*), recombination (*Bleu Shut*), or external alteration (*Diploteratology*), serves to expose the omnivorously synthetic aspect of photographed images as it de-emphasizes that quality of "immediate seeing" canonized by Brakhage and others (cf. P. Adams Sitney's *Visionary Film*) during the fifties and early sixties. These are films at several removes (at least) from the convincing reproduction of actuality and, more important, equally distant from any subjective reification of a world seen either by the eye or the subconscious mind. That is, "interiority" for these films consists of an awareness of projection as a frame-to-frame event, of the support (screen) as capable of sustaining or dispelling an illusion of depth, and speed of image assimilation as the agent of perceived motion.

Structurally, what we find in these films is the substitution of repetitive, additive, or other non-progressive schema for causal, associative or other evolutionary filmic structures (*Our Lady of the Sphere* is the exception here). This results in the devaluation of image to image "reading" or interpretation as a model for viewing and engenders, instead, a heightened receptivity to the temporal and physical elements of the cinema environment. In *T,O,U,C,H,I,N,G,* the rapid alternation of blank frames of color generates the illusion of rectangles of light leaping off the screen and activating the space between eye and flat support. In *69*, the animated forms that seem to revolve into and emerge from the off-screen space immediately adjacent to the borders of the frame develop a rich counterpoint between affirming the flatness of the support and staticity of the single frame and suspending these elements in a strong illusion of fluid movement into and out of the screen space. *Diploteratology* at times creates the sensation that the screen itself is melting or burning. *Bleu Shut,* in its direct address and implicit solicitation of its audience in a game of multiple choice, suggests a direct dialogue between spectator and image.

The responses described above share a common source in the frustration of identifying the film image as the mediation of a psychological eye, be it an eye recording an internal or external vision. With the retraction—or better, the displacement—of the ordering sensibility to accommodate the viewer's physical, perceptual, or cognitive idiosyncrasies, these

Runaway by Standish Lawder

135

Diploteratology or *Bardo Folly* by
George Landow

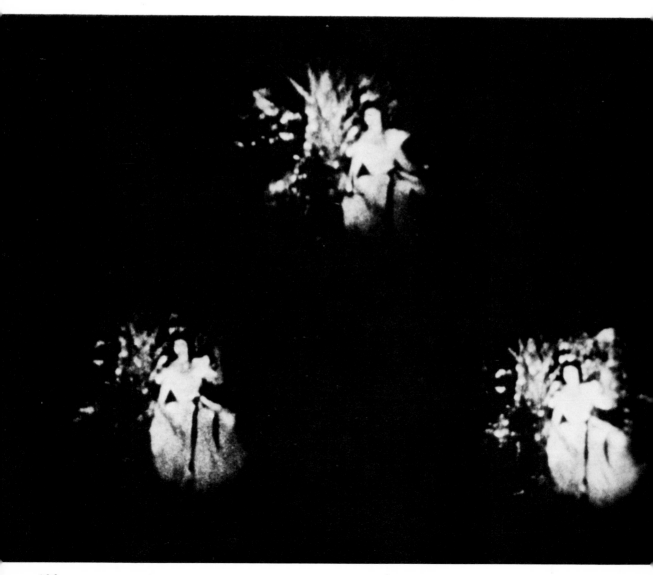

films evoke a paradoxical sense of subjectivity—paradoxical because of the degree to which they insist on their status as objects and refer us to the mechanical structural components of cinema.

Standish Lawder's *Runaway* contains perhaps the most simplified structure of the group. It is derived from four seconds of a commercial cartoon entitled *The Fox Hunt* in which a pack of dogs run across a field, prick up their ears, then race back in the opposite direction, stop and repeat the process. This single phrase of movement has been looped continuously into a Moebius strip and rephotographed. After an initial zoom into what looks like a video screen, the dogs continue to race back and forth until the filmstrip appears to tear and we see the jagged-edged strip careening wildly through the frame. The sound accompanying the loop is, at first, a few bars of looped organ music rhythmically interrupted by canned laughter (and at one point by sustained clapping). The visual track is subjected to constant, minute variations of light exposure (producing at times a flicker effect) and the imposition of (apparently artificial) horizontal scan bars reminiscent of video malfunctioning. These bars create a rhythm that interplays with the rhythm of exposure changes and the dogs' movement.

Towards the end, the sound of thunder followed by raindrops, is heard, suggesting an ironic metaphor as the darkened image is followed by a "storm" of horizontal bands. Once the basic repetitive phrase is set— and this occurs almost immediately—the viewer's attention is increasingly directed to the abstract qualities of movement (the utter banality of the cartoon reinforces this process). The image is one of entrapment—the dogs cannot escape the confines of the frame—but even this referential cue gives way to a perception of flat masses of dark and light oscillating in minimal patterns. The illusion of the torn strip breaks this pattern and explicitly recalls the mechanism of projection.

The process of abstraction of a "found" image occurs again in Landow's *Diploteratology* with a slightly different focus. The loop structure—roughly analogous in form to a serial painting by Andy Warhol—is the starting point for a didactic meditation on the nature of the film frame and light-sensitive emulsion. The film's title, *Diploteratology*—the study of severe malformations in growing organisms—posits the filmstrip as an organism composed of "cells," and refers to the filmmaker's procedure of rephotographing single frames of the original image as the plastic base expands and melts. A loop of a woman waving from a Cypress Gardens' tourist attraction is repeated for some minutes. This image splits into three, then two, small round cells similar to the telescopic iris. Her wave is seen discontinuously in the separate cells. The representational image of one cell changes to an abstract mass of colored bubbles (a magnified film frame) which dissolve and retreat off one side leaving a blank lighted circle, only to be replaced immediately by another melting form. One recognizes a consistency of color tonality and grainy surface in both abstract cell and remaining loop image—which soon becomes a second abstract mass. Further, the movement of the bubbles recapitulates in tempo and direction the languorous wave and gliding boat. The remainder of the film continues to juxtapose two burning cells that are replaced (near the end) by more regular images of water bubbles photographed with filters through a microscope.

As the succession of single frames is exposed, they reveal vestiges of the original loop while retaining a uniqueness in rate of dissolution or internal composition. In an unpublished essay, David Imber suggests that

Bleu Shut by Robert Nelson

this process resembles the way a star dies: the steady contraction of an interior mass and expulsion of matter into space.[2] The idea of a film frame as a cosmological entity, a comparison of the microcosmic with the macrocosmic, rehearses a level of filmic perception all but unseen in the normative viewing experience. The revelation—and animation—of a world of shape and texture within, rather than between, frames radically reconstructs the temporal scale of projection and confers on the image an aura of finite existence.

In his films since *Diploteratology,* Landow has continued to investigate the parameters of "commercial" images insofar as they encourage the perception of "false information" and regiment the learning experience. The ironic testing situation of *Institutional Quality* (1969) in which the spectator is instructed to place pencil marks on a booklet (actually the screen), induces a type of impossible audience response (we can make no concrete input to the flow of images) similar to that in *Bleu Shut.* Robert Nelson's film is structured like a television quiz game with commercial interruptions every other minute. A woman's off-screen voice informs us that the film will last 30 minutes and provides a partial itinerary of excitements: "At 5 minutes, 35 seconds comes the Johnny Mars Band. At 11:15, weiners. At 21:05, pornography. At 23:30, a duet." We are told to keep track of the elapsed time via a small clock in the upper right-hand corner of the screen.

The quiz sections consist of one-minute long, magazine-type stills (in lurid color) of gaudy boats with six possible names printed over them. Two off-screen voices proceed to guess which name fits the boat in question. There are eleven such interludes, and as Bob and Bill (the filmmaker and William Wiley) bumble from one wrong guess to another, the viewer naturally begins to test his acumen against that of the players while simultaneously ticking off the film's duration and anticipating the various introductory highlights. The commercial segments contain sequences from found films, home movies, and, perhaps, Nelson's unfinished projects. As P. Adams Sitney points out, each interval reiterates the testing situation in its presentation of problems in film perception. In some, the problem is temporal: recognition of the looped structure of a steaming hot-dog. In others, it is spatial—the filmmaker crawling through a mirrored room—or referential—the identification of the Hollywood movie from which a musical number has been extracted. The juxtaposition of a temporality that is consonant with the viewer's (the quiz sections) with a diversity of altered temporal schema (in the commercials) is paralleled by the alternation of flat images with spatially ambiguous ones. It is tempting to propose possible relations between the commercials—many have a tactile or sensual quality (the hot-dog, the pornography clip, the wide-angle bicycle ride) in opposition to the purely visual appeal of the boat images. But the structure finally seems more additive than progressive or organic. And it is precisely the disjunction between the two basic types of sequences and the different levels of response which they elicit that forms the core of the film. The viewer's self-conscious desire for a unified mode of response, the complex pattern of engagement/retreat, signals a highly sophisticated elaboration of the spectator to image relationship.

The substitution of one system of illusion for another, more conventional system (e.g., narrative continuity or deep-space) is one characteristic of recent New American Cinema. In *Bleu Shut,* the locus of illusionism is cognitive and manifest in the imaginary reciprocity between screen and observer. In Sharits' *T,O,U,C,H,I,N,G* the illusions generated

59 by Robert Breer

are of a perceptual nature, involving color, the production of retinal after-images, and the intrusion of the image into the space of the theater. Like his previous films, *T,O,U,C,H,I,N,G* has a distinctly symmetrical organization with six equal parts divided by a median section, each part occurring between the projected letters of the title. The images consist or ordered sequences of solid frames of color (dominated by lavender, blue, orange, and yellow) interspersed with four basic referential images. Once in each section, stills of a surgical procedure and sexual intercourse are alternated with a velocity that makes each difficult to identify. Sitney has described the other photographed images as follows: "Single frame shots of a shirt-less young man flash in positive and negative, both color and black-and-white. In some of the shots he holds his tongue in a scissors as if about to cut it off; in others a woman's fingernails are scratching his face."[3]

The soundtrack consists of a drumlike beat accompanying the rhythmic repetition of the word "destroy." At times, the rapid alternation of different positions of the scissors or flexed hand produce an illusion of movement. The color flashes induce after-images which blend and modulate the palette. On an aural level, the looped repetition of "destroy" tricks the ear into identifying different words or phrases: "the story," "it's off," "it's murder," "it's gory." In part, these variations are suggested by the content of the images and it is curious that in a film so highly abstracted, a fragment of narrative begins to take shape. Gradually, the scissors and hand seem to withdraw from the man's face and in the last section, his eyes are open. In this section, too, the interchanging of his image with interior rectangles of color create the illusion of a beam of light projected from the man's eyes to the spectator's eyes, as if he has ingested the confines of the screen and hypnotically redirected the color flicker outward. In this context, the turning away from tactile violence precipitates a purely optical "touching" in the illusion of a direct, concrete linkage between the viewer's eye and its mirror on the screen.

Much of Robert Breer's work also depends on the speed of alternating images to create its effects. Breer began as a painter (he continues to make kinetic sculpture) and was heavily influenced by the aesthetic of neo-plasticism. In *69*, as in several other films, one source of visual tension occurs between the movement of hard-edged geometrical forms and freely evolving line-drawings. The jamming together of dissimilar materials (graphic animation with object animation or live-action shots), a recurrent theme in Breer's work, takes place on a relatively minor scale in this film although the filmmaker is careful to include shooting "mistakes" (a single frame shot containing the animator's hand) and single frames of indecipherable images. The counterpoint of materials is here subsumed in a counterpoint of generating depth-illusions and exposing their mechanisms of creation. The film opens with the presentation of four rhythmically alternating outlined forms that seem to swing into and out of the depth of the frame: a hexagonal column (emerging from the lower left corner), a round column (upper left), a rectangular beam (lower right), and an upside down U (bottom center). A fifth shape, a spoked circle, traverses the screen space from right to left. At first, the phrases of movement fluctuate in different combinations. Frames of black leader (sometimes as much as 30 frames) interrupt the movement and gradually impose their own rhythmic cycle. At times, all five forms alternate in single frames producing a stuttering effect that flattens each form into separate increments of the previously fluid motion. In these moments, the illusion that the forms are disappearing into three-dimensional off-screen space is sus-

pended and the boundaries of the frame are affirmed.

Flat geometrical drawings and cartoon-like forms are introduced and juxtaposed with the more regular forms. Color emerges, first as a blue toned sequence then as replacement for either an outlined form or its surrounding background (leaving, say, the hexagonal column outlined in white). Single frame changes in color (blue, red, green, yellow, orange) again break up the fluid movement into discernible increments and their flashing sometimes creates slight after-images of the geometrical forms. In an interview with Jonas Mekas and P. Adams Sitney conducted in 1970, Breer traces the progression of *69:*

> "I think *69* goes from a kind of very deliberate, repetitive opening sequence that seems to be very locked in on itself, and gradually disintegrates, right? And it goes dark and ends dark . . . that was the analysis of the synthesis. They are all synthetic films, very much so, I mean frame by frame synthesis. . . I was analyzing the construction of the film. That's part of my idea about concreteness and exposing the materials of the film itself."[4]

The machine-like order and precision of the opening sections dissolves, revealing in the interstices of apparent motion and apparent depth the increasing traces of an idiosyncratic shaping sensibility. As in *T,O,U,C,H,I,N,G* and *Diploteratology,* the filmmaker found it necessary to assert, then defeat, the closed logic of mechanical order to reveal—albeit tentative and unemotive—his subjective presence.

Larry Jordan began making films at about the same time as Robert Breer in the early 1950's. And, like Breer, his principle mode of articulation is graphic animation. *Our Lady of the Sphere* (and several of his other films) was constructed from cut-outs of Victorian engravings, a procedure which almost inevitably generates radical juxtapositions of scale, spatial context, and the associative qualities of objects (Jordan had studied the collages of Max Ernst as a source for his technique). In an interview from 1970, Jordan speaks of trying to create a "limbo world . . . it's not Paradiso and it's not Purgatorio"[5]—in *Hamfat Asar* (a film employing the same materials) and this idea could pertain to *Our Lady of the Sphere* as well. Jordan constructs a consistent spatio-temporal context in which backgrounds, objects, and human figures float in and out, interact with each other, undergo transformations, and disappear. Sitney has commented on the fragility and evanescent quality of Jordan's images. They contain, as well, vague threads of narrative continuity and half-understood associative connections. While in no way put together by a psychoanalytic formula, the flow of images suggest explorations of a subconscious state subject to interpretative analysis. *Our Lady of the Sphere* is divided into two fairly evident sections. Following an introduction in which a variety of recurrent figures are introduced (and the filmmaker in the form of an engraving of a dandified gentleman reveals his guiding hand), the first section concerns the adventures of a young boy—with arms raised and a frightened or surprised expression—who tumbles (suspended) through a succession of scenes. As he does so, he seems to imagine or experience a series of events grounded in the themes of suspension and flight (human and cosmological). Acrobats turn into flashing stars; tour balloons, trapeze artists, jugglers, horseback riders enter from the sides of the frame, recede or move forward in depth (accomplished by zoom movements), explode in light emanations. This activity is mostly conjoined with calliope music or electronic tones. At the end of the first section, the boy falls at the feet of a circus juggler and is transformed into the fallen acrobat of the complete engraving.

The second section begins with a well-dressed lady with a balloon for a head walking into a background interior scene. Clocks and stars explode about her head. She wanders through different scenes—a waterscape, an urban street—and eventually gains a female companion attired like herself, loses her head, meets a figure in a metal diving suit and finally seems to resolve her endless search (perhaps for the fallen boy of the first part). Many other encounters and transformations take place along the way. If this description suggests a clear narrative evolution, it is only partially misleading. Despite the fact that most of the image condensations remain hermetic and opaque, Jordan maintains conventions such as matching screen direction and velocity as he develops motifs and thematic patterns. The spherical forms—clocks, compasses, balloons, planets—relate to the themes of suspension (both temporal and spatial) and submersion. Recurrent image-fragments such as a flower, a suitcase, the figure of Atlas, suggest at different times transiency and the task of the search. These elements are reinforced by rapid changes in color tinting (the dominant colors are red, yellow, light blue, and jade green) and by the soundtrack—which juxtaposes harp music, and electronic buzz, animal sounds, running water, etc. There are superimpositions and several varieties of camera movement which, in combination, produce a strong feeling of layered, amorphously mobile depth. In one sense, the strategies employed here would seem to conform with the illusion-producing/illusion-denying aesthetic of other films on this program. Jordan's vision, however, is more directed at the metaphysical than the concrete. It is true that *Our Lady of the Sphere* grants an awareness of the single frame as the unit of filmic structure and that the disjunction between static backgrounds and animated figures calls attention to the flatness of the screen surface; it is to the transcendence of these limitations that the film is addressed.

—Paul S. Arthur

Footnotes

1. Robert Morris. "Notes on Sculpture," *Minimal Art,* Gregory Battock, editor, New York: E. P. Dutton & Co., 1968, p. 234.

2. David G. Imber. "Temporal Referencing and Synthesis on *Bardo Follies*," New York: Bard College, 1975. (unpublished essay)

3. P. Adams Sitney. *Visionary Film,* New York: Oxford University Press, 1974, p. 425.

4. Jonas Mekas and P. Adams Sitney. "An Interview with Robert Breer," *Film Culture, No. 56-57,* Spring 1973, pp. 46–47.

5. P. Adams Sitney. "Larry Jordan Interview," *Film Culture No. 52,* Spring 1971, p. 82.

7

Serene Velocity (Ernie Gehr)
The Riddle of Lumen (Stan Brakhage)
Endurance/Remembrance/Metamorphosis (Barry Gerson)
Nostalgia (Hollis Frampton)

The technique of art is to make objects "unfamiliar," to make forms difficult, to increase the difficulty and length of perception because the process of perception is an aesthetic end in itself and must be prolonged. *Art is a way of experiencing the artfulness of an object; the object is not important.*

An image is not a permanent referent for those mutable complexities of life which are revealed through it; its purpose is not to make us perceive meaning, but to create a special perception of the object—*it creates a "vision" of the object instead of serving as a means for knowing it.*[1]

These statements by the Russian formalist critic Victor Shklovsky provide a theoretical base for the films of this program. Art is conceived of as primarily a form-giving act, and, as a consequence, the structure of the work is prominent and demands attention. In these four films the manipulation of material by the artist through framing, editing, use of the zoom, sound/image disjunction, and change of focus serves to radically alter the common perception of the object or space. This modification results in an increasing tendency towards abstraction: the representation of a space or object is circumscribed by the controlling formal strategies.

Moreover, the titles of these films suggest an interest in opening the films up to abstract and metaphorical readings. Problems, paradoxes, and riddles are posed by the films and their titles, encouraging the viewer to probe the material to discover the particular "'vision' of the object" which the artist presents. Indeed, it is strange that although these films (with the exception of *The Riddle of Lumen*) tend to conceal the artist's subjective intervention by maintaining a simple, fixed, almost autonomous structure, the transformation of spaces and objects leads one to attempt to define the controlling vision.

Ernie Gehr used a minimum number of structural components to make *Serene Velocity:*

1) fixed camera position,
2) frame by frame registration,
3) zoom positions altering every four frames,
4) uniform progression of zoom positions from the oscillation around the midpoint to the alternation of the end points of the zoom,
5) promotion of the pairs of zoom positions every sixty feet.

The rigorous maintenance of these few structural rules and the absence of characters and dramatic events tend to emphasize the autonomous, depersonalized stature of the work. The description of the mechanics of the film, however, does not account for the complexity of the viewer's response. Rather than experiencing the work as a succession of discrete units operating within a simple metrical system, the viewer becomes aware of an increasing complexity of various formal attributes.

Superimpositions and rhythmic patterns, nowhere apparent on the filmstrip itself, become a powerful factor in the viewing experience. The static quality of each image is undercut as the length between zoom positions increases. Walls appear to move laterally, the exit sign pushes towards and away from the upper edge of the screen, doors and objects along the wall seem to advance and retreat. The simultaneous play of these and other perceived movements affirms the four frame metric system while it establishes a more elaborate rhythm. Depending on the direction of one's glance or the dominance of a particular configuration or object (through scale, color, or vivid graphic composition), patterns of strong and weak beats are felt.

The central location of the camera in the corridor takes full advantage of the space's symmetry and representation of depth. The perception of the static quality of the image at the outset reinforces the normal tendency of perspectival lines to draw one's glance into the depth of the space. As the film progresses, the assertion of verisimilitude is challenged. As the zoom positions move further from the midpoint, the internal mechanism of the zoom (involving the regulation of the interrelationship of lenses) reduces the usual sense of perspective. The conventional relationship of foreground to background is subverted and the space appears flattened.

By alternately contracting and expanding the spatial field, the corridor is transformed into a purely optical space, one in which an illusion of three-dimensionality is destroyed. As the end points of the zoom are approached, the sense of abstraction increases: the lines of perspective become the graphic depiction of a large X, and identifiable objects become formal entities of shape and color.

Although as the film progresses, the flatness of the images becomes more apparent, another factor complicates the sense of two-dimensionality. As the objects and shapes retreat and advance, a tension begins to mount between the planes of the image and the screen. The image itself appears to encroach on the space of the audience. The increasing sense of two-dimensional surface is thus accompanied by a feeling of the image actually asserting its own volumetric dimension.

Serene Velocity can be categorized as a structural film "wherein the *shape* of the whole film is predetermined and simplified, and it is that shape that is the primal impression of the film."[2] By establishing a fixed, minimal structure which always makes itself felt, the film makes the viewer remain fundamentally apart from itself. Its thrust is guaranteed from the start, and is not subverted by anyone's creative or subjective impulse.

The apprehension of the separateness of *Serene Velocity* can never be experienced as such. Illusions of movement, depth and superimposition, which are created by the viewer during the film's projection, obscure the film's simple structure. Although a description of the film's structural components firmly establishes the priority of the stasis of the image, the experience of viewing the film challenges the assertion of stasis. This disjunction between apprehension of the object and experience of the projection arises from the activation of an optical principle known as *persistence of vision.* When images are projected at a certain rate of speed, this principle operates so that the retina retains the image for an instant after the light source has disappeared. It allows one to experience the projection of a succession of discrete images of consecutive movements as a continuous action.

In *Serene Velocity,* the rapidity of the alternation of shots and the sense of increasing distance between represented spaces creates images of superimposition. The viewer is presented with a situation which disturbs the normally subliminal apprehension of continuity by separating the components of the viewing process. The disjunction between the structure of the film as discrete units and the appearance of superimposition makes the viewer conscious of the distorting vision which causes the transformation.

The use of persistence of vision becomes the foundation for creating an analogy between the process of viewing film and that of consciousness. Just as the film object is filtered through a distorting mechanism, so all perceptions of the exterior are mediated by the individual's consciousness.

In an interview with Jonas Mekas in 1972, Gehr made repeated reference to the relationship between film and mental processes. His intentions in making *Serene Velocity* were:

> a desire less to express myself and more of making something out of the film material itself relevant to film for spiritual purposes. . . . What I mean by "spiritual" is sensitizing the mind to its own consciousness by allowing the mind simply to observe and digest the material, film phenomena presented, rather than manipulating it to evoke moods and sentiments.[3]

Gehr defines his task in terms of creating a film object which explores its own process of construction. The film structure functions as both an analogue and an instant of consciousness. One confronts certain notions of subjectivity through the exposition of the manner in which persistence of vision creates an illusion of depth and movement.

Gehr's choice of the zoom intensifies the analogy. The zoom lens accentuates the mediating nature of the photographic process. This lens and the human eye both impose their own vision upon perceived objects in a literal and figurative act of projection. The constant tension between the authority of the film object and the controlling, manipulating stance of the camera/viewer creates an experience which is paradigmatic of a particular conception of man's being in the world. This conception has perhaps been most precisely stated by Robbe-Grillet:

> Even if many objects are presented and are described with great care, there is always and especially, the eye which sees them, the thought which re-examines them, the passion which distorts them.[4]

. . . .

My *Riddle of Lumen* depends upon qualities of *LIGHT.* All films do, of course. But with *The Riddle of Lumen,* 'the hero' of the film is light/itself. It is a film . . . inspired by the sense, and specific formal possibilities, of the classical Eng.-lang. riddle . . . only one appropriate to film and, thus, as distinct from language as I could make it.[5]

The Riddle of Lumen by Stan
Brakhage

Without trying to establish exactly what Brakhage means by a "riddle of lumen," or to determine how a linguistic model can be transformed into a visual one, it is possible to examine certain concerns around which the film revolves in terms of the model Brakhage proposes. A riddle presents an enigma which acts as a kind of "rite of passage." One who answers the riddle, who passes the test attains a new, elevated status.

The test situation seems operant in the film on the two levels of perception and cognition. Perception of images is made difficult by frequent absence or change of focus, reduction of the context of an object through closeness of the camera, darkness, and by rapid editing and camera movements. The progression of images is non-linear. Connections between images or image clusters must be made by the viewer. For example, different images relating to childhood recur at different moments in the film. These moments can be synthesized as one possible progression. Other clusters of images revolve around flying, textures of materials, and plant life.

A riddle contains a catalogue of instances or metaphors of its subject. The layout must be analyzed and the parts examined in relation to one another in order to classify the material and discover how it "means." In *The Riddle of Lumen,* the subject is light. The problem to be explored is the ways in which the many images and their combinations are concerned with this subject.

The range of light that is visible is perceived as color. In the film, color has been given a privileged status. Between the poles of the more concrete representations such as a Kleenex box or a woman, both transformed by tints or special lighting, and the totally abstract movement of color across the surface of the screen, a myriad of subtle gradations appear. The predilection to build ambiguities by partially obliterating the representation clearly emphasizes the movement toward abstraction.

Indeed, when one examines the film it becomes clear that abstraction is given the dominant position. For example, the totally formal play between the colors blue and orange recurs during the film in the most varied and complex manner. Certain images present in microcosm this tendency toward abstraction. The focus mechanism is moved from one end point to another, establishing the clear representation at only one instant. Two observations can be made: the moment in which the object is recognized occupies only a fragment of a spectrum; and it is the manipulation of the film material which reduces the status of the concrete object and enhances the quality of abstraction.

Throughout the film, shots containing recognizable objects are surrounded by blurred images, shots of color, or black spaces interrupted by moving lights. In one section, there is a progression of shots each of which frames different combinations of electric lights. A change of framing or the introduction of camera light movement can transform what appears to be a totally abstract field into the mundane representation of traffic or an airport at night. The camera functions to instigate these instantaneous shifts of orientation.

> Imagine an eye unruled by man-made laws of perspective, an eye unprejudiced by compositional logic, an eye which does not respond to the name of everything but which must know each object encountered in life through an adventure of perception. How many colors are there in a field of grass to the crawling baby unaware of "Green?" . . . Imagine a world before the "beginning was the word."[6]

The Riddle of Lumen by Stan
   Brakhage

Endurance/Remembrance/
Metamorphosis by Barry
Gerson

The longing to return to the freedom of childhood, expressed as a quest for the resurgence of visual complexity, involves a process which requires stripping the conventional and the learned from the act of perception. The relinquishing of the conventional for the uncommon mode of perception is required to understand Brakhage's riddle as well as a linguistic one. Ironically, the visual task is one which requires the rejection of an association with language since the acquisition of language is the primary means used by children to learn conventional methods of perception and conception.

Within *The Riddle of Lumen* there are several images of childhood which are structured to assert the viewer's distance from the event. A space containing a child's wagon is traversed by a dog running in slow motion; blurred forms of blue represent children playing, a childhood figure is glimpsed behind trees. Each time a filmic strategy is used to deny access to a world of past innocence.

The first shot which introduces the subject of childhood is that of a reading primer. Two pages which contain drawings of a house and a bird are depicted with absolute clarity. The abstraction of the drawings results from an extreme schematization and reduction of subject matter. The visual distinction between this shot and those described above is startling. The early image of the primer establishes the relationship between the acquisition of language and the loss of complexity and freedom of vision. The later shots of childhood are interwoven with others to create a web of images of various degrees of abstraction. The childhood images are themselves an integral part of the web.

The preeminance of abstraction and the return to images of childhood are joined in one process. The reaffirmation of the multiplicity of vision creates an approximation of childhood vision. Since it is impossible to complete a return to the vision of childhood, an approximation, rather than a duplication of that vision is established. Therefore the images of childhood are transformed by certain filmic techniques and can never be recorded directly.

The last shot of the film re-establishes the sense of the object, but it has been transformed. An object gradually comes into focus in the center of an open field. However, its significance is baffling; it is impossible to name. Objecthood has regained a sense of mystery.

Endurance/Remembrance/Metamorphosis is a film composed of three parts of equal duration. Each part consists of a single shot of a minimal space. In *Endurance,* a section of a dark room is framed so that a reflection of a window with a curtain blowing is balanced by the curtain which moves on and off screen. Occasionally the camera seems to mimic the gentle movements of the curtain as it slowly advances and retreats.

A view of a lawn scene is taken from an interior space in *Remembrance.* Reflections of the interior space appear on the window which mediates the camera's view of the exterior, and the frequent readjustments of camera position call attention to the frames of the window and the image.

The third section, *Metamorphosis,* examines a cluster of plants by shifting focus so that the image is in constant flux. Layers materialize and vanish very gradually. Perspectival foreground/depth relationships are abandoned for the perpetual reconstitution of a surface. The camera moves frequently, but its movements never reveal the scene's spatial coordinates or clarify the suggestion of a frame on the left edge of the screen.

Each of the three sections of the film creates an ambiguous sense of space. In *Endurance,* the camera is positioned in the room to frustrate immediate recognition that a curtain is swaying on the left. The strange angle invites a misreading that the camera is not directed downward to the reflection on the floor but upward in order to glance out of a window. The ambiguities would not be experienced if the rest of the space were not engulfed in darkness. The blackness obscures the boundaries between wall and floor, thereby obfuscating the spatial context.

A similar ambiguity occurs in *Remembrance* where it is difficult to discern whether certain forms exist outside the window or are reflections of objects in the room. There is an essential difference, however, between the two segments of the film. In *Endurance,* with a certain amount of visual adjustment, the eye can discriminate between reflection and object, whereas in *Remembrance* this clarity is not possible until the camera moves. The camera tilts and pans to accentuate the disparity between foreground, the reflections on glass, and background, the exterior view.

With *Metamorphosis,* a qualitative change occurs, and the ambiguity is never resolved. Neither the eye nor the movements of the camera are able to unmesh the layers of surface which the internal focus mechanism makes visible. The constant manipulation of the space also makes it difficult to ascertain its scale and the constitution of its parts.

Each four minute segment of the film incorporates a unique set of strategies to create its special character. *Endurance* establishes a balance of forces by spatially separating the reflection from the curtain, balancing them by repeating the undulating rhythm in counterpoint. The camera is synthesized within the contrapuntal structure since its movement mimics that of the curtain.

In *Remembrance,* camera movement does not mimic object movement. Nothing in the field is mobile. Instead, the camera asserts its function as framer. As the camera rotates laterally and advances and retreats from the framed window, the objects change in relation to one another. As the camera moves, one senses a special effort to maintain the window's frame within the shot. The act of imitation does not occur on the level of movement, but on that of frame: the frame of the window mimics the frame of the image. This inclination is accentuated as the camera maneuvers to isolate the reflection of an antique lamp superimposed on a tree, enclosing the image on three sides by the window frame.

The primary structural strategy in *Metamorphosis* is not mimicked by an element of the visible field. The focusing apparatus is totally hidden within the body of the camera, but it enforces its way of seeing with such force that the objects recorded are radically diminished in terms of their reference to the phenomenal world. Whereas the first two sections of the film establish a certain ambiguity between object and reflection, the last one dematerializes the object so that the terms of that dichotomy are themselves abandoned. Established in its place is a new vision where the objects represented are subordinated to and reflect the "eye" of the camera.

Finally, one may ask, what do the titles of these parts indicate? At the very least, they direct the viewer to experience or interpret the sections as instances or analogical forms of endurance, remembrance, and metamorphosis. A suggested method or model of investigation is never indicated. I will briefly suggest a possible direction.

The repetition of undulating movements and the balance of the parts in *Endurance* impress one with the sense of continuity and stability.

Nostalgia by Hollis Frampton

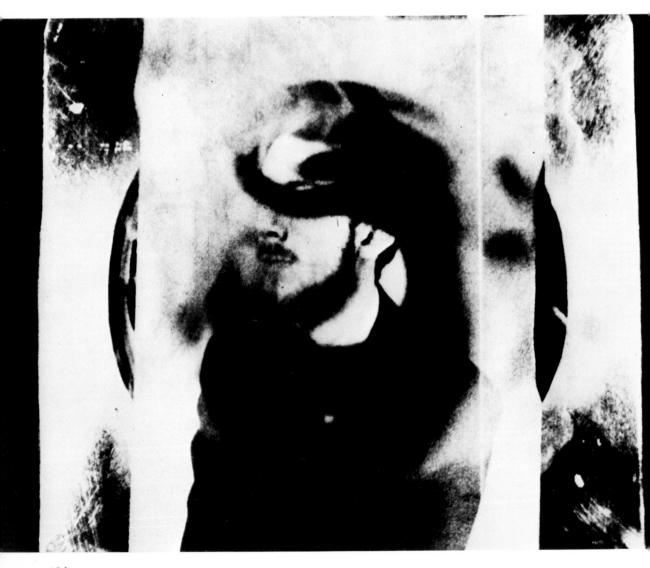

States of reflection and objecthood, interiority and exteriority, are held in perpetual equilibrium by the mediating agent which establishes and reinforces the situation.

In *Remembrance* the camera actively structures a transformation from a generalized field to a particular arrangement of two of its components. The postulation of the window as eye, directing the vision simultaneously out to the exterior landscape and back into the space which houses it, suggests that the movement toward the final image is indicative of a movement of consciousness. Indeed, the movement mirrors a possible instance of the mind in the act of recollection. A particular organization of material is selected by the eye from general impressions and the act of attention engendered triggers the recollection of past experiences.

The constant state of flux in *Metamorphosis* operates to totally transform the field of vision from moment to moment. The simultaneous representation of reflection and object gives way in this section to a movement between the visible and the invisible. The poles of exteriority and interiority merge: layers of space appear on the surface and retreat from it, creating a situation whereby the interior is continually exteriorized.

Each segment of *Endurance/Remembrance/Metamorphosis* presents a framed field of vision and its manipulation through the use of certain filmic strategies. The progression from a balance of parts through superimposition to an ongoing series of transformations on a single plane depends upon this careful selection and organic interaction of the materials of the environment and film.

In his article "Incisions in History/Segments of Eternity," Hollis Frampton postulates the notion of historic time as a human convention, a man-made fabrication to confer meaning, legibility, and purpose on human experience.

> Historic time is the time of mechanistic ritual, of routine, automatic as metabolism. It is composed of sequential, artificial, isometric modules which are related to one another, in language, by the connective phrase: "and then." This sort of connection, like that between links in a chain, is capable of transmitting energy only under the tension of implied causality.[7]

According to Frampton, through the structure of language the wild and haphazard heaping of events within a person's or culture's life are harnessed to a finite, sequential, narrative model. The strictness of its grammar, the hierarchies of dependent and independent clauses, its successive, additive nature, and, perhaps especially, the explicit temporal distinctions indicated by tense make language a major focus of attack for an artist trying to recapture the complex experience of temporality.

The structure of *Nostalgia* combats the concept of linear experience with the creation of a disjunction between image and language. On the image track, a sequence of photographs is presented. Each one undergoes a similar transformation of being destroyed by fire. On the sound track, a voice describes the photographs and circumstances in which they were taken, and then introduces reminiscences triggered by the images. The disjunction is crucial to the film experience: the voice track consistently lags behind the image track by one photograph. Thus each time one hears the description, one anticipates the appropriate image, and simultaneously, each photograph directs one into the past to the previous description. One is unable to locate the present moment. The sound/image disjunction requires the spectator to look within, not beyond, the boundary of the film to analyze the interrelationships, ambiguities, and contradictions which are a direct result of this non-coincidental structure. Although certain elements direct one's attention to time periods beyond the limits of the film, that pull is frustrated by the circuitous structure which so strongly emphasizes its own nature as self-contained and self-propelled.

It is interesting that each track, if isolated, is totally comprehensible as a linear progression, yet each points to temporal moments beyond the consecutive order. One of the properties of language is the ability to incorporate indices of the past and future within an ongoing discourse. Instantaneous shifts of tense do not confuse one; they are all subordinated to the temporality of the act of telling.

Photographs also refer to different moments in time. The moment of looking at a photograph is always divorced from the moment of recording. Through the burning of the photographs, another temporal level is incorporated. The gradual transformation which directs the consciousness simultaneously back toward its incipience and ahead toward its decay is a representation of the most fundamental temporal mode—that of mortality. The process can certainly be incorporated into the situation of the photograph without disturbing its status as an object existing in "real" time.

The image/sound disjunction creates two non-synchronous levels of discourse which provoke intricate labyrinths of contradictory messages. The voice establishes its position in time at the outset by blowing into the microphone and chatting about the recording situation. On viewing the film, one realizes that the establishment of the time of recording contradicts the time of the completed work. By using such phrases as "do you see what I see" or "as you can see," Frampton establishes a form of direct address which is violated by the non-congruence of image and word. Direct address becomes transformed in the viewing situation into the tense of the future perfect: "you will have seen." The constant split between the assumption and denial of presentness establishes the essential circular bind in which the viewer is situated. By using mundane speech and representations, and manipulating only the location of the moment of discourse, those elements of language which establish its character of succession and linearity are revealed to be purely conventional.

In Frampton's article mentioned at the outset, he distinguishes between the historic and ecstatic experience of time. The ecstatic experience involves both the escape from linear time and also, as he says, an "imperviousness to language." *Nostalgia* is certainly structured to embody these qualities.   The final description of the narrator points to an image which one never witnesses: it is the image of terror which calls forth an ecstatic experience. Here the moment of ecstasy is mocked: instead of the promised image, one finds oneself at the end of the film. The anticipation is thwarted and one is once again returned to the intricate circular form of the film.

The rift between a direct experience and one mediated by language can never be closed since the former requires an escape from the shackles of language as well as its cohort, linear time. *Nostalgia* refers to the two poles of the duality. They cause mutual reverberations, but remain poised in a stance of irreconcilable separateness. Jorge Luis Borges, likewise concerned with the human experience of time, wrote of the eternal division between the ecstatic and historic times. After an ecstatic experience, he explained the frustration of trying to recapture the moment through the mediation of language:

> Thus, this half-glimpsed idea remains an anecdote of the emotions, and the true moment of ecstasy and the possible insinuation of eternity—which that [ecstatic experience] lavished on me—are confined, in confessed irresolution, to this sheet of paper.[8]

—Ellen Feldman

Footnotes

1. Victor Shklovsky. "Art as Technique," *Russian Formalist Criticism: Four Essays,* editor, Lee Lemon and Marion Reis, Lincoln: University of Nebraska Press, 1965, pp. 12, 18.

2. P. Adams Sitney. "Structural Film," in *Film Culture Reader,* P. Adams Sitney, editor, New York: Praeger Publishers, 1970, p. 327.

3. Ernie Gehr and Jonas Mekas, "Ernie Gehr Interviewed by Jonas Mekas, March 24, 1971," *Film Culture No. 53-54-55,* 1972, pp. 26–27.

4. Alain Robbe-Grillet. *For a New Novel,* New York: Grove Press, Inc., 1965, p. 137.

5. Stan Brakhage. "Metaphors on Vision," *Film Culture No. 30,* 1963, opening statement.

6. Stan Brakhage. Notes on *The Riddle of Lumen, Film-Makers' Cooperative Catalogue,* no. 6, 1975, p. 32.

7. Hollis Frampton. "Incisions in History/Segments of Eternity," *Artforum,* Vol. XIII, no. 2, 1974, p. 42.

8. Jorge Luis Borges. "A New Refutation of Time," in *A Personal Anthology*, Anthony Kerrigan, editor, New York: Grove Press, Inc., 1967, p. 56.

Catalog List

The organization of this exhibition has followed a chronological line. It has avoided thematic groupings, such as those suggested by Sitney, in favor of a history which, in each of the seven programs, represents the variety of concerns within each period covered. Certain central works of the avant-gard could not be included because of their long running times; these include Ken Jacobs' *Tom, Tom, the Piper's Son* and Stan Brakhage's *Scenes from under Childhood*. In addition, certain filmmakers could not be represented because their films were not available; these include the works of Andy Warhol, Jack Smith and Gregory Markopoulos. Still other important filmmakers whose works are listed in the chronology could not be represented because of the time limitations of the programs. (J. G. H.)

CATALOG LIST
(All films are 16mm, sound, 24 fps and on loan from the artist unless otherwise noted.)

1 1943-1948

Meshes Of The Afternoon
Maya Deren and Alexander Hammid
1943, 18 minutes, black & white
silent, 24 fps
Camera, Alexander Hammid;
Lent by Grove Press, Inc.

Geography Of The Body
Willard Maas
1943, 7 minutes, black & white
Commentary by George Barker; Camera, Marie
    Menken;
Lent by Grove Press, Inc.

Early Abstractions (#1-#5, #7 and #10)
Harry Smith
1939-57, 22.5 minutes, color

Fireworks
Kenneth Anger
1947, 15 minutes, black & white
Camera assistant, Chester Kessler; Music by Respighi;
Filmed in Hollywood; Cast: Kenneth Anger (Dreamer),
Gordon Gray (First Sailor), Bill Seltzer (Second Sailor).

A Study In Choreography For Camera
Maya Deren
1945, 4 minutes, black & white
Dancer, Talley Beatty;
Lent by Grove Press, Inc.

Mother's Day
James Broughton
1948, 23 minutes, black & white
Assistant director, Kermit Sheets; Camera, Frank
Stauffacher; Music, Howard Brubeck.

2 1949-1958

The Lead Shoes
Sidney Peterson
1949, 18 minutes, black & white
Lent by Grove Press, Inc.

Bells Of Atlantis
Ian Hugo
1952, 9.5 minutes, color
Assisted by Len Lye; Narrated and acted by Anaïs Nin;
Electronic music by Louis and Bebe Barron;
Lent by Film Images.

The Wonder Ring
Stan Brakhage
1955, 4 minutes, color
silent, 24 fps
Theme suggested by Joseph Cornell.

Bridges-Go-Round
Shirley Clarke
1958, 8 minutes, color
Version #1: Electronic soundtrack by Louis and
Bebe Barron; Version #2: Jazz soundtrack by Ted
Macero; Both versions to be projected together.

A Movie
Bruce Conner
1958, 12 minutes, black & white

Recreation
Robert Breer
1956, 2 minutes, color
Spoken text by Noël Burch.

Anticipation Of The Night
Stan Brakhage
1958, 40 minutes, color
silent, 24 fps

3 1959-1963

Science Friction
Stan Vanderbeek
1959, 9 minutes, color

Prelude, Dog Star Man
Stan Brakhage
1961, 25 minutes, color
silent, 24 fps

Notebook
Marie Menken
1963, 10 minutes, color
silent, 24 fps
Lent by Stephen Maas.

Little Stabs At Happiness
Ken Jacobs
1959-63, 18 minutes, color
Featuring Jack Smith.

Mass For The Dakota Sioux
Bruce Baillie
1963-64, 24 minutes, black & white

4 1963-1966

Scorpio Rising
Kenneth Anger
1963, 29 minutes, color
Music by Little Peggy March, The Angels, Bobby
Vinton, Elvis Presley, Ray Charles, The Crystals, The
Ran-Dells, Kris Jensen, Claudine Clark, Gene
McDaniels, The Surfaris; Filmed in Brooklyn and
Manhattan; Cast: Bruce Bryon (Scorpio), Johnny
Sapienza (Taurus), Frank Carifi (Leo), John Palone
(Pinstripe), Ernie Allo (Joker), Barry Rubin (Fall
Guy), Steve Crandell (Blondie), Bill Dorfmann (Back),
Johnny Dodds (Kid).

Fire Of Waters
Stan Brakhage
1965, 6.5 minutes, black & white

Window
Ken Jacobs
1964, 12 minutes, color
silent, 16 fps
Originally filmed in 8mm.

The Flicker
Tony Conrad
1966, 30 minutes, black & white
Sound on separate magnetic tape.

5 1966-1967

Samadhi
Jordan Belson
1967, color, 6 minutes
Lent by Pyramid Films Corporation.

**Film In Which There Appear Sprocket Holes, Edge
Lettering, Dirt Particles, Etc.**
George Landow
1965-66, 4 minutes, color
silent, 24 fps

Castro Street
Bruce Baillie
1966, 10 minutes, color and black & white

Notes On The Circus
Jonas Mekas
1966, 12 minutes, color

Lapis
James Whitney
1963-66, 10 minutes, color

Wavelength
Michael Snow
1966-67, 45 minutes, color

6 1967-1970

T,O,U,C,H,I,N,G
Paul Sharits
1968, 12 minutes, color
Lent by Castelli-Sonnabend Tapes and Films, Inc.

Runaway
Standish D. Lawder
1969, 5.5 minutes, black & white

69
Robert Breer
1968, 4.5 minutes, color

Diploteratology Or Bardo Folly
George Landow
1967, 20 minutes, color
silent, 24 fps
Formerly known as *Bardo Follies.*

Our Lady Of The Sphere
Larry Jordan
1969, 10 minutes, color

Bleu Shut
Robert Nelson
1970, 33 minutes, color
Soundtrack by R. Nelson, Diane Nelson, Wm. T. Wiley.

7 1970-1972

Serene Velocity
Ernie Gehr
1970, 23 minutes, color
silent, 16 fps

The Riddle Of Lumen
Stan Brakhage
1972, 14 minutes, color
silent, 24 fps

Endurance/Remembrance/Metamorphosis
Barry Gerson
1970, 12 minutes, color
silent, 16 fps

Nostalgia
Hollis Frampton
1971, 36 minutes, black & white
(*Hapax Legómena I.*)

Filmographies

Kenneth Anger

Who Has Been Rocking My Dream Boat? (1941, 11 min.)
Tinsel Tree (1941, 6 min.)
Prisoner Of Mars (1942, 20 min.)
The Nest (1943, 30 min.)
Escape Episode I (1944, 45 min.)
Drastic Demise (1945, 12 min.)
Escape Episode II (1946, 40 min.)
Fireworks (1947, 15 min.)
Puce Women (1948, unfinished.)
Puce Moment (1949, 7 min.)
The Love That Whirls (1949, unfinished.)
The Lune Des Lapins (Rabbit's Moon) (1950, 15 min.)
Maldoror (1951-52, unfinished.)
Le Jeune Homme Et La Mort (1953, 25 min.)
Eaux D'Artifice (1953, 13 min.)
Inauguration Of The Pleasure Dome (1954, 38 min.)
Thelema Abbey (1955, 35 min.)
Scorpio Rising (1963, 29 min.)
Kustom Kar Kommandos (1965, 3½ min.)
Invocation Of My Demon Brother (1969, 11 min.)
Lucifer Rising, Part I (1974, 25 min.)
Lucifer Rising, Part II (1976, 30 min.)

Bruce Baillie

On Sundays (1960-61, 26 min.)
David Lynn's Sculpture (1961, 3 min., unfinished.)
Mr. Hayashi (1961, 3 min.)
The Gymnasts (1961, 8 min.)
Friend Fleeing (1962, 3 min., unfinished.)
Everyman (1962, 6 min.)
News #3 (1962, 3 min.)
Have You Thought Of Talking To The Director? (1962, 15 min.)
Here I Am (1962, 10 min.)
A Hurrah For Soldiers (1962-63, 4 min.)
To Parsifal (1963, 16 min.)
Mass For The Dakota Sioux (1964, 24 min.)
The Brookfield Recreation Center (1964, 5 min.)
Quixote (1964-65, 45 min., revised 1967.)
Yellow Horse (1965, 8 min.)
Tung (1966, 5 min.)
Castro Street (1966, 10 min.)
All My Life (1966, 3 min.)
Still Life (1966, 2 min.)

Termination (1966, 6 min.)
Port Chicago Vigil (1966, 9 min.)
Show Leader (1966, 1 min.)
Valentin De Las Sierras (1967, 10 min.)
Quick Billy (1970, 60 min.)

Jordan Belson

Transmutation (1947)
Improvisations #1 (1948)
Mambo (1951, 4 min.)
Caravan (1952, 3½ min.)
Mandala (1953, 3 min.)
Bop Scotch (1953, 3 min.)
Flight (1958, 10 min.)
Raga (1959, 7 min.)
Seance (1959, 4 min.)
Allures (1961, 9 min.)
Re-Entry (1964, 6 min.)
Phenomena (1965, 6 min.)
Samadhi (1967, 6 min.)
Momentum (1969, 6 min.)
Cosmos (1969, 6 min.)
World (1970, 6 min.)
Meditation (1971, 6 min.)
Chakra (1972, 6 min.)
Light (1974, 7 min.)
Cycles (1975, 11 min.)

Stan Brakhage

This filmography essentially reproduce the one compiled by Joyce Rheuban in the January, 1973 issue of Artforum. *Several corrections have been made and the list of films has been updated to the present.*

Interim (1952, 25 min.)
Unglassed Windows Cast A Terrible Reflection (1953, 35 min.)
The Boy And The Sea (1953, 2 min., lost first film photographed by Brakhage.)
Desistfilm (1954, 7 min.)
The Extraordinary Child (1954, 10 min.)
The Way To Shadow Garden (1954, 10 min.)
In Between (1955, 10 min.)
Reflections On Black (1955, 12 min.)
The Wonder Ring (1955, 4 min., theme suggested by Joseph Cornell; Brakhage's "out-takes" became Cornell's *Gnir Rednow.*)

"Tower House" (1955, 10 min., film photographed for Joseph Cornell under the working title "Bolts of Melody," then "Portrait of Julie," finally becoming Cornell's "Centuries of June.")

Untitled film of Geoffery Holder's Wedding (1955)

Zone Moment (1956, 3 min., lost.)

Flesh Of Morning (1956, 25 min.)

Nightcats (1956, 8 min.)

Daybreak And Whiteye (1957, 8 min.)

Loving (1957, 6 min.)

Anticipation Of The Night (1958, 40 min.)

Wedlock House: An Intercourse (1959, 11 min.)

Window Water Baby Moving (1959, 12 min.)

Cat's Cradle (1959, 5 min.)

Sirius Remembered (1959, 12 min.)

The Dead (1960, 11 min.)

Thigh Line Lyre Triangular (1961, 5 min.)

Films By Stan Brakhage: An Avant-Garde Home Movie (1961, 5 min.)

Blue Moses (1962, 11 min.)

Silent Sound Sense Stars Subotnick And Sender (1962, 2 min., lost.)

Oh Life—A Woe Story—The A Test News (1963, 5 min.)

"Meat Jewel" (1963, incorporated into *Dog Star Man: Part II*.)

Mothlight (1963, 4 min.)

Dog Star Man (1961-1964)
　Prelude: Dog Star Man (1961, 25 min.)
　Dog Star Man: Part I (1962, 35 min.)
　Dog Star Man: Part II (1962, 7 min.)
　Dog Star Man: Part III (1964, 11 min.)
　Dog Star Man: Part IV (1964, 5 min.)

The Art Of Vision (1961-65, 270 min., incorporates *Dog Star Man*.)

Three Films includes *Blue White, Blood's Tone, Vein* (1965, 10 min.)

Fire Of Waters (1965, 10 min.)

Pasht (1965, 5 min.)

Two: Creeley/McClure (1965, 5 min., also incorporated in *15 Song Traits*.)

Black Vision (1965, 3 min.)

The Horseman, The Woman, And The Moth (1968, 19 min.)

Lovemaking (1968, 36 min.)

Songs (1964-1969)
　Song 1 (1964, 4 min., 8mm)
　Songs 2 and 3 (1964, 7 min., 8mm)
　Song 4 (1964, 5 min., 8mm)
　Song 5 (1964, 6 min., 8mm)

Songs 6 and 7 (1964, 6 min., 8mm)

Song 8 (1964, 5 min., 8mm)

Songs 9 and 10 (1965, 9 min., 8mm)

Song 11 (1965, 5 min., 8mm)

Song 12 (1965, 5 min., 8mm)

Song 13 (1965, 5 min., 8mm)

Song 14 (1965, 5 min., 8mm)

15 Song Traits (1965, 47 min., 8mm)

Song 16 (1965, 7 min., 8mm)

Songs 17 and 18 (1965, 8 min., 8mm)

Songs 19 and 20 (1965, 14 min., 8mm)

Songs 21 and 22 (1965, 10 min., 8mm)

23rd Psalm Branch (1966-67, 100 min., 8mm)
　Part I (1966)
　Part II and Coda (1967)

Songs 24 and 25 (1967, 10 min., 8mm)

Song 26 (1968, 8 min., 8mm)

My Mountain Song 27 (1968, 26 min., 8mm)

Song 27 (Part II) Rivers (1969, 36 min., 8mm)

Song 28 (1969, 4 min., 8mm)

Song 29 (1969, 4 min., 8mm)

American 30's Song (1969, 30 min., 8mm)

Window Suite Of Children's Songs (1969, 24 min., 8mm)

Scenes From Under Childhood (1967-1970)
　Scenes From Under Childhood: Section No. 1 (1967, 30 min.)
　Scenes From Under Childhood: Section No. 2 (1969, 40 min.)
　Scenes From Under Childhood: Section No. 3 (1969, 27½ min.)
　Scenes From Under Childhood: Section No. 4 (1970, 46 min.)

The Weir-Falcon Saga (1970, 29 min.)

The Machine Of Eden (1970, 11 min.)

The Animals Of Eden And After (1970, 35 min.)

Sexual Meditation No. 1: Motel (1970, 6 min., 8mm)

Wecht (1971, 2 min., original in Carnegie Museum Film Department.)

Eyes (1971, 35½ min.)

Deus Ex (1971, 33¼ min.)

The Act Of Seeing With One's Own Eyes (1971, 32 min.)

Fox Fire Child Watch (1971, 3 min.)

Angels' (1971, 2 min.)

Door (1971, 1¾ min.)

Western History (1971, 8¼ min.)

The Trip To Door (1971, 12¼ min.)

Sexual Meditation: Room With View (1971, 3 min.)

The Peaceable Kingdom (1971, 7¾ min.)
Eye Myth (1972, 190 frames, begun in 1968 as sketch for *The Horseman, The Woman, And The Moth.)*
Sexual Meditation: Faun's Room Yale (1972, 2 min.)
Sexual Meditation: Office Suite (1972, 3 min.)
The Process (1972, 8 min.)
The Riddle Of Lumen (1972, 13½ min.)
The Shores Of Phos: A Fable (1972, 10 min.)
Sexual Meditation: Hotel (1972, 5 min.)
The Presence (1972, 2½ min.)
The Wold-Shadow (1972, 2½ min.)
Gift (1972, 2½ min., Super 8mm) (also available in 16mm.)
Sexual Meditation: Open Field (1972, 5¾ min.)
Eye Myth Study Film (1973, 4 min.)
Sincerity: Reel No. 1 (1973, 27 min.)
The Women (1973, 2¼ min.)
Skein (1974, 4 min.)
Aquarien (1974, 2¼ min.)
Hymn To Her (1974, 2½ min.)
Star Garden (1974, 20¾ min.)
Flight (1974, 4¾ min.)
Dominion (1974, 4 min.)
"He Was Born, He Suffered, He Died" (1974, 7½ min.)
Clancy (1974, 4¼ min.)
The Text Of Light (1974, 67 min.)
Eye Myth Loop (1974, 9 seconds, made in 1968 but first distributed in 1974.)
The Stars Are Beautiful (1974, 18½ min.)
Sincerity: Reel 2 (1975, 40 min.)
Short Films (9) (1975, 40 min., not to be released until 1978.)

Commercial Work

Martin Missil Quarterly Reports (1957)
"Opening" for G.E. Television Theatre (1958, 30 sec.)
Untitled film on Pittsburgh (1959, 35 mm, 45 min.)
The Colorado Legend And The Ballad Of The Colorado Ute (1961)
Mr. Tomkins Inside Himself (1962)
Film on Mt. Rushmore, photographed for Charles Nauman's Part II Film on Korczak Ziolkowski, Film on Chief Sitting Bull (1963–65)
Brakhage also photographed James Broughton's wedding in December, 1961. The footage was later edited into Broughton's *Nuptiae*.

Robert Breer

Form Phases I (1952, 2 min.)
Form Phases II and III (1953, 7½ min.)
Form Phases IV (1954, 4 min.)
Image By Images I (1954, endless loop.)
Un Miracle (1954, 1 min.)
Image By Images II and III (1955, 7 min.)
Image By Images IV (1956, 3 min.)
Motion Pictures (1956, 3 min.)
Cats (1956, 1½ min.)
Recreation I (1956-57, 2 min.)
Recreation II (1956-57, 1½ min.)
Jamestown Baloos (1957, 6 min.)
A Man And His Dog Out For Air (1958, 3 min.)
Par Avion (1958, 3-4 min.)
Cassis Colank (1958-59, 5 min., unfinished.)
Eyewash (1959, 5 min.)
Trailer (1959, 1 min., 35 mm.)
Homage To Jean Tinguely's "Homage To N.Y." (1960, 10 min.)
Inner And Outer Space (1960, 4 min.)
Blazes (1961, 3 min.)
Kinetic Art Show–Stockholm (1961, 15 min.)
Pat's Birthday (1962, 13 min.)
Horse Over Tea Kettle (1962, 6 min.)
Breathing (1963, 6 min.)
Fist Fight (1964, 11 min.)
66 (1966, 5 min.)
69 (1968, 5 min.)
PBL I And II (1968, 2 min.)
70 (1970, 5 min.)
Gulls And Buoys (1972, 6 min.)
Fuji (1974, 8 min.)
Etc. (1975, 10 min.)

James Broughton

Mother's Day (1948, 23 min.)
Adventures Of Jimmy (1950, 11 min.)
Loony Tom, The Happy Lover (1951, 10 min.)
Four In The Afternoon (1951, 15 min.)
The Pleasure Garden (1953, 38 min.)
The Bed (1968, 20 min.)
Nuptiae (1969, 14 min.)
The Golden Positions (1970, 32 min.)
This Is It (1971, 9½ min.)
Dreamwood (1972, 45 min.)
High Kukus (1973, 3 min.)
Testament (1974, 20 min.)

Shirley Clarke

Dance In The Sun (1953, 7 min.)
In Paris Parks (1954, 13 min.)
Bullfight (1955, 9 min.)
A Moment In Love (1957, 10 min.)

Brussels "Loops" (1958, twelve 2½ min. loop films.)
Bridges-Go-Round (1958-9, 8 min.)
Skyscraper (1959, 20 min.)
A Scary Time (1960, 20 min.)
The Connection (1961, 100 min.)
The Cool World (1963, 100 min.)
Man In Polar Regions (1967, eleven screen film for Expo '67.)
Portrait Of Jason (1967, 105 min.)

Bruce Conner

A Movie (1957, 12 min.)
Cosmic Ray (1961, 4 min.)
Looking For Mushrooms (1961-67, 3 min.)
Report (1963-67, 13 min.)
Ten Second Film (1965, 10 sec.)
Vivian (1965, 3 min.)
The White Rose (1965-67, 7 min.)
Breakaway (1966-67, 5 min.)
Liberty Crown (1967, 5 min.)
Permian Strata (1969, 4 min.)
Five Times Marilyn (1973, 13½ min.)
Crossroads (1974-75, 36 min.)
Take The 5:10 To Dreamland (1975, 6 min.)

Tony Conrad

The Flicker (1966, 30 min.)
Coming Attractions (with Beverly Grant Conrad, 1970, 78 min.)
Straight And Narrow (with Beverly Grant Conrad, 1970, 10 min.)
Four Square (with Beverly Grant Conrad, 1971, 18 min.)
Ten Years Alive On The Infinite Plain (1972, 20 to 200 min.)
Yellow Movie (1972, a series.)
Film Of Note (1973, 45 min.)
Loose Connection (1973, 55 min.)
Deep Fried 7360 (1973)
4-X Attack (1973, 2 min.)
Electrocuted 4-X, Brine Damaged (1973, 2 min.)
Curried 7302 (1973)
Deep Fried 4-X Negative (1973, 2 versions.)
7302 Creole (1973)
Deep Fried 7360 (1973, 200' version.)
Raw Film (1973)
7360 Sukiyaki (1973)
Third Film Feedback (1974, 18 min.)
Electrocuted 4-X (1974, 8 min., second series.)
Pickle Wind (1974, 4 min.)
Kalvar Processing Attack (1974, 4 min.)
Photochromic Emulsion Loop (1974)
Bowed Film (1974)

7360 Sukiyaki (1974)
Pickled 3M-150 (1974, 12 realizations.)
First Film Feedback (1974, 18 min.)
Flicker Matte (1974)
Boiled Shadow (1974, 4 min.)
Roast Kalvar (1974, 2 realizations.)
Articulation of Boolean Algebra For Film Opticals (1975, 71 min.)
Aquarium (1975, 7 min.)
Shadow File (1975)
Moment Propagation (1975, 25 min.)

Maya Deren

Meshes Of The Afternoon (with Alexander Hammid, 1943, 18 min.)
At Land (1944, 15 min.)
A Study In Choreography For Camera (1945, 4 min.)
Ritual In Transfigured Time (1946, 15 min.)
Meditation On Violence (1948, 12 min.)
The Very Eye Of Night (1959, 15 min.)

Hollis Frampton

Manual of Arms (1966, 17 min.)
Information (1966, 4 min.)
Process Red (1966, 3½ min.)
States (1967/revised 1970, 17 min.)
Heterodyne (1967, 7 min.)
Snowblind (1968, 5½ min.)
Maxwell's Demon (1968, 4 min.)
Surface Tension (1968, 10 min.)
Palindrome (1969, 22 min.)
Carrots & Peas (1969, 5½ min.)
Lemon (for Robert Huot) (1969, 7½ min.)
Prince Ruperts Drops (1969, 7 min.)
Works and Days (1969, 12 min.)
Artificial Light (1969, 25 min.)
Zorns Lemma (1970, 60 min.)
Hapax Legomena: complete (1971-72, 202 min.)
Hapax Legomena I: (Nostalgia) (1971, 36 min.)
Hapax Legomena II: (Poetic Justice) (1972, 31½ min.)
Hapax Legomena III: (Critical Mass) (1971, 25½ min.)
Hapax Legomena IV: (Travelling Matte) (1971, 33½ min.)
Hapax Legomena V: (Ordinary Matter) (1972, 36 min.)
Hapax Legomena VI: (Remote Control) (1972, 29 min.)
Hapax Legomena VII: (Special Effects) (1972, 10½ min.)
Appartus Sum (1972, 2½ min.)

Tiger Balm (1972, 10 min.)
Yellow Springs (1972, 5 min.)
Less (1973, 1 min.)
Straits of Magellan: Autumnal Equinox (1974, 27 min.)
Straits of Magellan: Winter Solstice (1974, 33 min.)

Ernie Gehr

Morning (1968, 5½ min.)
Wait (1968, 7 min.)
Reverberation (1969, 23 min.)
Transparency (1969, 11 min.)
History (1970, 40 min.)
Serene Velocity (1970, 23 min.)
Field (1970, 19 min.)
Still (1971, 55 min.)

Barry Gerson

The Neon Rose (1960-64, 41 min.)
Automatic Free Form (1968, 20 min.)
Evolving (1969, 17 min.)
Group I: Grass/Ice/Snow/Vibrations (1969, 16 min.)
Group II: Water/Contemplating (1969, 16 min.)
Generations (1969, 4 min.)
Group III: Sunlight/Floating/Afternoon (1970, 23½ min.)
Group IV: Breaded Light/Dissolving/Beyond (1970, 12¼ min.)
Group V: Endurance/Remembrance/Metamorphosis (1970, 12 min.)
Movements (1971, 4 min.)
Group VI: Converging Lines/Assimilation (1971, 18 min.)
Group VII: Portrait of Diana/Portrait of Andrew Noren (1970-72)
Shadow Space (1973, 6 min.)
Inversion (1973, 12 min.)
Luminous Zone (1973, 28 min.)
Translucent Appearances (1975, 22 min.)
Celluloid Illuminations (1975, 32 min.)

Ian Hugo

Ai-Ye (1950, 24 min.)
Bells Of Atlantis (1952, 9½ min.)
Jazz Of Lights (1954, 18 min.)
Melodic Inversion (1958, 8 min.)
Venice Etude No. 1 (1961, 7½ min.—later incorporated into *The Gondola Eye*.)
The Gondola Eye (1963, 28 min.—The film was re-edited in 1967 and shortened to 18 min.

It was re-edited again in 1971 and further shortened to 16½ min.)
Ian Hugo: Engraver and Filmmaker (1968, 10 min.—revised in 1972 and shortened to 7 min.)
Through The Magiscope (1969, 10 min.)
Apertura (1970, 6 min.)
Aphrodisiac I (1971, 6 min.)
Aphrodisiac II (1972, 6 min.)
Levitation (1972, 6½ min.)
Transmigration (1973, 6 min.)
Transcending (with Yass Hakoshima. Made in Video for Channel 13 and later transferred to film, 1974, 16½ min.)
"Work In Progress" (with Arnold Eagle, 1975, 15 min.)

Ken Jacobs

Orchard Street (1956, 15 min., abandoned.)
Saturday Afternoon Blood Sacrifice: TV Plug: Little Cobra Dance (1957, 9 min.)
Star Spangled To Death (1957, approx. 180 min., unfinished.)
Little Stabs At Happiness (1959-63, 18 min.)
Blonde Cobra (with Bob Fleischner and Jack Smith, 1959-63, 28 min.)
The Death Of P'Town (1961, 7 min.)
Baud'larian Capers (1963-64, 20 min., revised in 1975.)
Window (1964, 12 min., originally 8mm.)
The Winter Footage (1964, 20 min., 8mm.)
We Stole Away (1964, 30 min., 8mm.)
Lisa And Joey In Connecticut: "You've Come Back!" "You're Still Here!" (1965, 12 min., originally 8 mm.)
The Sky Socialist (1965, approx. 120 min., 8mm., unfinished.)
Naomi Is A Dream Of Loveliness (1965, 4 min.)
Airshaft (1967, 4 min.)
Soft Rain (1968, 12 min.)
Tom, Tom, The Piper's Son (1969, 115 min., revised in 1971.)
Nissan Ariana Window (1969, 21 min.)
Posthumous Works: Azazel (1972, for analytical projector, 3-D.)
Excerpts From The Russian Revolution (1973, 20 min., 3-D.)
Urban Peasants: An Essay In Yiddish Structuralism (with Stella Weiss, 1975, 45 min.)
A Good Night For The Movies: The 4th Of July By Charles Ives By Ken Jacobs (1972, 24 hrs., shadow cinema work.)

A Man's Home Is His Castle Films: The European Theater Of Operations/Urban Peasants (1975, approx. 150 min.)
The Impossible: Chapter One, Southwark Fair (1975, approx. 90 min., 3-D performance for two analytical projectors.)

Larry Jordan

One Romantic Venture Of Edward (1952-64, 7 min.)
The Child's Hand (1953-54, 7 min.)
Morningame (1953-54, 9 min.)
Man Is In Pain (1954, 4 min.)
Trumpet (1954-56, 4 min.)
Undertow (1954-56, 7 min.)
3 (1954-56, 6 min.)
Visions Of A City (1956, 15 min.)
Waterlight (1957, 9 min.)
Triptych In Four Parts (1958, 12 min.)
The Studio: A Fable (1959-60, unfinished.)
Finds Of The Fortnight (1959-60, dismantled.)
The Soccer Game (1959-60, 6 min.)
Minerva Looks Out Into The Zodiac (1959-60, 6 min.)
Hymn In Praise Of The Sun (1960, 9 min.)
The Soccer Game: The Forty And One Nights, or *Jess's Didactic Nickelodeon,* also called *Heavy Water* (1960-61, 6 min.)
Portrait Of Sharon (1960, 9 min.)
The Herb Moon (1960, 5 min.)
The Seasons' Changes: To Contemplate (1960, 7 min.)
Four Vertical Portraits (1960-61, unfinished.)
The Movie Critic (1961, 4 min., unfinished.)
The Monkey (1961, 4 min., unfinished.)
Circus Savage (1961, 150 min., unfinished.)
Duo Concertantes (1961-64, 9 min.)
Enid's Idyll (1962, 9 min.)
Shomio (1963-64, 2 min.)
Pink Swine (1963-64, 3 min.)
The Dream Merchant (1963-64, 3 min.)
Rodia-Estudiantina (1963-64, 3 min.)
Big Sur: The Ladies (1963-64, 3 min.)
Johnnie (1963-64, 3 min.)
Jewel Face (1963-64, 3 min.)
Hamfat Asar (1965, 15 min.)
Cornell 1965 (1965, 9 min.)
The Old House Passing (1965-66, 40 min.)
Three Moving Fresco Films (1960-68, 28 min.) (*Enid's Idyll, Portrait of Sharon, Hymn In Praise Of The Sun.*)
Gymnopedies (1966, 6 min.)
Hildur And The Magician (1969, 70 min.)
Our Lady Of The Sphere (1969, 70 min.)

Living Is Dying (1970, 30 min.)
Sacred Art Of Tibet (1970, 28 min.)
Once Upon A Time (1972, 12 min.)
Orb (1972, 4½ min.)
Plainsong (1972-73, 11 min.)
Fireweed (1973, 3 min.)
The Apparition (1973)

George Landow

Fleming Faloon (1963-64, 7 min.)
Studies And Sketches (1963-65, 17 min.)
Film In Which There Appear Sprocket Holes, Edge Lettering, Dirt Particles, Etc. (1965-66, 4 min.)
Film In Which There Appear (Sprocket Holes, Edge Lettering, Dirt Particles, Etc. (1966, 10 min. wide screen.)
Diploteratology or Bardo Folly (1967, 20 min.)
The Film That Rises To The Surface Of Clarified Butter (1968, 9½ min.)
Institutional Quality (1969, 5 min.)
Remedial Reading Comprehension (1970, 5 min.)
What's Wrong With This Picture? (1971, 7 min.)
What's Wrong With This Picture? (1972, 3 min.)
Thank You Jesus For The Eternal Present: 1 (1973, 5½ min.)
Thank You Jesus For The Eternal Present: 2 (1974, 10 min.)
Wide Angle Saxon (1975, 22 min.)
"No Sir, Orison" (1975, 3 min.)

Standish D. Lawder

Sunday In Southbury (1968, 7 min.)
Eleven Different Horses (1969, 3 min.)
Headfilm (1969, 6 min.)
Necrology (1969, 6 min.)
Runaway (1969, 5½ min.)
Roadfilm (1969, 1½ min.)
Catfilm For Ursula (1969, 3 min.)
Corridor (1970, 22 min.)
Dangling Participle (1970, 16 min.)
Color Film (1971, 3 min.)
Construction Job (1972, 6 min.)
Raindance (1972, 15 min.)
Catfilm For Katy And Cynnie (1973, 4 min.)
Intolerance (Abridged) (1973, 12 min.)

Willard Maas

Coney Island (1942, 10 min., unfinished.)
Geography Of The Body (1943, 10 min.)
Image In The Snow (1943-48, 30 min.)

Merry-Go-Round (with Ben Moore, 1948, unedited)
Mechanics Of Love (with Ben Moore, 1955, 7 min.)
Narcissus (with Ben Moore, 1956, 48 min.)
Four American Artists (1957, unedited/lost.)
Excited Turkeys (1966, 9 min.)
Orgia (1967, 8 min.)
Radiator (1967, 5 min., unfinished.)

Note: An unpublished filmography by Maas himself in 1963 conflicts with the above as to certain dates and running times. However, the filmography above is a synthesis of two published *filmographies of Maas:* Filmwise #5-#6 (1967) *and* Film Comment *(Fall 1971).*

Jonas Mekas

Guns Of The Trees (1961, 75 min.)
Film Magazine Of The Arts (1963, 20 min.)
The Brig (1964, 68 min.)
Award Presentation To Andy Warhol (1964, 12 min.)
Report From Millbrook (1966, 12 min.)
Hare Krishna (1966, 4 min.)
Notes On The Circus (1966, 12 min.)
Cassis (1966, 4 min.)
Diaries, Notes And Sketches (1968, 180 min.)
Time & Fortune Vietnam Newsreel (1969, 4 min.)
Reminiscences Of A Journey To Lithuania (1972, 82 min.)
Diaries, Notes And Sketches (Years 1949-1965) (1975, 240 min.)

Marie Menken

Visual Variation On Noguchi (1945, 7 min.)
Hurry! Hurry! (1957, 4 min.)
Glimpse Of The Garden (1957, 4 min.)
Dwightiana (1959, 3½ min.)
Eye Music In Red Major (1961, 5½ min.)
Arabesque For Kenneth Anger (1961, 5 min.)
Bagatelle For Willard Maas (1961, 5½ min.)
Mood Mondrian (1961, 6½ min.)
Notebook (1962, 10 min.)
Moonplay (1962, 5 min.)
Here And There With My Octoscope (1962, 4 min.)
Go! Go! Go! (1963, 12 min.)
Drips And Strips (1961-65, 2½ min.)
Sidewalks (1961-66, 6½ min.)
Lights (1964-66, 8½ min.)
Watts With Eggs (1967, 2 min.)
Excursion (1968, 5 min.)

Robert Nelson

Plastic Haircut (1963, 15 min.)
Thick Pucker (1965, 11 min.)
Oiley Peloso The Pumph Man (1965, 14 min.)
Oh Dem Watermelons (1965, 12 min.)
Confessions Of A Black Mother Succuba (1965, 16 min.)
The Awful Backlash (1967, 14 min.)
Superspread (1967, 12½ min.)
The Off-Handed Jape (1967, 9 min.)
Grateful Dead (1967, 7½ min.)
Penny Bright And Jimmy Witherspoon (1967, 3 min.)
Hot Leatherette (1967, 5½ min.)
Half Open And Lumpy (1967, 2 min.)
The Great Blondino (with Wm. Wiley, 1967, 41 min.)
Blondino Preview (1967, 2½ min.)
War Is Hell (1968, 28 min.)
Bleu Shut (1970, 33 min.)
King David (with Mike Henderson, 1970, 16 min.)
No More (1971, 70 min.)
Worldly Woman (1973, 6½ min.)
Rest In Pieces (1974, 8½ min.)
Deepwesturn (1974, 4 min.)

Sidney Peterson

The Potted Psalm (with James Broughton, 1946, 24½ min.)
The Cage (1947, 31 min.)
Horror Dream (1947, 10 min.)
Clinic Of Stumble (1947, 18 min.)
Ah Nurture (with Hy Hirsch, 1948, approx. 20 min.)
The Petrified Dog (1948, 19 min.)
Mr. Frenhofer And The Minotaur (1948, 21 min.)
The White Rocker (1949, approx. 20 min.)
The Lead Shoes (1949, 18 min.)
Adagio For Election Day (1949, 18 min.)

The Following Films for Orbit Films:

Blunden Harbor (1952, 20 min.)
Chocolate Factory (1952, 20 min.)
Doll Hospital (1952, 20 min.)
Vein Stripping (surgical procedure, 1952, 25 min.)

The following three films were made for The Museum of Modern Art:

Architectural Millinery (bldg. tops in N.Y., 1954, 7 min.)
Manhole Covers (1954, 9 min.)

Japanese House (1955, 20 min.)
(*MOMA* scripts prepared for an animated series to be called *They Became Artists* included *The Cow Is Me* (Chagall, 1954) and *The Invisible Moustache of Raoul Dufy.* The Dufy script was produced by UPA as part of a similar series in 1955.)

Scripts for United Productions of America (UPA) animated films (35mm.):

The Invisible Moustache Of Raoul Dufy (1954–55)
The Merry-Go-Round In The Jungle (on the Douanier Rousseau, 1956)
The Day Of The Fox (on Sharaku, 1956)
Columbus Discovers America (1956)
A Woman's Place (Belle Starr, 1956)
The Twelve Days Of Christmas (1956)
Rome Burns (Nero fiddling, 1956)
The Greeks Take Troy (1956)
Lady Godiva (1956)
Grimaldi (1956)
The Night Watch (Rembrandt, 1956)
The Farm (Miro, 1956, script and storyboard.)

Script and storyboard for Disney:

Fantasia II (1957–58)

Paul Sharits

Ray Gun Virus (1966, 14 min.)
Word Movie/Flux Film 29 (1966, 3¾ min.)
Piece Mandala/End War (1966, 5 min.)
Razor Blades (1965–68, 25 min.)
N:O:T:H:I:N:G (1968, 36 min.)
T,O,U,C,H,I,N,G (1968, 12 min.)
S:TREAM:S:S:ECTION:S:ECTION:S:S: ECTIONED (1968–70, 42 min.)
Inferential Current (1971, 8 min.)
Axiomatic Granularity (1973, 20 min.)
Color Sound Frames (1974, 25 min.)
Apparent Motion (1975, 32 min.)

Harry Smith

Early Abstractions (Films #1– #5, #7 & #10) (1939–1957, 23 min.)
Heaven And Earth Magic Feature (Film #12) (1957–1962, 66 min.)
Late Superimpositions (Film #14) (1965–68, 31 min.)

Note: It is notoriously difficult to date the films of Harry Smith. Each statement made by Smith on the subject contradicts the other; as do the attempts of film his- *torians to situate his works in time. This must therefore be read as an approximation and should be probably be acknowledged as such.*

Michael Snow

A To Z (1956, 6½ min.)
New York Eye And Ear Control (A Walking Woman Work) (1964, 34 min.)
Short Shave (1965, 4 min.)
Wavelength (1967, 45 min.)
Standard Time (1967, 8 min.)
←——► (1969, 52 min.)
One Second In Montreal (1969, 26 min.)
Dripping Water (with Joyce Wieland, 1969, 10½ min.)
Side Seat Paintings Slides Sound Film (1970, 20 min.)
La Region Centrale (The Central Region) (1970–71, 190 min.)
Breakfast (Table Top Dolly) (1972 and 1976, 10 min.)
Rameau's Nephew By Diderot (Thanks To Dennis Young) By Wilma Schoen (1974, 285 min.)

Stan Vanderbeek

What, Who, How (1957, 8 min.)
Mankinda (1957, 10 min.)
Astral Man (1957, 1-1/3 min.)
Yet (1957–58, 2 min.)
Ala Mode (1958, 5 min.)
Wheeels No. 1 (1958, 5 min.)
Wheeels No. 2 (1959, 5 min.)
Dance Of The Looney Spoons (1959, 5 min.)
Science Friction (1959, 9 min.)
Achoo Mr. Keroochev (1959, 1¾ min.)
Skullduggery (1960, 5 min.)
Blacks and Whites, Days and Nights (1960, 5 min.)
Snapshots Of The City (1961, 5 min.)
The Human Face Is A Monument (1963, 10 min.)
Summit (1963, 12 min.)
Breathdeath (1964, 15 min.)
Phenomenon No. 1 (1965, 7 min.)
Poem Field No. 2 (1966, 6 min.)
See, Saw, Seems (1967, 6 min.)
Poem Field No. 1 (1967, 4 min.)
Man And His World (1967, 1 min.)
Panels For The Walls Of The World (1967, 8 min.)
Poem Field No. 5: Free Fall (1967, 7 min.)

Spherical Space No. 1 (1967, 5 min.)
The History Of Motion In Motion (1967,
    10 min.)
T.V. Interview (1967, 13 min.)
Newsreel Of Dreams No. 1 (1968, 8 min.)
Poem Field No. 7 (1967, 4½ min.)
Vanderbeekiana (1968, 29 min.)
Oh (1968, 10 min.)
Super-Imposition (1968, 17 min.)
Will (1968, 4¾ min.)
Newsreel Of Dreams No. 2 (1969, 8 min.)
Found Film No. 1 (1968–70, 6-1/3 min.)
Film Form No. 1 (1970, 10 min.)
Film Form No. 2 (1970, 10 min.)
Transforms (1970, 3 min.)
Symmetricks (1972, 7 min.)
Videospace (1972, 7 min.)
Who Ho Ray No. 1 (1972, 8 min.)
You Do, I Do, We Do (1972, 14 min.)
Computer Generation (1973, 29 min.)

James Whitney

Twenty-Four Variations (alternate title: *Varia-
    tions*) (with John Whitney, 1939–40, 5 min.,
    8 mm.)
Film Exercise No. 1 (with John Whitney, 1943,
    5 min.)
Film Exercises No. 2 and 3 (with John Whitney,
    1944, 4 min.)
Film Exercises No. 4 and 5 (with John
    Whitney, 1945, 12 min.)
Yantra (1950–55, 7 min.)
Lapis (1963–66, 10 min.)

Bibliographies

General Books and Catalogues

Battcock, Gregory. *The New American Cinema.* New York: E.P. Dutton & Co., 1967.

Castelli-Sonnabend Videotapes and Films. New York: Castelli-Sonnabend Tapes and Films, Inc., 1974.

Curtis, David. *Experimental Cinema.* New York: Delta, 1971.

Dwoskin, Stephen. *Film Is.* Woodstock, New York: The Overlook Press, 1975.

Film-Makers' Cooperative Catalogue No. 6. New York: Film-Makers' Cooperative, 1975.

Hein, Birgit. *Film Im Underground.* Berlin: Verlag Ullstein, 1971.

Kardish, Laurence. *Reel Plastic Magic.* Boston: Little, Brown & Co., 1972.

Mekas, Jonas. *Movie Journal.* New York: Collier Books, 1972.

Michelson, Annette. editor. *New Forms in Film.* Montreux, 1974.

Renan, Sheldon. *An Introduction to the American Underground Film.* New York: E.P. Dutton & Co., Inc., 1967.

Russett, Robert and Cecile Starr. editors. *Experimental Animation.* New York: Van Nostrand and Reinhold, 1976.

Sitney, P. Adams. editor. *Film Culture Reader.* New York: Praeger Publishers, 1970.

Sitney, P. Adams. *Visionary Film, The American Avant-Garde.* New York: Oxford University Press, 1974.

Tyler, Parker. *Underground Film—A Critical History.* New York: Grove Press, Inc., 1969.

Vogel, Amos. *Film as a Subversive Art.* New York: Random House, 1974.

Wheeler, Dennis. editor. *Form and Structure in Recent Film.* Vancouver: The Vancouver Art Gallery, 1972.

Youngblood, Gene. *Expanded Cinema.* New York: E.P. Dutton & Co., Inc., 1970.

Kenneth Anger

Alexander, Thomas Kent. "San Francisco's Hipster Cinema," *Film Culture No. 44,* 1967, 70-74.

"An Interview with Kenneth Anger," *Spider Magazine,* Vol. I, no. 13, 1965, 5-11, 14-16.

Anger, Kenneth. *Hollywood Babylon.* San Francisco: Straight Arrow Books by arrangement with The Stonehill Publishing Co., 1975.

___. *Magick Lantern Cycle: A Special Presentation in Celebration of The Equinox Spring 1966.* New York: Film-makers' Cinematheque, 1966.

"Anger at Work," *Cinema Rising #1,* April, 1972, p. 17.

Cornwell, Regina. "On Kenneth Anger," *December,* Vol. X, no. 1, 1968, 156-158.

Dietsfrey, Harris. "Two Films and An Interlude by Kenneth Anger," *Artforum,* 1965, 48-50.

Kelman, Ken. "Appendix to Thanatos in Chrome," *Film Culture No. 32,* 1964, p. 11.

___. "Thanatos in Chrome," *Film Culture No. 31,* 1964, 6-7.

Kunden, Art. "Anger at the 3rd Los Angeles Filmmakers Festival," *Canyon Cinema News,* November, 1964, 13-14.

Markopoulos, Gregory. "'Scorpio Rising,'" *Film Culture No. 31,* 1964, 5-6.

Martin, Bruce and Joe Medjuck. "An Interview with Kenneth Anger," *Take One,* Vol. I, no. 6, 12-15.

Mekas, Jonas, P. Adams Sitney and Richard Whitehall. "Three Notes on *Invocation of My Demon Brother,"* *Film Culture No. 48-49,* 1970, 1-6.

Micha, René. "Le Nouveau Cinéma," *Les Temps Modernes,* no. 214, 1964, 1717-1728.

Rayns, Tony. "Lucifer: A Kenneth Anger Kompendium," *Cinema,* no. 4, 1969, 23-31.

Sitney, P. Adams. "The Avant-Garde Film: Kenneth Anger and George Landow," *Afterimage,* no. 2, 1970, 22-28.

Bruce Baillie

Baillie, Bruce. "An Interview with Bruce Baillie," *Film Comment,* Vol. 7, no. 1, (Spring 1971), 24-32.

Polt, Harriet. "The Films of Bruce Baillie," *Film Comment,* Vol. 2, no. 4, (Fall 1965), 51-53.

Whitewall, Richard. "An Interview with Bruce Baillie," *Film Culture, No. 47,* 1969, 16-20.

Jordan Belson

Callenbach, Ernest. "Phenomena and Samadhi," *Film Quarterly,* (Spring 1968), 48-49.

Sturhahn, Larry. "Experimental Filmmaking: The Art of Jordan Belson-An Interview with Jordan Belson," *Filmmakers' Newsletter,* Vol. 8, no. 7, May, 1975, 22-26.

Stan Brakhage

Arthur, Paul. "Stan Brakhage: Four Films," *Artforum,* Vol. XI, no. 5, January, 1973, 41-45.

Brakhage, Stan. *The Brakhage Lectures.* Chicago: The Good Lion, 1972.

___. "Letter from Brakhage: On Splicing," *Film Culture No. 35,* 1964-5, 51-56.

___. "Letter to Yves Kovacs." *Yale Literary Magazine,* Vol. CXXXIII, no. 4, March, 1965, 33-37.

___. "Metaphors on Vision," *Film Culture No. 30,* 1964.

___. *A Motion Picture Giving and Taking Book.* West Newbury, Mass: Frontier Press, 1971.

___. "On Dance and Film," *Dance Perspectives,* no. 30, (Summer 1967), 36-38.

___. "Sound and Cinema," *Film Culture No. 29,* 1963, 81-102. (An exchange of letters with James Tenney and Gregory Markopoulos.)

Camper, Fred. *"The Art of Vision,* A Film by Stan Brakhage," *Film Culture No. 46,* (Autumn 1967), 40-44.

___. *"Western History* and *The Riddle of Lumen,"* *Artforum,* Vol. XI, no. 5, January, 1973, 66-71.

Clark, Dan. *Brakhage.* New York: Film-Makers' Cinematheque Monograph, Series No. 2, 1966.

Cohen, Phoebe. "Scenes from under Childhood," *Artforum,* Vol. XI, no. 5, January, 1973, 51-55.

Frampton, Hollis. "Stan and Jane Brakhage Talking," *Artforum,* Vol. XI, no. 5, January, 1973, 72-79.

Michelson, Annette. "Camera Lucida/Camera Obscura," *Artforum,* Vol. XI, no. 5, January, 1973, 72-79.

Richie, Donald. *Stan Brakhage–A Retrospective.* New York: The Museum of Modern Art, 1970.

Tyler, Parker. "Stan Brakhage," *Film Culture No. 18,* 1958, 23-25.

Robert Breer

Breer, Robert. "On Two Films," *Film Culture No. 22-23,* 1961, 63-64.

——. "Robert Breer on his Work," *Film Culture No. 42,* 1966, 112-13.

Burch, Noël. *"Images by Images, Cats, Jamestown Balooes, A Man and His Dog Out for Air* (films by Robert Breer)," *Film Quarterly,* Vol. XII, no. 3 (Spring 1959), 55-57.

Coté, Guy. "Interview with Robert Breer," *Film Culture No. 27,* (Winter 1962-63), 17-20.

Cummings, Paul. "Tape Recorded Interview with Robert Breer," *Archives of American Art.* New York: Smithsonian Institution, July 10, 1973.

Hammen, Scott. *"Gulls and Buoys,* An Introduction to the Remarkable Range of Pleasures Available from the Films of Robert Breer," *Afterimage,* Vol. 2, no. 6, December, 1974.

Mekas, Jonas and P. Adams Sitney. "An Interview with Robert Breer," *Film Culture No. 56-57,* (Spring 1973), 39-55.

James Broughton

Aigner, Hal. "San Francisco Letter," *Take One,* Vol. 3, no. 5, May-June, p. 32.

Broughton, James. "The Bed," *Filmagazine,* Vol. 1, no. 1, 1968, 33-34.

——. "Excerpts from Script Writing Seminar at The San Francisco Art Institute," *Canyon Cinema News,* no. 5, 1974, 9-13.

——. "Film as a Way of Seeing," *Film Culture No. 29,* 1963, 19-20.

——. "The Gardener's Son," *Sequence,* no. 14, 1952, p. 22.

——. "Knokke-le-Zoute," *Film Quarterly,* Vol. 17, no. 3, 1964, 13-15.

——. *A Long Undressing.* New York: Jargon Society, 1971.

——. "A Manifesto: Concurrent Theater," *Los Angeles Free Press,* March 15, 1968.

——. *The Playground.* San Francisco: The Centaur Press, 1949.

Broughton Issue. *Film Culture No. 61,* (Winter 1975).

Callenbach, Ernest. "Review," *Film Quarterly,* Vol. 21, no. 4, 1968, 52-53.

Kazan, Nick. "The Rejection is Mutual," *San Francisco Sunday Examiner & Chronicle,* July 11, 1971, 24-31.

Mayoux, Michel. "Trois Créatures: Préambule à un Cinéma Poétique," *Cahiers Du Cinéma,* no. 10, 1952, 18-26.

Sitney, P. Adams. editor. *The Essential Cinema.* New York: University Press, 1975.

Smith, Deborah. "The Bed," *Filmagazine,* Vol. 1, no. 1, 1968, p. 33.

Vogel, Amos. "The Avant-garde of the Seventies," *Film Comment,* Vol. II, no. 3, May-June, 1975, p. 35.

Shirley Clarke

Berg, Gretchen. "Interview with Shirley Clark," *Film Culture No. 44,* 1967, 52-55.

Blue, James. "Entretien avec Shirley Clarke," *Objectif,* no. 31, February-March, 1965, 12-19.

Breitrose, Henry. "The Films of Shirley Clarke," *Film Quarterly,* Vol. XIII, no. 4, (Summer 1960), 57-58.

Clarke, Shirley. *"Bridges-Go-Round," "Bullfight," "A Moment in Love,"* Catalogue entries for the 1958 International Experimental Film Competition. Brussels, Belgium: Royal Film Archive, 1958, nos. 130, 071, 060, respectively.

——. "A Conversation–Shirley Clarke and Storm de Hirsch," *Film Culture No. 46,* 1967-68, 44-54.

——. "The Expensive Art," *Film Quarterly,* Vol. XIII, (Summer 1960), 19-34.

——. "A Statement on Dance and Film," *Dance Perspectives,* no. 30, (Summer 1967), 20-23.

Delahaye, Michael. "Entretiens–Le depart pour Mars," *Cahiers du Cinéma,* no. 205, October, 1968, 20-33.

El-Kaim, Arlette. "The Connection," *Les Temps Modernes,* no. 191, Avril, 1962, 1578-1582.

Madsen, Axel. "Recontre avec Shirley Clarke," *Cahiers du Cinéma,* no. 153, March, 1964, 20-26.

Rice, Susan. "Shirley Clarke: Image and Images," *Take One,* Vol. 3, no. 2, November-December, 1971, 20-22.

Bruce Conner

Belz, Carl I. "Three Films by Bruce Conner," *Film Culture No. 44,* 1967, 56-59.

Brown, Robert K. "Interview with Bruce Conner," *Film Culture No. 33,* 1964, 15-16.

Conner, Bruce. "Bruce Conner," *Film Comment,* Vol. 5, no. 4. (Winter 1969), 16-25.

——. "Bruce Conner Makes a Sandwich," *Artforum,* September, 1967.

——. "I Was Obsessed. . .," *Film Library Quarterly,* Vol. II, no. 3. (Summer 1969), 23-27.

Mosen, David. "Report," *Film Quarterly,* Vol. XIX, no. 3, (Spring 1966), 54-56.

Tony Conrad

Conrad, Tony. *Flexagons.* Baltimore: Research Institute for Advanced Study, 1962.

——. "The Flicker," Anthology Film Archives.

——. "Inside the Dream Syndicate," *Film Culture No. 41,* 1966.

——. "Letter to Peter Yates," *Arts and Architecture,* February-March, 1966.

——. "Shadow File," *Luminous Realities.* Dayton, Ohio: Wright State University, 1975.

——. *The Theory of the Flexigon.* Baltimore: Research Institute for Advanced Study, 1960.

——. "Tony Conrad on *The Flicker,*" *Film Culture No. 41,* 1966, 5-8.

Cornwell, Regina. "Some Formalist Tendencies in the American Avant Garde Film," *Studio International,* October, 1972.

Freyer, Ellen. "Film," *Craft Horizons,* December, 1973.

Kelman, Ken. *"The Flicker,"* New Cinema Bulletin, May, 1967.

LeGrice, Malcolm. "Vision," *Studio International,* July-August, 1974.

Preston, Richard. "Voyeurama," *East Village Other,* October 25, 1968.

Schillaci, Anthony. "Film As Environment," *The Age of Communication,* 1970.

Schultz, Victoria. "Independent Film," *Changes,* June, 1972.

"Sprockets," *East Village Other,* October 25, 1968.

Maya Deren

Deren, Maya. "Adventures in Creative Film-making," *Home Movie Making,* 1960, 26-33, 76-81.

___. *An Anagram of Ideas on Art, Form and Film.* New York: Alicat Book Shop, 1946.

___. "Chamber Films," *Filmwise,* no. 2, 1962, 37-40.

___. "Choreography for Camera," *Dance,* October, 1943.

___. "Cinema as an Art Form," *Introduction to the Art of the Movies.* Edited by Lewis Jacobs. New York: Noonday Press, 1960, 252-265.

___. "Cinematography: The Creative Use of Reality," *Daedalus: The Visual Arts Today,* 1960, 150-167.

___. "The Cleveland Lecture," *Film Culture No. 29,* 1963, 64-69.

___. "Creative Cutting. Parts I and II," *Movie Makers,* May-June, 1947, 190-191, 204-206.

___. *Divine Horsemen: Voodoo Gods of Haiti.* New York: Chelsea House Publishers, 1970.

___. "Meditation on Violence," *Dance Magazine,* December, 1948.

___. "Notes, Essays, Letters." *Film Culture No. 39,* 1965, 1-86.

___. "Poetry and the Film: A Symposium," *Film Culture No. 29,* 1963, 55-63.

___. "A Statement on Dance and Film," *Dance Perspectives,* no. 30, 1967, 10-13.

___. "Tempo and Tension," *The Movies as Medium.* Edited by Lewis Jacobs. New York: Farrar, Strauss & Giroux, 1970, 144-150.

Cornwell, Regina. "Maya Deren and Germaine Dulac: Activists of the Avant-Garde," *Film Library Quarterly,* Vol. 5, no. 1, 1971, 29-38.

Filmwise, no. 2, 1961. (An entire issue on Maya Deren.)

Sitney, P. Adams. "The Idea of Morphology," *Film Culture No. 53-54-55,* 1972, 1-24.

Hollis Frampton

Bershen, Wanda. *"Zorns Lemma," Artforum,* Vol. X, no. 1, September, 1971, 41-45.

Cornwell, Regina. "Some Formalist Tendencies in the Current American Avant-Garde Film," *Kansas Quarterly,* Vol. IV, no. 2, (Spring 1972), 60-70.

Field, Simon. "Interview with Hollis Frampton," *Afterimage,* no. 4, (Fall 1972), 44-77.

The Films of Hollis Frampton. Minneapolis: Walker Art Center, November 16-18, 1972.

Frampton, Hollis. "Digressions on the Photographic Agony," *Artforum,* Vol. IX, no. 3, November, 1972, 43-51.

___. "Eadweard Muybridge: Fragments of a Tesseract," *Artforum,* Vol. IX, no. 7, March, 1973, 43-52.

___. "For a Metahistory of Film: Commonplace Notes and Hypotheses," *Artforum,* Vol. X, no. 1, September, 1971, 32-35.

___. "Incisions in History/Segments of Eternity," *Artforum,* Vol. XIII, no. 2, October, 1974.

___. "Meditations Around Paul Strand," *Artforum,* Vol. 10, no. 6, February, 1972, 52-57.

___. "(Nostalgia): Voice-Over Narration for a Film of that Name, Dated 1/8/71," *Film Culture No. 53-54-55,* (Spring 1972), 103-113.

___. "Notes on (Nostalgia)," *Film Culture No. 53-54-55,* (Spring 1972), p. 114.

___. "A Pentagram for Conjuring the Narrative," *Form and Structure in Recent Film.* Dennis Wheeler, editor, Vancouver: The Vancouver Art Gallery, 1972.

___. "Poetic Justice," Rochester, New York: The Visual Studies Workshop, 1973.

___. "Stan and Jane Brakhage, Talking," *Artforum,* Vol. XI, no. 5, January, 1973, 72-79.

___. "To the editor," *Artforum,* Vol. XIII, no. 7, March, 1975, p. 9.

___. "The Withering Away of the State of Art," *Artforum,* Vol. XIII, no. 4, December, 1974, 50-55.

Francastel, Pierre. "Seeing . . . Decoding," *Afterimage,* no. 5, (Spring 1974), 4-21.

Rayns, Tony. "Lines describing an impasse: Experimental 5," *Sight and Sound,* Vol. 44, no. 2, (Spring 1975), 78-80.

Resnick, Douglas. "Hollis Frampton." Catalogue entry, *Options and Alternatives: Some Directions in Recent Art,* (an exhibition, organized by The Yale University Art Gallery), April 4- May 16, 1974.

Segal, Mark. "Hollis Frampton's *Zorns Lemma,*" *Film Culture No. 52,* (Spring 1971), 88-94.

Simon, Bill. "New Forms in Film," *Artforum,* Vol. XI, no. 2, October, 1972, 79-84.

Sitney, P. Adams. "Hollis Frampton," *The American Independent Film.* Boston: Boston Museum of Fine Arts, (Spring 1971).

Snow, Michael. "Hollis Frampton Interviewed by Michael Snow," *Film Culture No. 48-49,* (Winter-Spring 1970), 6-12.

Ernie Gehr

Cornwell, Regina. "Some Formalist Tendencies in the Current American Avant-Garde Film," *Kansas Quarterly,* Vol. IV, no. 2, (Spring 1972), 60-70.

Cowan, Bob. "Letter from New York," *Take One,* Vol. 4, no. 1, September-October, 1972, 36-37.

Cuthell, David. "Ernie Gehr." Catalogue entry, *Options and Alternatives: Some Directions in Recent Art,* (an exhibition organized by The Yale University Art Gallery), April 4-May 16, 1974.

Field, Simon. "New Film Forms," *Art & Artists,* November, 1974, 24-27.

Gehr, Ernie. "Program Notes for a Film Showing at The Museum of Modern Art, New York City, February 2nd, 1971 at 5:30 pm," *Film Culture No. 53-54-55,* (Spring 1971), 36-38.

Mekas, Jonas. "Ernie Gehr Interviewed on March 24, 1971," *Film Culture No. 53-54-55.* (Spring 1971), 25-36.

Simon, Bill. "New Forms in Film," *Artforum,* Vol. XI, no. 2, October, 1972, 79-84.

Barry Gerson

Cowan, Bob. "Letter from New York," *Take One,* Vol. 2, no. 7, September, 1970, 26-27.

Gerson, Barry. "A Statement by Barry Gerson, 1973," *Bulletin for Film and Video Information,* Callie Angell and Hollis Melton, editors, Vol. 1, no. 3, June, 1974.

Simon, Bill. "New Forms in Film," *Artforum,* Vol. XI, no. 2, October, 1972, 79-84.

Ian Hugo

Hugo, Ian "Animal Close-ups: Were easy to Film in a Mexican Zoo," *Films in Review,* Vol. I, no. 8, November, 1950, 13-15.

——. *"Melodic Inversion," "The Gondola Eye,"* Catalogue entries for the Third International Experimental Film Competition. Brussels, Belgium: Royal Film Archive, 1964, Nos. 075, 081.

——. "Notes on *Venice Etude Number One,*" *Scenario,* Vol. III, no. 2, March-April, 1962, 3-4.

Nin, Anaïs, "Poetics of the Film," *Film Culture No. 31,* 1963-64, 12-14.

Ken Jacobs

Breer, Robert. "Letter from Robert Breer to Jonas Mekas, 5/25/70," *Film Culture No. 56-57,* (Spring 1973), 69-70.

Brown, J.F. "Stereoptical viewing," *The Drama Review,* no. 65, March, 1975, p. 95.

Cornwell, Regina. "Some Formalist Tendencies in the Current American Avant-Garde Film," *Kansas Quarterly,* Vol. IV, no. 2, (Spring 1972), 60-70.

Field, Simon. "Art is. . . ?" *Art and Artists,* Vol. 6, no. 9, London, December, 1971, 24-29.

Frot-Coutaz, Gerard. "Programme 'Underground'," *Cinema 74,* no. 183, January, 1974.

Jacobs, Ken. "The Day the Moon Gave up the Ghost," *Form and Structure in Recent Film.* edited by Dennis Wheeler, Vancouver: Vancouver Art Gallery, October 29-November 5, 1972.

——. "Filmmakers vs MOMA," *Filmmakers' Newsletter* Vol. II, no. 7, 1969, 1-2.

Mendelson, Lois and Bill Simon. *"Tom, Tom, the Piper's Son,"* *Artforum,* Vol. X, no. 1, September, 1971, 46-52.

Pam, Dorothy. "The Apparition Theatre of Ken Jacobs," *The Drama Review,* no. 65. March, 1975.

Rayns, Tony. "Ken Jacobs," *Sight and Sound,* Vol. 43, no. 1, (Winter 1973-74), 18-19.

Sitney, P. Adams. "The Avant-Garde Film: Ken Jacobs, *Afterimage,* no. 2 (Autumn 1970), 19-22.

Whiteman, Priscilla. "Ken Jacobs," *Options and Alternatives: Some Directions in Recent Art,* (An Exhibition organized by the Yale University Art Gallery), April 16-May, 1973.

Yalkut, Jud. "The Work and Words of Ken Jacobs; 'I am Very Much Interested in the Personality of a Light Bulb,'" *New York Free Press,* March 28, 1968.

Larry Jordan

Sitney, P. Adams. "Larry Jordan Interview," *Film Culture No. 52,* (Spring 1971), 77-88.

George Landow

Arthur, Paul. "The Calisthenics of Vision: Open Instructions on the Films of George Landow," *Artforum,* Vol. X, no. 1, September, 1971, 74-80.

Camper, Fred. *"Remedial Reading Comprehension,"* *Film Culture No. 52,* (Spring 1971), 73-77.

Kelman, Ken. *"The Tibetan Film of the Dead,"* *Film Culture No. 47,* 1969, 12-13.

Sitney, P. Adams. "Interview with George Landow," *Film Culture No. 47,* 1969, 1-12.

Standish D. Lawder

Locke, John W. "Standish Lawder," *Artforum,* Vol. XII, no. 9, May, 1974, 50-53.

Willard Maas

Gruen, John. *The Party's Over Now: Reminiscences of the Fifties: New York's Artists, Writers, Musicians, and Their Friends.* New York: Viking Press, 1972, 84-90.

Maas, Willard. "Avant-Garde: a letter to the editors," *Sight and Sound,* Vol. 27, no. 6, (Autumn 1958), 328-329.

——. "A Love Affair: I Talk to Myself About Stan Brakhage," *Filmwise,* no. 1, 1962, 32-34.

——. "Memories of My Maya," *Filmwise,* no. 2, 1962, 23-29.

——. "Poetry and Film: A Symposium," *Film Culture,* no. 29, 1963, 55-63.

——. "Shadows of Evening: A Short Film for Gerard Malanga," *Filmwise,* no. 5-6, 1967, 43-45.

——. "Marie Menken and Willard Maas," *Filmwise* no 5-6, 1967.

Semsel, George. "Willard Maas: An Interview," *Film Comment,* Vol. 7, no. 3, (Fall 1971), 60-64.

Tyler, Parker. "Willard Maas." *Film Culture No. 20,* 1959, 53-58.

Jonas Mekas

Mekas, Jonas. "A Call for a New Generation of Film-Makers," *Film Culture No. 19,* 1959, 1-3.

——. "Notes on Some New Movies and Happiness," *Film Culture No. 37,* (Summer 1965), 16-20.

Simon, Bill. "New Forms in Film," *Artforum,*" Vol. XI, no. 2, October, 1972, 79-84.

Tomkins, Calvin. "Profile: All Pockets Open," *The New Yorker,* Jan. 6, 1973, 31-49.

Marie Menken

Filmwise, No. 5-6, 1967 (Special issue devoted to Menken and Willard Maas).

Mekas, Jonas. "Movie Journal," *The Village Voice,* Jan. 4, 1962.

Robert Nelson

"Robert Nelson on Robert Nelson," *Film Culture No. 48-49,* (Winter-Spring 1970), 23-30.

Sidney Peterson

Harrington, Curtis. "Note sur les films de Sidney Peterson," *Age du Cinéma,* no. 6.

Peterson, Sidney. *A Fly in the Pigment.* Sausalito: Contact Editions, 1961.

___. "An Historical Note on the Far-out West," *Contact,* Vol. III, no. 3, August, 1962, 7-11.

___. "The Museum and TV." (A report to The Museum of Modern Art in fulfillment of the requirements of a Rockefeller Grant, 1955.)

___. "A Note on Comedy in Experimental Film," *Film Culture No. 29,* 1963, 27-29.

___. "Philippe—Or the Future of Dance Movies," *Anthology of Impulse 1951-1966,* Dance Horizons, Inc., 79-83.

___. "A Statement on Dance and Film," *Dance Perspectives,* no. 30, (Summer 1967), 16-19.

___. "You Can't Pet a Chicken," *The Atlantic,* March, 1963, Vol. 211, No. 3, 126-129.

Tarshis, Jerome. *"The Potted Psalm* and other Local Legends." *San Francisco.* April, 1974, 84-87.

Tyler, Parker. "Sidney Peterson." *Film Culture No. 19, 1959,* 38-43.

Paul Sharits

Cornwell, Regina. "Illusion and Object," *Artforum,* Vol. X, No. 1, September, 1971, 56-62.

Krauss, Rosalind. "Stop Time," *Art Forum,* April, 1973.

Michelson, Annette. "Paul Sharits and the Critique of Illusionism: An Introduciton." Minneapolis: Walker Art Center, 1974.

Sharits, Paul. "Blank Deflections: Golden Cinema," *Film Culture No. 48-49,* (Spring-Winter 1970), 20-22.

___. "Notes on Film," *Film Culture No. 47.*

___. "Words Per Page," *Afterimage,* no. 4, (Fall 1973), 26-42.

Harry Smith

Berge, Carol. "Dialogue Without Words: The Work of Harry Smith," *Film Culture No. 37,* 1965, 2-4.

Cohen. "A Rare Interview with Harry Smith," *Sing Out The Folk Song Magazine,* "Part One"—Vol. 19, no. 1, April-May, 1969, 2-11, "Part Two"—Vol. 19, no. 2, July-August, 1969, 22-28.

Kelman, Ken. "Death and Transfiguration," *Film Culture No. 34,* 1964, 51-53.

"Harry Smith Interview," *Cantrills Filmnotes,* no. 19, October, 1974, 6-13.

Noquez, Dominique. "'Les Quatre Mille Farces du Diable'—Le Cinema de Harry Smith," *L'Art Vivant,* no. 56, March-April, 1974, p. 41.

"Seventh Independent Film Award," *Film Culture No. 37,* 1965, p. 1.

Sitney, P. Adams. "Animating the Absolute: Harry Smith," *Artforum,* Vol. X, no. 9, May, 1972, 60-71.

Michael Snow

Farber, Manny. *Negative Space.* New York: Praeger Publishers.

Mekas, Jonas, and P. Adams Sitney. "Conversation with Michael Snow," *Film Culture No. 46,* 1967, 1-4.

Michelson, Annette. "Toward Snow," *Artforum,* Vol. IX, no. 10, June, 1971, 30-37.

Skoller, Donald. "Aspects of Cinematic Consciousness: Suspense and Presence/Disillusion/Unified Perceptual Response," *Film Comment,* Vol. 8, no. 3, September-October, 1972, 41-51.

Snow, Michael. "Letter from Michael Snow," *Film Culture No. 46,* 1967, 4-5.

___. *A Survey.* Toronto: Art Gallery of Ontario, 1970.

Stan Vanderbeek

Mener, Jacques. "Breathdeath," *Script,* nos. 10-12, March, 1964, 68-69.

Vanderbeek, Stan. "A Letter to Lenny Lipton," *Film Culture No. 48-49,* 1970, 37-40.

___. "Anti-Dotes for Poisoned Movies," *Film Culture No. 25,* 1962, 71-72.

___. "A Statement on Dance and Film," *Dance Perspectives,* no. 30 (Summer 1967), 30-32.

___. "Compound Entendre," *Film: A Montage of Theories.* Edited by Richard Dyer MacCann. New York: Dutton, 1966, 329-32.

___. "'Culture: Intercom' and Expanded Cinema," *Film Culture No. 40,* 1966, 15-18.

___. "If the Actor Is the Audience," *Film Culture No. 24,* 1962, p. 92.

___. "Interview: Chapter One," *Film Culture No. 35,* 1964-65, 20-22.

___. "Media Wrap Around or a Man with No Close," *Filmmakers' Newsletter,* Vol. 4, no. 5, March, 1971, 20-25.

___. "Movies . . . Disposable Art—Synthetic Media—& Artificial Intelligence," *Take One,* Vol. 2, no. 3, January-February, 1969, 14-16.

___. "On *Science Friction,"* *Film Culture No. 22-23,* 1961, 168-69.

___. "Re Computerized Graphics," *Film Culture No. 48-49,* 1970, 35-36.

___. "Re-Vision," *Perspectives on the Study of Film.* Edited by John Stuart Katz. Boston: Little, Brown, 1971, 227-233.

___. "Simple Syllogism," *Film Culture No. 29,* 1963, p. 11.

___. "Social-Imagistics: What the Future May Hold," *American Film Institute Report,* Vol. 4, no. 2, May, 1973, 54-56.

___. "The Cinema Delimina: Films from Underground," *Film Quarterly,* Vol. 14, no. 4 (Summer 1961), 5-15.

___. "The Future Is Not What It Used To Be," *Film Culture No. 48-49,* 1970, 34-35.

James Whitney

Brick, Richard. "John Whitney Interviewed by Richard Brick," *Film Culture No. 53-54-55,* (Spring 1972), 39-73.

Teramaye, T., "Towards Being Choicelessly Aware—The Immanent World of James Whitney," 1974. (Unpublished).

Illustration credits:

Anthology Film Archives, Francene Keery: pp. 34, 53, 56, 58, 62, 68, 76, 88, 122, 127, 156

Larry James Huston: p. 142

Francene Keery: pp. 71, 72, 74, 78, 80, 81, 82, 86, 90, 94, 95, 96, 102, 103, 104, 105, 106, 107, 110, 111, 112, 113, 114, 118, 120, 130, 135, 136, 138, 140, 150, 152, 153

Babette Mangolte: p. 146

Peter Moore ©1974: p. 43

The Museum of Modern Art/Film Stills Archive: pp. 22, 30, 32, 33, 52, 53, 58, 65

Nationalmuseum, Munich, Courtesy George Eastman House: p. 28

Robert Parent: p. 42

Walker Art Center, Eric Sutherland: p. 42

Film Distribution Sources

The American Federation of Arts
41 East 65th Street
New York, New York 10021

Canadian Filmmakers' Distribution Center
406 Jarvis Street
Toronto 181, Canada

Canyon Cinema Co-Op
Room 220
Industrial Center Building
Sausolito, California 94965

Castelli-Sonnabend Tapes and Films, Inc.
420 West Broadway
New York, New York 10012

Center Cinema Co-Op
School of the Art Institute of Chicago
Michigan Avenue at Adams Street
Chicago, Illinois 60603

Cooperative Cineastes Independants
2026 Ontario East
Montreal 133, Canada

Creative Film Society
7237 Canby Avenue
Reseda, California 91335

Film Images
17 West 60th Street
New York, New York 10023

Film-Makers' Cooperative
175 Lexington Avenue
New York, New York 10016

Grove Press Films
196 West Houston Street
New York, New York 10014

Impact Films, Inc.
144 Bleecker Street
New York, New York 10012

Intermedia Film Co-Op
1972 West 4th Street
Vancouver 9, Canada

The Isaacs Gallery, Ltd.
832 Yonge Street
Toronto, Ontario
Canada M4W 2H1

Macmillan Films Inc.
34 MacQuesten Parkway South
Mount Vernon, New York 10550

Monument Film Corp.
43 West 16th Street
New York, New York 10011

The Museum of Modern Art
Department of Film
11 West 53rd Street
New York, New York 10019

New Cinema Enterprises Corp. Ltd.
35 Britain Street
Toronto, Ontario M5A 1R7

New Yorker Films
43 West 61st Street
New York, New York 10023

New Line Cinema Corporation
853 Broadway
New York, New York 10003

Pyramid Films
Box 1048
Santa Monica, California 90406

Serious Business Company
1609 Jaynes Street
Berkeley, California 94703

Visual Resources, Inc.
1 Lincoln Plaza
New York, New York 10023